G

AM I

Memoirs of an Accompanist

*

Normally the most considerate of accompanists, on this occasion Gerald Moore
too often overwhelmed the singer.

Daily Telegraph, 8 May 1961

PENGUIN BOOKS

in association with Hamish Hamilton

Penguin Books Ltd, Harmondsworth, Middlesex, England
Penguin Books Australia Ltd, Ringwood, Victoria, Australia

—

First published by Hamish Hamilton 1962
Published in Penguin Books 1966
Reprinted 1968, 1974

—

—

Made and printed in Great Britain
by C. Nicholls & Company Ltd
Set in Linotype Pilgrim

TO ENID

Acknowledgements

For permission to reprint photographs, the publishers wish to thank: Georges Maiteny (Yehudi Menuhin); John Vickers (Solomon); Fayer, Vienna (Elisabeth Schwarzkopf and Irmgard Seefried); Angus McBean (Victoria de los Angeles); Cecil Beaton (Kathleen Ferrier); Lotte Meitner-Graf (Elisabeth Schumann); Dorothy Wilding (John McCormack and Elena Gerhardt); Eschen, Berlin (Dietrich Fischer-Dieskau).

Contents

7

CONTENTS

I

Birth and Background

'I DON'T know what will become of the boy: he's no good at school and no good at games. It isn't as if he even had any hobbies.' So that indomitable woman, my mother, frequently addressed my father: in my hearing of course. I can see how right she was. From my ninth to fourteenth birthday my worried parents, despite increasing financial difficulties, showered me with fretwork sets, carpentering tools, painting materials, magic lantern, Plasticine modelling sets, stamp albums, etc., and I can see myself opening these parcels in my nursery, looking at them with lack-lustre eyes, breathing the while through my mouth, for I was adenoidal, and quietly and patiently stuffing the bewildering impedimenta out of sight.

But it was the 'no good at sport' which fanned some spark in my sluggish nature to high endeavour. I had been presented with a pair of ice skates one Christmas and with a great show of resolution I slung them over my shoulder on a cold January morning, prepared to risk life and limb, and marched through the streets of Watford to the pond which, I had been told, was completely frozen. My pilgrimage was not unobserved. The shining new skates attracted the attention of a couple of curious urchins who followed me at a respectful distance. Such cat-calls as 'Swank!' and 'Wot does 'e think 'e's doin' of' accompanied my progress so that presently my original pair of ragamuffins was joined by other and similar types of both sexes. By the time I arrived at this confounded pond I had a retinue of jeering attendants who were not sparing with their advice. I gingerly approached the edge of the pond and with one foot on terra firma tested the ice with the other. It was one eighth of an inch thick and would not have borne the weight of a cat. Edmond Dantès, when he unearthed his treasure on the Isle of Monte Cristo, did not turn his eyes more thankfully to heaven than did I in this moment of divine

9

deliverance. With heaving chest and terrible courage I seized those cursed skates, whirled them round my head like a flail, and attacked my tormentors who scattered as did the Philistines before Samson. The skates were lost in the mêlée. To this day I can boast that I have never put on a pair.

My angling career was as stillborn as my skating. A fishing-rod, which as soon as it was given me I had successfully hidden for two years at the bottom of a cupboard, was at last brought to light. I was told to use it. I collected worms from the garden – I am not afraid of worms, I am a lion with worms – and then with unusual forethought I rehearsed putting the rod together. This was beyond me. My father rigged it up for me at home. Wisely not dismantling it, and ready for immediate action, I proceeded through the streets with a can of worms in one hand and a twelve-foot rod in the other.

Why is it that today when I need it so badly in my professional career I have lost that personal magnetism I seemed to have as a child? No sooner did I emerge from the house than once again I attracted a train of raucous-voiced attendants. I had to face fifteen minutes of purgatory during my walk to the River Colne before I was able to sink my bait in the bosom of the stream. Once this was done there was little of interest to be seen and, to my great delight, my audience rapidly dwindled. This was all I was waiting for. For at least an hour I had been standing there with my mouth open, having seen no sign of piscatorial life but longing to be alone. What a world of difference is hereby shown between the amateur angler and the professional pianist for the latter cannot give vent to his feelings; whether his audience is five thousand or fifty he accepts the situation with seeming equanimity; if he is ever tempted to shove his pianoforte over the edge of the platform on to the front row of the stalls, he resists the urge. I had no such paltry inhibitions with my fishing tackle. No sooner had the last of my 'dead heads' disappeared (a 'dead head' in the language of the concert world is one who does not pay for his ticket) than I cast my rod upon the waters and stole silently away. After lying in pitch darkness in the recesses of a cupboard for two years my rod had tasted the fresh air for exactly one hour and twenty minutes before it sank to its last resting place.

My best game was fives, and I was not bad at football and cricket. I still feel that I had potential genius for cricket and, properly handled, could have developed into a second Jack Hobbs. To me a cricketer is a god ; you can have all your actors, statesmen, scientists. I sit, to this day, in the Long Room at Lord's watching the players file past me with my eyes agog ; Denis Compton, Tony Lock, Evans, May – I could stretch out my hand and touch them and can scarcely refrain from doing it. As for C. B. Fry's dictum that if a cricketer were a mouse he would be unable to find his way back to his own hole, I scout it. He is a child of the sun. A distinguished visitor to Rossall School saw the name of Thomas Beecham on the list of Captains of Cricket and asked with incredulity if that were the famous conductor ; upon being told it was he was heard to mutter, 'Hm, he can't be such a bad chap after all.' And yet when I told Yehudi Menuhin a month or two ago that his shipmates on his voyage to South Africa would be the England cricket eleven, he did not know what I was talking about. I suppose cricket is a mania. When I first took Enid, my wife, to Lord's she said after fifteen minutes that she had reached the conclusion that everybody in the ground, with the exception of herself, was a lunatic.

Although an absolute dud at them, I have always loved games. With that great man Solomon, the pianist, my intimate friend for nearly forty years, I used to play tennis at 7 a.m. for an hour, two or three times a week. He was a very fine player and sometimes succeeded in beating me. Golf, with advancing years, took the place of tennis. To squeeze in eighteen holes with him before breakfast, living in the heart of London as we were, necessitated an early start, and in the summer months we have been known to arrive on the first tee soon after dawn. Now golf has been thrown overboard and my physical exercises are confined to watching cricket, playing bridge and gardening.

But looking back, I can honestly say that I cannot remember when I could not play the piano. I dislike the term 'at the piano', so often used on posters and programmes to designate the accompanist, yet in my case the term is not inappropriate for it seems to me that as soon as I could toddle I was seized and flung, literally, at the piano. I had my first lessons when I was six or seven. Whatever proficiency I may now have is due entirely to the determination of my mother, for my approach, as usual, was lackadaisical. How I ever learned anything I cannot imagine for I was as obstinate as a mule when it came to practising. My mother, bless her heart, stood over me and I dug away with pretended diligence or I should have been knocked off the stool. My *Nunc Dimittis* from these painful sessions – the light at the end of the tunnel – came in sight when I was commanded to 'play that page once more and breathe through your nose'.

But it would be stupid to deny that I had talent. It was discovered in my school days that I had perfect pitch – I had a remarkably quick ear and a retentive memory. In my holidays, having been taken to a Gilbert and Sullivan operetta or concert-party troupe at the seaside, I would come home and play the tunes I had heard – not merely picking out the air with one finger but harmonizing unhesitatingly. This trick had its disadvantages in that it was easier for me to hear my piano teacher in Watford – Wallis Bandey – play a passage of music and then sit down immediately and imitate what he had done than it was for me to look at the score and read the notes. The ears defeated the eyes – I was a poor sight-reader. But I adored music and my head was haunted by good, bad and indifferent tunes. If my mother had not stood over me as I tried to learn my piece, I would happily have spent my practising time in improvising, at which I was adept. Reckoning me as the average whining schoolboy – but certainly no infant prodigy – it could be said that I had an unusual keyboard facility.

Harold Holt, the impresario, a charming man personally, but one whose knowledge of and liking for music were non-existent, used to say that good accompanists were born but not made. This old cliché is constantly applied to anybody in any walk of life and is, in my opinion, absolute nonsense. Surely it is just as fatuous to say that a man is a born diplomat,

a born leader of men, or a born drunkard. It must be environ-
ment, training, experience which, creating the opportunity,
make the man. The use he makes of all these determines
whether he turns diplomat or rises to the dizzy heights of
accompanying. I cultivated a taste for the art in the same way
that an epicure cultivates a taste for good wine and cigars.

I was born at Watford, Hertfordshire, in 1899 and can
boast that I have lived in six reigns. Watford was a small
market town in those days, bordered by Bushey, Cassiobury
Park, Aldenham, Elstree, where it was very pleasant to walk,
cycle, and picnic. Is it a sign of old age when I protest that
things are not as they were in the dim and distant past? I am
glad to by-pass the town in these days or look at it from an
express train, for the surroundings now are arterial roads,
factories; the fields and pretty lanes have become housing
estates.

We are told that the Welsh are inherently musical, but beyond the fact that my mother came from Wales I cannot say
in all fairness that she had any great love for the divine Muse.
What possessed her to drive me on to the keyboard? It sounds
a spiteful observation since I owe everything to my mother,
but a daughter of one of our near neighbours showed quite an
aptitude for the piano and I believe my fond parent was spurred
on by the thought of keeping up with Mrs Allen. There was a
close friendship between the two mothers but an intense rivalry
below the surface. First one would gain the upper hand and
then the other. Our side lost face considerably when I made
my first public appearance, aged eight, at the local school of
music. An audience numbering at least twenty souls, consist-
ing of pupils and their escorts, assembled for this important
affair. Eventually the announcement came, 'Master Gerald
Moore will play a sonatina by ...' (Was it Gurlitt, Dussek,
Loeschhorn?) I was no prima donna in those days. At the
sound of my name I burst into tears. With a kind smile, be-
lying the cold gleam in his eyes, the major-domo intimated that
perhaps Master Moore would consent to play later. 'Make no
mistake, you are going to play,' muttered my implacable guard-
ian. Perhaps, on reflection, I was a prima donna already and

13

instinctively realized that an appearance in the latter part of the programme was tactically much stronger. Be that as it may, I failed to rise to the occasion when my name was called a second time. My sobs were clearly heard and caused the greatest amusement to everybody. To everybody, that is, save two. These two now rose; or rather one of them rose, carrying the other by the scruff of the neck and the seat of the trousers, and advanced to the platform where the Gurlitt sonatina was duly executed. It was like a tandem. I steered, impelled from behind. This was indeed a setback for the Moores. Father was informed over the tea table that we should be the laughing-stock of the town, and 'can you imagine what Mrs Allen will say?'

In my kindergarten days I drove to school in a horse-drawn bus with straw-covered floor, and longed each journey to set eyes again on our lovely schoolmistress, black hair – masses of it – blue eyes, rosy cheeks, who was unfortunately an old lady of twenty-one. I loved her. She shared my heart with one of the senior girls, aged nine, whom I can see in my mind's eye to this day and realize now that she, unlike the teacher, was not pretty at all with her snub nose, red face and uneven teeth, but oh! the thrill to be near her: when we played 'tag' I always allowed this enchantress to catch me for the pleasure of being touched by her. The amorous impulse of those spacious Edwardian days had spread its contagion, it seems, even to me in my infancy.

I had also at this time a very great liking for our cook. She was a very large woman – broad rather than tall (all hammered-down, Damon Runyon would have said) – who 'gave' so agreeably when I hugged her, a sensation I found quite absorbing. Waking early in the morning, creeping along the passage on bare feet, and stealing into her room, was a delicious adventure, for you slid into the bed beside her and her back was like a large warm wall. Only one stipulation was strictly observed: she must not be touched by your icy feet. I am convinced that so long as she was with us no fresh air was ever admitted to her room for her window was closed summer and winter. The stuffiness was indescribable. I adored it. But the cook, the snub-nosed girl, were side-issues: it was my raven-haired teacher, Miss Griffith, that I really loved. Only the chilblains on her hands were offensive to me. In the winter my passion for her waned as the chilblains waxed – in the summer she was perfect.

From the childish paradise I was removed to the sterner and more manly grammar school – where perforce I had to abandon my mistress. I came home one day and reported to mother that Mrs Allen's boy, along the road, had been publicly reprimanded at our school luncheon by the headmaster who had called out to him in stentorian tones: 'Do not bite your bread. Break it.' This gave great satisfaction at home, it was one up for our side.

At our splendid new school building on the Rickmansworth road I was the first boy to break a window. One evening, the last boy to leave the school – I was continually being kept behind in the detention class for woolgathering – I was throwing my tennis ball against the wall when, calamity, it smashed through a window. My name was written on the ball and, to make matters worse, the caretaker was cleaning in that very room. I saw in the distance the headmaster mowing his lawn. With a mien truly angelic and without delaying a moment I walked over to him and addressed him in this wise: 'Sir, I have a confession to make. I have broken a window in the physics laboratory.' My calculations worked out just as I anticipated, I was praised for my straightforwardness in owning up and was told to go to the Head's study and copy out 200 lines from Spenser's *Faerie Queene*. Thanking my lucky stars that I had escaped so lightly I took his beautifully bound book home with its copious marginal notes in the Head's own hand and promptly spilled a bottle of ink over it. Next morning I returned the book to his library, making sure he was otherwise engaged at the time, and then proceeded to hand in my imposition. My desecration of this precious volume was only discovered when I was thousands of miles away.

This episode has some bearing on my future career. I look back with shame on my deceitful behaviour but I am more inclined to be tolerant for I see that this youngster must already have shown signs of tact; a tact which was to stand him in good stead much later in his adopted career.

The inky *Faerie Queene* played on my mind somewhat, it was not remorse, but fear of the consequences. My father, however, had more urgent worries: for some time he had been losing heavily in speculations on the Stock Exchange. We were now living beyond our means so it was decided to pull up stakes and depart. In 1913 my parents with their three sons, Gerald, Trevor and Basil, emigrated to Canada.

2

Arrival in Canada

I SUPPOSE it is natural, in a country which is strange to you, to be on your best behaviour, especially if you are as excessively modest as I am. You feel like a new boy at school; you do not answer back. Visiting Australia for the first time in 1953, I had been in the country only a couple of hours when my taxi-cab driver electrified me by turning his back on the road – allowing the car to steer itself – and informed me that there was no doubt that Sydney was the logical capital of the British Commonwealth, it was the centre of the world geographically, industrially and culturally, and that if he were Winston Churchill he would evacuate England and bring the entire population to Australia. After a four-day flight from England I felt too tired to enter into an argument; I merely felt frightened, paid my fare and sent my missionary away to other and more productive fields.

Civic pride is without doubt a laudable trait. It shone brightly in Toronto in 1913. Today it is a splendid city and I am very fond of it, but in my boyhood its virtues were somewhat exaggerated. Rupert Brooke in his *Letters from America* found that groups of citizens were seen on every corner, their theme of conversation being 'Oh, what a beautiful city.'

English people were not popular in Canada at this time, and with good reason. Failures by the hundred poured into the Dominion and instead of being humble or subdued, they were loud-mouthed braggarts wanting to show Jack Canuck how John Bull did it. 'This is the way we do it at home.' No wonder that they were disliked. Looking in the newspaper under *Situations Vacant* (to my joy I was not sent to school, it was necessary for me to look for work to help the family finances) I would repeatedly see the sign, 'No English need apply'.

Happily this state of affairs no longer exists; the emigrating

Englishman is not so cocky and the Canadian is infinitely more broadminded and tolerant.

I obtained employment in a department store at a weekly salary of three dollars and fifty cents. I was then fourteen. My lean and hungry look must have been mistaken for asceticism for I was installed in the book department, my duties being to take the customers' purchases, wrap them up and return with their change. But I also had to dust the shelves and sweep the floor, and this was most disagreeable to me. I found it far less arduous to camouflage myself behind piles of books, where I would read to my heart's content. Cries for the cash boy were ignored, I was immersed in Charles Dickens. When my hide-out was discovered a new plan had to be made; I therefore locked myself in the lavatory several times a day and thus remained for half an hour at a stretch. In undisturbed conditions I sat there enjoying *Great Expectations*. But 'leaving the room' is the world's oldest excuse for an artful dodger and I was soon forbidden to do this under any pretext whatsoever.

Pecuniary vicissitudes did not deter my mother in her determination to make me go on with my music. She took me with a friend of hers, whose company I was going to regret, to Heintzman's on Yonge Street to buy a piano. The salesman was electrified when the small boy cascaded up and down the keyboard and played his party pieces; he must take me that very evening to play to Michael Hambourg who would give me a scholarship. This seemed the most exciting thing that had ever happened to me. Unfortunately, mother's acquaintance now felt that she should join in the fun and to show her pleasure asked the man in the most dulcet tones, 'Are you English?' The tone of her interrogation plainly indicated that being so extremely nice he must be English. If we had not been buying a piano this ill-timed remark, intended though it was to be ingratiating, might well have given such umbrage to our new friend that his interest in me would have evaporated. Fortunately he contented himself by replying with some heat, 'Madam, I am a Canadian, but if you would prefer someone else to introduce the boy to Professor Hambourg, I will arrange it.'

The Hambourg brothers Mark, Jan and Boris were known to all musicians, but Mark, the most famous, was the family champion, a pianist with an international reputation. Jan, the violinist, was an epicure; his interests were bestowed in equal proportions on Bach, Burgundy, the French impressionists and racehorses. The violoncellist Boris, a man of a particularly sweet and gentle nature, was devoted to chamber music and was a member of the Hart House String Quartet. It was their father, Michael, who now took me under his wing by offering me a scholarship. The conditions, extraordinarily generous, were that I undertook to pay back to the professor ten per cent of my first two years' earnings when I became a professional.

My parents were never the ones to do things by halves; they immediately withdrew me from my employment as 'reader' so that I might devote myself to my piano. I can see now that this sacrifice on their part was unjustified for I made only a pretence of practising. I still had to be coaxed to the piano. I look back now, having turned sixty, and realize that if I had really worked in those days I might have become a good pianist. When I think of boy prodigies like Heifetz, Elman, Menuhin, Josef Hoffman, Solomon, who had the passion, resolution and concentration to work and work and work away at their instruments, I come much nearer to understanding the expression 'born musician'. I was most certainly not in this category. Michael Hambourg was in despair, and with good reason! He could not force the horse to drink. The truth is that another interest was pushing my piano into second place. I rather fancied myself in a biretta. I had a mania: religion.

Brought up in the 'low' Church of England, I found later that the ritual of the 'high' Church had glamour and appealed more to my sense of theatre. Confirmed when I was eleven, I soon became an acolyte and was never happier than when I was carrying the crucifix at the head of a procession or genuflecting before the altar. I wore such a convincing cloak of piety that my mentor the vicar, back in those Watford days, was convinced I was destined to take Holy Orders. I felt a halo round my head, and it was a large size in haloes. My devotions, night and morning, were so lengthy and repetitive that they were a torture to me. I would fall asleep on my knees at night in my icy bedroom, wake up with a jerk and, for penance, begin my prayers all over again. These religious or superstitious exercises gave birth to great weeping and wailing and beating of the breast; manifestations which were viewed, to my annoyance, with unconcern by my six-year-old brother Trevor, who shared my bedroom. In a later and less archaic period he would simply and accurately have described me as 'nuts'.

In Toronto I looked for a similar type of Anglican church to the one I had left behind and found it in St Thomas's on Huron Street. Here, my voice still unbroken, a ghastly quality of soprano, I became a choirboy fascinated by Holy Eucharist settings of Stanford, Macpherson, Healey Willan, etc. And again I became an acolyte.

Our music director at the church, Richard Tattersall, decided to teach me the organ. Again I had to pay no fee for this tuition, the understanding between us being that I was to be his substitute during his four or six weeks' summer holiday.

Towards the end of 1915 that dear old gentleman, Michael Hambourg, a picturesque personality with his big benevolent presence, his white moustache and imperial, died. He died of a heart attack shortly after giving me a lesson. Boris the 'cellist, and a tenor, Redfern Hollinshead, were planning a joint recital tour of Western Canada about this time and I was glad to be able in some measure to repay the kindness the professor had shown me, and accepted their invitation to be accompanist at these concerts for the sum of forty dollars. Since there were forty engagements, my fee worked out at one dollar per concert. Clad in an Eton suit I was billed as 'The remarkable English boy pianist'.

Between Winnipeg and Calgary we roamed into townships of Manitoba, Saskatchewan, Alberta, which I have never been able to find on a map. Earl Grey, Lanigan, and a score of other gatherings on the prairie, all looked alike with their grain elevators, their clapboard houses and their surrounding flat blanket of snow. Yes, and their outdoor sanitation. Chick Sale, the specialist, would have done a roaring trade here and I am convinced many a good man, under duress, has been lost in a blizzard going down the garden.

As my travelling and hotel expenses were paid for me, I made up for this barnstorming when we came to the larger cities. At big hotels like the Palliser at Calgary, the Macdonald at Edmonton, the Fort Garry at Winnipeg, I developed a taste for expensive dishes. The *table d'hôte* menu I despised – everything had to be *à la carte*. One freezing February morning – the earth so dead and frore – I breakfasted on strawberries and cream, a cereal, kidneys and bacon, muffins; luncheon consisted of a dozen oysters, wild duck and crêpes suzette. Boris begged me to curb my appetite, it was undermining the tour, biting into the profits. With tears in his eyes he told me it was lovely to have me with him, 'but don't eat so much, my boy'.

Throughout our entire itinerary we adhered to the same programme of music – I opened the first half with a Chopin Scherzo, the second half with a Liszt Rhapsody, and with each succeeding concert these pieces became more and more of a scramble. I have never been able to play them since. But I greatly enjoyed accompanying the 'cello pieces and the songs.

On my return from this expedition I came down to earth with a bump; it was necessary for me to pay my keep.

At St Thomas's Church I resumed my place in the choir on my first Sunday at home, and during that very week the Rector invited me to take charge of the church's choral services. Whoever thinks that Canada is lacking in openings and opportunities for the young can take note that I found myself translated in the twinkling of an eye from a sixteen-year-old choirboy to organist and choirmaster. Services, so to speak, as usual during alterations. My first brush occurred at the full rehearsal on a Friday evening when my bass soloist, very much the rococo type and engaged on a professional basis, interrupted me while I was talking, objecting to my reference to the tenors and basses as 'men'. 'Address us as gentlemen, please,' he boomed. With a smile masking my hatred I replied, 'Very well then. Gentlemen – or, if you prefer it – bearded boys.' Yes, for a long time I had nursed a hearty dislike for this red-complexioned, buck-toothed bully: it was he, during the summer months when I had substituted for Mr Tattersall, who had repeatedly brandished his hymn book up and down, using it like a conductor's baton beating the time, to indicate to me and all beholders that I was playing the hymns too slowly. I was determined to rid myself of this squalid pest at the first opportunity. My chance came one Saturday. Seated that day at the organ, I was not weary but decidedly ill at ease and practising for dear life. Who should creep up silently behind me, unheard above the din I was creating, tap me on the shoulder making me jump out of my skin (the church was supposed to be haunted, I never forgot this when I was alone in it), but my *bête noire*. He wore the most conciliatory of smiles. The following conversation ensued:

'Wouldn't you be well advised, Mr Moore, to let me take all responsibility for directing the choir and so leave you free to concentrate on your organ?'

'But you cannot read music.'

'My dear boy, with your lack of experience you will be quite unable to—'

'You may judge for yourself tomorrow when you sit down there in the nave.'

'Sit down in the congregation? What do you mean?'

'I mean' – very quietly and coldly – 'you will not be sitting in the choir.'

What a magnificent diapason tone that organ had! It now surged in such a mighty *crescendo* that his protests went unheard. Of course the fellow went immediately and complained to the Rev. C. Ensor Sharpe, but that strong man was solidly behind me.

My official title at this time, I suppose, was organist, choirmaster and – I must not neglect to add – caretaker. This last honour I would gladly have waived since it meant rising at six-thirty each morning to open the church for service at seven; it meant mowing acres of lawn, sweeping the church and dusting the pews, but I had not the conscience to turn it down since the Rector knew I was hard up, and in any case it was only for the summer months.

What with my absorption in some of the splendid settings of the Holy Eucharist, my frantic gesticulating, my muttered imprecations and my glarings at the choir during the most sacred moments of the service in trying to rouse its members to greater endeavour, the religious fever from which I had suffered so long subsided. It was a healthier condition of mind. Yet when I spoke to Mr Sharpe about this he admitted that when he had a sermon to preach he found it difficult to pay proper attention to the service that preceded his arrival in the pulpit, being too busy going over and over again in his mind what he wanted to say. I was much happier anyway, no longer jogged by superstitious dread of catastrophe if I failed to spend lengthy vigils on my knees ; moreover I was able of nights to jump into bed much quicker and with never a care.

After a few weeks I began to feel that my caretaking chores were hardly in keeping with the dignity of my position. I emerged from church on Sunday, having concluded the service with a brilliantly executed voluntary by Guilmant or Widor, to be pounced on by an irate gentleman, a pillar of the church. This man invariably lagged half a beat behind the rest of the congregation in the responses, letting us all know he was there, watchful and critical. His 'Amen' rang threateningly round the church at least one second after everyone else had turned hopefully to the next prayer. When the time came for him to join the great majority he would without doubt be numbered among the blessed. If there is a police force in heaven this man is a centurion in the force. He now informed me that when he had retrieved his silk hat from beneath his seat, its underbrim was coated with dust. I was resolved there and then to resign my regalia of the lawn mower, duster and broom to worthier hands.

Fortune once again turned my way. I applied for and obtained a post as cinema organist in the down-town district, the theatre-land of Toronto. This was better for all concerned, it more than made up for my caretaking emoluments, it did not interfere with my church appointment, and was more hygienic for the worshippers' silk hats.

In those far-off days of the silent film the larger cinemas employed twenty- or twenty-five-piece orchestras in addition to the ubiquitous cinema organ on which I had to play what was quaintly called 'relief'. In fact my duty was to relieve the orchestral players between their afternoon and evening sessions.

This instrument of torture, the cinema organ, not to be confused with the church organ, shares pride of place for sheer horror with the saxophone, the harmonica and the concertina. They are all incapable of producing other than ignoble sounds. But I was in my teens and at first wallowed in the vulgarity of it by experimenting with the different stops which were able to reproduce [sic] the tones of the celesta, chimes, bells, whistles, drums, xylophones, motor horns and what not. Not bothering to look at the film, I sat convulsed with merriment as I listened to the extraordinary succession and mixture of noises I was able to evoke from my machine. During one tender love scene, of which I was oblivious, the astonished audience heard a fife and drum band marching in splendid rhythm, getting louder and louder as it approached: my *chef-d'œuvre* here was to give the impression of a motor-car which, tooting deafeningly on its horn, scattered and finally silenced the band. I was justly proud of this improvised *scena*. In another and frightfully tense scene where a murder was about to be committed I was wafted away on angels' music compounded of the harp and celesta. This was all great fun until I was suddenly aware of a voice hissing 'Ssssst' in my ear. It was the manager – how green and menacing his face seemed in the eerie gloom – 'What the thunder are you doing?'

But the most important stop of all on this sordid box of tricks is the tremolo. So sickened was I by its giant palpitations that I stilled its shuddering by shoving the offending stop home to rest. Once again came a complaint from the management – did they never go home? – intimating that the tremolo must be used at all times. Coupled with the vox humana it produced a noise like the bleatings of a flock of sheep. I employed this combination *ad nauseam*.

With my console situated at an oblique angle to the picture screen, it was impossible to view the films or follow the action ; magnificent creatures like Theda Bara or Wallace Reid became

24

tall out of all proportion and thin as wafers. I stuck, therefore, to my winning combination and to offset my boredom read novels by the light of my desk lamp. I held down this job for months and months. Everyone was delighted with me. You cannot go wrong with the tremolo and the vox humana.

Apart from my tedium at the cinema I enjoyed life. There were parties and dances with lots of pretty girls for which Toronto is famous, and there was, invariably, the usual accompaniment of drinks. I was more than partial to the charms of Venus and to Bacchus.

Yes, I had learned to drink, or rather how not to drink, in the Wild West when I was a 'Remarkable Boy' in an Eton suit. Prohibition did this to me. Often a visitor backstage on my forty-dollar tour would produce a pocket flask of rye whisky, half-fill a tumbler with it and add a dash of water, with the injunction that I must down it quickly. I felt it would be manly to comply but my first drink nearly tore me in half: only time and perseverance enabled me to master the situation.

Distinguished musicians paid periodical visits in those days. I heard Paderewski, that king amongst pianists, the brilliant Josef Hoffmann and the immortal Eugene Ysaÿe; saw Pavlova; and it was here that I first heard a singer whom I was one day to accompany, Maggie Teyte. She was performing in Gounod's *Faust*, a worn-out old chestnut of an opera but which at the time thrilled me. Maggie sang gloriously and so did her Mephistopheles, a Spanish bass, José Mardonez. But when Pablo Casals and Harold Bauer, names to conjure with, came to give a recital of violoncello and piano sonatas at the Massey Hall with its capacity of nearly three thousand, only about five hundred people bothered to come and hear them. Periodically the Philadelphia Orchestra under Leopold Stokowski paid a visit and their playing was a revelation to me. They combined forces frequently with the Toronto Mendelssohn Choir in the Ninth Symphony, *Messiah* and other choral works. This was a fine body of voices formed and trained by Dr A. S. Vogt who was head of the Toronto Conservatory and a worthy musician deserving of gratitude. But when a local wealthy patron of music expressed his opinion that it was beyond understanding why Mr Paderewski did not avail himself of the opportunity while in the city of having one or two lessons from Dr Vogt I began to understand what it meant to be provincial. Perhaps that taxi driver who told me so many years later in Australia that Sydney was the centre of the world was the reincarnation of Dr Vogt's enthusiastic supporter.

But it was here that I first made the acquaintance of Schubert's song cycles *Die Winterreise* and *Die schöne Müllerin*. James Campbell McInnes, a well-known singer from England and a friend of Hamilton Harty, settled down in Toronto and when he asked the Hambourg Music School (it functioned for many years after the Professor's death) if they could recommend a young pianist to accompany him, my name was put forward. I really believe the music of these marvellous songs laid the seeds of my future career. Playing them and loving them, the thought came to me then, 'This is the life for me.'

My parents were glad to get some help from me. I was earning between sixty and seventy dollars weekly, but they could see I was in a rut. They were convinced their son was an embryo Paderewski, although I was secretly aware that my playing had gone to pot, and they came to the conclusion, rightly enough, that no future as a concert pianist could be realized in a small city such as the Toronto of 1919. With great unselfishness and at a sacrifice they determined I must go elsewhere to study: London, England, was finally decided on. There Mark Hambourg lived and had signified he would accept me as a pupil; there, too, were uncles and aunts who would welcome the long-lost sheep with open arms.

Off I went and my boat train from Liverpool to London was met at Euston by a life-long friend of my father, with his little daughter Enid. This child of nine putting her arms round my neck and welcoming me so warmly was, after much persistence on my part, after many refusals from her, in fact after another quarter of a century, to become my wife.

3

Return to London

UPPER NORWOOD, a suburb on the south-east borders of London, would have been described by estate agents of the Victorian age as a desirable residential area; even in the first decade of the present century this would have been no misnomer. Successful City merchants, who were referred to as carriage people, dwelt there in large houses with pleasant gardens. I still bear a sentimental attachment to the place though only the husks of those once fine houses now remain, being split up into flats or boarding establishments, their gardens overgrown with weeds.

Decidedly it was once a superior locality but even in my youth I found the title 'Upper' suspect, having a suggestion of smugness, a jejune idea reinforced much later when James Agate wrote caustically to the *Sunday Times* from America that the ladies at a New York cocktail party were attired as if for an Upper Norwood tennis club dance. I preferred the name of Crystal Palace, for it was on the Norwood heights that this great glass building was erected. It sparkled in the sunshine. I knew and owned every nook and cranny of this amusement centre and its grounds, since my uncle and aunt invariably had me to stay with them on my school holidays and gave me a season ticket. But the red-letter day of the week was Brock's Firework Display in the Palace grounds, with its rockets, catherine wheels and set pieces. (The Crystal Palace's own funeral pyre when it was burned to ashes in a few rip-roaring moments was the finest firework display it ever gave, eclipsing anything Messrs Brock had ever contemplated. Many years later, in 1936, dining in Bayswater, I could see the blaze fifteen miles away. My feelings were wounded when my hostess exclaimed, 'And a good thing too, the place was a positive eye sore.')

Here on my return to England my relatives received me as if I were the Prodigal Son. How fascinating London was with its hansom cabs and open-topped omnibuses. Winter and summer, wet or fine, I would sit on the upper deck of a bus on my visits to Mark Hambourg's house in Regent's Park and soon caught the Englishman's perpetual cold in the head. I would arrive for my piano lesson with frozen fingers.

Mark taught me for a considerable period without fee. But I still had not found out for myself how to practise and could not be roused from my lethargy. To wake me up Mr Hambourg – as I naturally addressed him – would roar at me ; in an endeavour to spur me he would manifest utter impatience. I am convinced that he finally made a nominal charge for his tuition for my own good, because he found me so unrewarding a pupil.

After a year or so I found the small savings I brought with me from Canada had dwindled to nothing. I needed money. Youngsters take everything for granted and I was no exception. Nobody, I was apt to say to myself, helps me ; other students are sent by some wealthy patron to Cortot in Paris, to Schnabel in Berlin, but nobody ever gives me a penny. I see now how much I have to be thankful for ; first of all the sacrifices my parents made for me, then the lessons from the dear old Professor in Toronto, then the organ lessons, and finally the generosity of Mark beneath whose gruff Brahmsian manner beat one of the kindest hearts.

On the recommendation of Mark Hambourg I was engaged as accompanist on the Mossel tour. Max Mossel, an indifferent violinist but a first-class business man, ran a series of subscription concerts in Birmingham, Cheltenham, Liverpool, Glasgow and Edinburgh, and made a fortune out of them. His tactics with me, as no doubt with others, were to say he was losing money and I was engaged for five guineas per concert, paying my own travelling and hotel expenses. But Mossel was a unique personality and a wit. He liked relating how he wanted Harold Bauer on his tour and, finding his fee very high, told him that he would cable him in America when arrangements with other artists had been settled ; he would then know if he could budget for the great pianist. He did, finally, afford to have Bauer and cabled him, 'Book dates as arranged for x pounds. Mossel.' From the U.S.A. came the laconic reply, 'Guineas. Bauer', to be answered the following week by 'Pounds. Mossel.' These cables, 'Guineas' – 'Pounds', were exchanged weekly across the Atlantic for several months at no little cost to the senders.

But I only made a pound or two profit out of these concerts and was jubilant when I was offered from another source a tour of forty concerts at a bigger fee. I was booked at the time for a tour under Mossel and could not take them both. I begged Mossel, giving him three months' notice, to release me from my contract with him but he furiously declined to do so, telling me that if it became known that I behaved in this fashion my reputation would suffer. I had the impudence to write back, 'You are threatening me. I therefore refuse to play for you.' This was very wrong of me, of course, and Mossel never forgave me or spoke to me again ; if we accidentally passed on the street he would look right through me.

Yet it was while playing at a Max Mossel concert that Sir Landon Ronald first heard me. A famous figure in England's musical life, Ronald was then Principal of the Guildhall School of Music and a fine conductor. In his younger days he had been an accompanist, which perhaps was why he listened to the man at the piano with interest. 'Why be a solo pianist ?' he asked me. 'The world is overstocked with them. Stick to accompanying, it is one of the most delightful of all tasks in music and you seem to me to be extremely promising at it.' I have never regretted following his advice.

I still languished in the suburbs which was all wrong despite my affection for my kin. After all, I came to the world's busiest concert city in order to absorb its orchestras and chamber music, its piano and song recitals, and it was essential I live within approachable distance of the West End.

My first digs were at Swiss Cottage, Hampstead, and one of my fellow lodgers was a music enthusiast, not to say maniac. He gave singing lessons at which I accompanied, and at any and every opportunity when receiving or visiting friends, he sang. His voice, poor fellow, was excruciatingly painful to listen to. It had the effect on me then that the chewing of water-cress or the scraping of a knife on a plate has for me now. His intonation was intriguing and I would liken it to

that of Mrs Foster Jenkins, a wealthy amateur American soprano, who drew packed houses to hear her sing out of tune.
Together we went to all the concerts that were to be heard at
that time, but I soon tired of his companionship; he was too
aggressive for my taste and talked too much and too loudly. He
would deflate me by saying – his tone and tempo increasing
violently with each word – 'Just imagine if I, with my brain,
my temperament, my musicality, had your fingers—' and with
a shout and eyes glistening, 'Doesn't it dazzle you!' I did not
enthuse. In fact I did not like it. He, on his side, resented my
lukewarm reception of his ephemeral ideas. I removed myself
to Kilburn.

In this inspiring arrondissement my landlady was a kindly
home-loving German married to an Englishman, scion of a fine
old family. He too was so home-loving that he never left the
house. He was a retired dipsomaniac, his imprisonment self-
imposed: 'It reduces temptation, my boy.' Physical fitness was
his fetish though he never tasted the fresh air. Washing dishes,
cleaning furniture, hewing firewood, were his tasks, a routine
he performed wearing nothing but a white beard, wire spectacles, and a loin-cloth. Had it not been for the spectacles, held
together by a piece of string, he might have stepped straight
out of an El Greco. Sometimes he tied to his waist heavy iron
dumb-bells and with these he would stride bare-footed about
his menial chores loudly singing Handel arias. A fine-looking
figure of a man when you got used to it, he had the physique
of a forty-year-old though nearly seventy. His conversation,
cultivated and interesting, was frequently salacious. He was
never known to bathe.

As I say, one had to get acclimatized, but delivery boys and
such like, startled when he received them, were unwontedly
quiet and awed in his presence. Strange to the place, a man
repairing the kitchen range saw the charwoman donning her
coat and bonnet and muttered, 'Crikey, if you're going 'ome
I'm orf too. I'm not staying alone in the 'ouse with 'im.'

Even I was apprehensive when my landlord crept bare-
footed into my music-room brandishing a carving knife. But his
intentions were pacific, he only wanted to know if I were

practising Mozart or early Beethoven. I did not flinch too conspicuously as I answered, but I kept my weather-eye on the knife.

One afternoon a piercing scream reverberated through the house. Mine host had confined himself to his room for a week in order to write an essay on semi-precious stones. During this period when he was not seen by human eye (trays of food deposited three times daily outside his door) a new domestic had been engaged. It had been considered politic to keep this young woman in ignorance of the mysteries of the *ménage* and she was probably under the impression that the occupant of the top room was a bedridden invalid. On this particular day and believing herself virtually alone in the house with me, she was quietly dusting in the lower hall. Suddenly the silence from above was broken by loud and violent curses. Casting her eyes upstairs she fainted from fright at what she saw. I heard her scream above my practising and bounded to the scene to find her in a heap at the bottom of the stairs like Amy Robsart. Her alarm was not unreasonable: my friend had decided to emerge from his hibernation and was carrying the table he had used for a writing-desk down the stairs; unfortunately one of its legs had got caught and wedged in a balustrade, hence the vitriolic language. Thinking the house empty save for me, he was stark naked. True, his torso and head were hidden from the girl's view by the table, it was what she saw exposed beneath the table that gave rise to her concern. The old man was nothing if not considerate and quickly wrapping a towel round his middle he helped me to revive her. Alas, her return to consciousness gave her a first glimpse of the grizzly beard, the steel-rimmed spectacles, the white torso, and she sought refuge once again in oblivion. I twitted the old fellow about it later when the household had settled down by telling him he had made a complete exhibition of himself. 'I cannot deny it, dear boy' – with utmost good humour – 'but please to remember I did it by instalments.'

Twice a year my landlady gave a party. In formal fashion one sat round the room and friends diverted the company with songs, duets and violin selections. (How descriptive that word

'selections' !) Eventually cake was served – this was the mag-
net for it was unquestionably a gorgeous one – and a little red
wine. I only played once for her, being otherwise engaged
when subsequent soirées were held during my régime. But I
felt I was following in the right footsteps when my hostess informed me that at one of her parties – years previously – the
accompanist was Hamilton Harty and his fee one guinea.

These idylls from my sojourn in the precincts of Kilburn
Priory were but sidelights for, during this 'cave-man' period,
big changes came into my life generated by three new influ-
ences, not to say stimuli : I was heard by and engaged to play
for the Yorkshire tenor John Coates ; I met and became a
friend of Solomon, great man and pianist ; and lastly I paid my
first visit to the Gramophone Company and started recording.

4

John Coates

THE concert tour through the British Isles, referred to earlier, which most unethically I had accepted in the face of Mossel's objections, was with Peter Dawson. We became good friends and he engaged me on every possible occasion. Peter's sturdy frame and ruddy complexion belong to an open-air type of man : this was his nature and it came out in his singing. True he gave one or two Wigmore Hall recitals with me, singing Schubert, Brahms and the finer type of English songs most creditably, but his *métier* was the ballad – *Songs of the Sea*, *The Open Road*, *The Floral Dance*. I do not think anybody could sing such songs better than he, for he possessed a voice of fine manly quality, had a good technique, thanks to his early days under Sir Charles Santley, and these straightforward songs came to him naturally without him having to think about them or spend any time on their study. With the possible exception of John McCormack he was one of the finest sight-readers of any singer I have met and would take up a copy of a new song, seize immediately on its salient features, and be ready and willing to perform or record it forthwith. Songs of this nature, it may be argued, do not deserve time wasted on them, but it will be conceded that a man must be endowed with great facility and self-confidence to dare to mete out such cavalier treatment by way of preparation for a performance.

Peter was much happier pottering than practising ; his delight was to spend his day tinkering in his house or garden, or making a cabinet. With a more mature outlook, with industry, he could have become a serious artist, but as it was he settled down as a star turn in Variety where he had an easy and instantaneous success. I played for him several times at the London Palladium and, sitting in a dressing-room comfortable as a scullery, waiting for my call, would vaguely wonder if I were making any progress. But it was a salutary and toughening experience and did me no harm at all except in the Birmingham Palace of Varieties, where I finished the week's engagement with a sore shoulder. Here we shared the bill with a group of wrestlers with whom we became quite friendly and whose antics and tumbles we watched open-mouthed from the wings. Absorbed one evening in the spectacle of two giants tying one another into knots. I was gripped from behind by a little Japanese ju-jitsu expert, half my size, and thrown away over his head. He laughingly and most politely raised me to my feet. It was all in fun, and in a week or so I felt none the worse for it.

The English singer who impressed me more than any other at that time was John Coates the Yorkshire tenor. I had had several opportunities of listening to Coates who, accompanied brilliantly by Berkeley Mason, gave many recitals in the Chelsea Town Hall. They were a strangely assorted pair, the singer with his pink, cherubic and smiling face, the accompanist saturnine, dour and thin. Was there ever a singer with a wider repertoire than 'Arch-Chanter John' as Sir Edward Elgar dubbed him? He was equally at home in the Lieder of Beethoven, Schubert and Schumann as he was with the early English songs of Arne, Byrd and Purcell; he championed the songs of Bax, Ireland, Howells, Warlock, and was abreast of the younger school; the chansons of Weckerlin, Bruneau, Lully, tripped as easily off his tongue as did Fauré and Duparc. In Germany they called him the ideal Siegfried and Lohengrin. He had played many roles at the Royal Opera House, Covent Garden, under Sir Thomas Beecham, and it is a moot point whether he or Gervase Elwes was the finest Gerontius of that era.

Peter Dawson told me at rehearsal one day that Coates had heard me play and wanted me to visit him at his home in Chelsea. Thus began a long association. For four or five years Coates had no other accompanist but me. I was free, according to our arrangement, to accept other engagements so long as he was consulted. This was the nearest I have ever come to being tied up with one person. Many artists – Jascha Heifetz, Isaac Stern, Marian Anderson – have their accompanist under contract and he plays for no one else. No doubt this is lucrative for the accompanist otherwise he would not accept such an arrangement, but it seems to me he almost becomes the property of the other. It is a convenient arrangement for the violinist or singer, though it narrows the scope of the accompanist's work. When you are a free-lance you study not the programmes of one but of dozens of artists, you are not confined to violin music or the programme of an individual singer, your repertoire becomes endless – singers and instrumentalists of all schools pass through your hands and leave their imprint on your mind. Hard work it most certainly is, but your horizon is immeasurably widened, your repertoire and interests vastly enriched.

Though the road was hard, I look back on my John Coates days as being the most valuable, musically, of my life. He taught me all I know about accompanying. No pianist himself, he was yet able to convey to me the *meaning* of the piano part to a song and *how* to express that meaning in my playing. He would listen carefully and critically to every note in my part. It was a tough school; after two hours of slogging study he would say it was now time to start work. 'You play that as if you had never been in love' or 'Have you no zest for living?' 'This is angry, all venom, and you sound like a blancmange.' All this was hurled at me with scorn and acidity. Many a time I felt like revolting under the lash of his tongue but, thank God, I stuck it.

Coates sought me out originally because Berkeley Mason was prevented by commitments at home from undertaking a proposed visit to the U.S.A. with him. I therefore took Mason's place and became his accompanist for a year prior to this scheduled tour. No opportunity was neglected to rub in the fact that I was a poor substitute.

During this year Coates had me reduced to such a state of nervousness that I could hardly play the introduction to the simplest song at the start of a programme without wrong notes ; my fingers quivered as if with ague, my heels rat-tatted on the floor. Such was my state of mind that playing the piano was a torture to me. Bowing to his audience after his first song, under the noise of the applause he would turn and snarl at me with smiling moveless lips but with a baleful glitter in his eyes which only I could see: 'Come along, come along, wake up, man, what's the matter with you!' White of face I sat there wondering what *was* the matter with me. Yet, to my surprise, my accompanying received most favourable comments from the Press. When in self-defence I timidly mentioned this fact to Coates he would snort with indignation, 'The critics! What do they know about it!' As for visitors to the artists' room, their praises should go in one ear and out the other. 'Anyone coming round after the concert has *got* to say something nice.'

How could I at twenty-five, with any pretensions to manhood, submit to this treatment? Necessity. Necessity wielded a whip as cruel as the Coates lash. I was afraid of failure. I felt that this was my chance to make good; if I did not grasp it I was lost.

Of course we had been working like mad for months on the hundred and fifty songs we were taking to the States. Even on the eve of our sailing, after a half-hour broadcast from Savoy Hill, we repaired to another studio in the building for frenzied rehearsal and would probably have worked all night if Coates had had his way. Fortunately we were stopped when our whereabouts were discovered by some worried official, for the room was not sound-proof: we were breaking in on advertised programmes; owners of crystal sets wondered what on earth was happening.

The adenoidal tendencies of my youth still persisted to some extent. Our English love of living in draughts, of ensuring that our bathrooms are like refrigerators, of sitting on top of a bus (buses were exposed to all the elements in those days and I loved London so much I sat there in rain, snow and fog, drinking it all in – summer and winter – which was the kiss of death) and the thousand other ways that we court disaster in our island home made me subject to colds in the head. And it was with a particularly rich and noisy specimen that I climbed the gangway of our vessel bound for America. Coates was terrified, justifiably. Here was a singer setting off on a tour of concerts with a companion who might generously pass dangerous germs on to him. A singer with a cold is no good and if he tries to sing over his cold he risks being laid up for several weeks. He is a runner with a sprained ankle – helpless. If I were the greatest accompanist in the world, Coates said, no singer would put up with me if I were perpetually sneezing and coughing. However, he took every precaution and in the dining-saloon the two of us occupied a table for four – we sat not quite *vis-à-vis* so that I saw him out of the corner of my eye rather as a pawn on the chessboard looks at a knight. But as usual with a Coates sermon, I took it seriously to heart and for the benefit of any singer who might be fearful of coming into contact with me I pronounce myself as no longer in a dangerous condition. I am as careful as if I were a singer and at the slightest symptom of a cold I am most un-English ; I am not supine and say, 'What is to be is to be' ; no, I fight it tooth and nail and generally most success-fully.

At sea we rehearsed in the public lounge daily, and when we were not rehearsing I was practising on my own. It mattered not if an audience of two or three came to listen, the work went on and I would be corrected or chided in front of them. Very much the little boy. Owing to the rough seas the old hulk, on which we celebrated Christmas Day, sprang a leak and developed a pronounced list. It limped past the Statue of Liberty three days overdue. Had it taken a plunge beneath the waves it would have gone down to the sound of our rehearsing.

Every city we visited on this American-Canadian tour would see me following the same routine: scouring the town for Coates's favourite influenza mixture – never being able to get it – and then going direct to a piano in the hotel or the concert hall or some studio and practising feverishly. For I had now learned how to practise under any conditions. I could work in a hall where vacuum cleaners made as much din as I, where chairs would be shoved squeaking over the floor, where stage hands or janitors would stare curiously at me and try to engage me in conversation.

The only fresh air I tasted was, as I have said, the trotting here and there, through snow and slush, to every known drug-store in North America to find medicines or preventatives for

37

the great man. Save that it kept me from my piano, however, I did not grudge the drug-trudge, for Coates at the time was in the late sixties. This is a ripe period for a singer to undertake a strenuous concert tour.

That he had enormous success proves he had a wonderful vocal technique. He must have had amazing vitality, too, since there seemed no limits to his zest and stamina. Pianists and violinists have undertaken concert tours at a more advanced age than Coates, but not many singers; certainly I can think of no artist who has made at his time of life what was to all intents and purposes a début, for it was his first nation-wide American tour and despite his 'rave notices' (as they are called in America) his last.

Though I chafed under the iron musical discipline of Coates, I felt a firm loyalty towards him and did all I could to make conditions easier for him by looking after our travel arrangements, having the luggage weighed, tipping the porters – and the hotel staff. We would have a grand settling up once we were ensconced in our drawing-room on the Pullman.

I also assumed the role of protector. At nearly every town, especially in Canada, there would be a Society of Yorkshiremen anxious to visit and talk with this distinguished son of Bradford. They constituted a major problem for they pursued Coates with characteristic, kindly intentioned tenacity. In Winnipeg, Manitoba, Coates, exhausted and chilled after a long train journey from Chicago, decided to spend the day of the concert in bed. I sat in the sitting-room connecting our bedrooms to answer the telephone and put off reporters and visitors.

One man from Bradford telephoned six times between breakfast and noon, claiming to be an old friend: he refused to be put off. In vain I pleaded that Coates was ill, that he had to conserve his energy for a heavy recital programme that evening. 'It is his duty to see me and mine to see him. I shall be knocking on the door at midday.'

I begged the old gentleman to remain in bed and receive his visitor there but he would have none of it; he rose – bathed – shaved – dressed – and chatted with this old friend for an hour. When Coates finally ushered him to the door I heard him ask

his visitor if he were coming to the concert that evening. My
hackles rose when I heard this inconsiderate nuisance answer,
without apology, that he would have to give it a miss as he
would be refereeing a billiards competition at his club. This, to
my mind, was the last straw. As Coates quietly closed the door
he saw my fury and the comical side of it dawned on him. He
painstakingly lowered himself to the floor and sat with his back
against the door, blinking at me.

'How many years have you known your old friend?' I asked.

'We were never even acquainted, but he informed me he
used to see me on the Bradford tram when I was a boy of fifteen,' whispered Coates from his recumbent position.

This episode, trivial in itself, typifies the layman's lack of
understanding of the artist's work. From various remarks made
to me I gather that the musician is pictured as rising late in the
morning, taking the air at noon, lunching at his club, resting in
the afternoon and leisurely proceeding to his concert in the
evening. It is as simple as that. Few people on the fringe of the
music world – even managers or concert promoters – have
much idea of the slogging preparation, the nervous anxiety, the
problems of public performance.

On our return to England Coates and I were on far more
friendly terms. 'The American tour', he confided to me, 'was
going to kill or cure you, and I think it has effected a cure.' He
certainly remodelled me as an artist. He was not called the
Chelsea Potter for nothing. Rival tenors said of him that he
could make a poor song sound convincing; could take a rough
stone and turn it into a jewel. I do not claim to be a jewel but
I was certainly transformed by Coates.

If I had to sum up in one word all that Coates taught me I
would say – to work.

When I met the great man in 1925 I was an accompanist with
some experience behind me. I was good enough for accompanying ballads or battering down the keys for recording purposes.
I was, in fact, an average accompanist and my standard was
such as you will hear today at half the recitals you attend. The
critics called me 'sympathetic' or 'discreet' or 'able'. They still
hand out these epithets to me occasionally which shows, after

all, that either they or I have not made much progress.

An average accompanist, however, was not good enough for Arch-Chanter John. He went to work on me in a big way. He made the accompaniment a vital singing force with deepest meaning. He taught me how to listen to myself with fierce, unflagging concentration. He gave me my technique such as it is.

Coenraad V. Bos, a superb artist, tells us in his book *The Well-tempered Accompanist* that in his young days he played for Raymond von zur Mühlen and how, after their first few concerts together, zur Mühlen gave him no praise or encouragement whatsoever but, on the contrary, criticized him severely. After their fifth concert Bos was told, 'You must have played well today for I did not notice you.'

Coates would never have uttered so patronizing a remark as this. To him the accompanist was a partner sharing equally with him the mood of the composer. Joy, sadness, passion, exultation, serenity, rage, must be experienced by each of them. How can the singer project an emotion to the listener if the accompanist holds back self-effacingly from the scene? The accompanist whose chief recommendation is modesty or unobtrusiveness would have been no use to Coates. I have no time for him either. The accompanist should be a source of inspiration, and his playing must shine out in the marvellous introductions and postludes he has to perform. The serene glow of some, the passion of others should say something to the singer; his imagination should be loosened, galvanized by them. Far from not noticing, I would assert that the good singer gives the closest attention to the accompaniment – relies on it. Could such an undoubtedly fine artist as von zur Mühlen fail to notice the accompaniment to *Erlkönig* or, indeed, any accompaniment of any Schubert, Schumann, Wolf, Brahms song? Of course not, and he only spoke in this strain from the heights of his own ego to belittle the important role of his young colleague and to maintain the status of Mastersinger to that of Bos's respectful Apprentice. The fact that Bos recounts this experience in a book published near the end of his long, honourable and distinguished career is in itself an unconscious tribute to his own unspoiled nature, to his absence of ego.

Comparing myself to Coeny, as his friends called him, I can see that he was a much sweeter and nicer person than I. The reader, however, will have grasped that fact already.

Coates and I parted company over a matter of two or three guineas. We were engaged to appear at the Grotrian Hall, Wigmore Street, by Miss Gladys Crook of the Imperial Concert Agency. By this time Mr Coates (he was always Mr Coates to me) had moved fifteen miles away to Northwood, Middlesex. He christened his house 'The Coterie' and thither I had to travel for our work. Coates was to sing two groups; in addition I was to accompany May Harrison the violinist, and another singer whose name I cannot recall. My fee was about ten guineas. I told Mr Coates that two rehearsals would be enough for me but he answered, 'Enough for you but not enough for me. I shall have to get extra rehearsals with another accompanist and you will have to pay him out of your fee.' I would not agree. This was the last concert that we ever did together. We did not quarrel but I found it impossible to make time to get out to Northwood twice a week to rehearse, for I now had numerous concerts with Albert Sammons, England's premier violinist, with Beatrice Harrison, a superb 'cellist, and with many prominent British singers. There was also in the offing – and this was frightening to a young man still in his twenties – the possibility of my accompanying the mighty Feodor Chaliapin.

I cannot help regretting that our long and – to me – valuable partnership should have foundered over a few paltry guineas.

Although Coates and I saw nothing of one another for a year or so, there was no ill-will between us and I was sure we were good friends at heart: even so I was charmed – prior to my departure for a tour of South Africa with Marie Hall, violinist, in 1929 – when he asked me to dine with him at the Savile Club and talk over old times.

*

Coates's family life was serene. He had an adorable wife and fine sons and daughters, and yet I would not describe him as a happy man. He bubbled over with good humour at times, but a set-back such as he had in his action against the Performing Rights Society preyed on his mind for years. The gist of his case was that it seemed to him unfair that he should have to pay for the privilege of performing a song in public which the composer had brought in manuscript to him and which, by the very fact that he was going to sing it, induced the publishers to publish it. The costs of this case which he lost were heavy; Harry Plunket Greene and one or two other contemporary singers, though they did not see eye to eye with Coates, wished to contribute towards his expenses. He would have none of it and it cost him dear. In fact where Ben Davies, though he did not bear comparison with Coates as an artist, laughed his way through life – John Coates worried. He worried about his work, he worried about his voice, his rehearsing. Perhaps worry is always tapping on the door of your true artist. He had turned thirty years of age when, having made his mark as a baritone, he decided he was a tenor. He had the courage to throw up all his engagements and, studying tenor parts for all he was worth, started his career all over again in opera, oratorio and recital. Then, bless his heart, when he had turned seventy we find him worrying again : he turned out his old operatic costumes and started to slim with the extravagant idea of reappearing in opera. His physique, splendid though it was, rebelled : anaemia seized him. He lay on his deathbed in 1940 worrying over the fact that he could do nothing to help his beloved England in her struggle for existence (he had served with distinction in the 1914–18 war when already over military age) and it was while he was lying there helpless that I tried to express in a half-hour broadcast, with the help of some of his gramophone records, all the gratitude I felt for this man. He listened to me, and dictated to his daughter a letter to me signed by his shaking hand.

14 July 1940

My dear Gerald

Thank you for a great treat and for the charming and generous way in which you spoke of me. I appreciate it deeply, as I am sure you will believe me. Your playing comes out wonderfully. I can only say it was quite satisfying; even *I* am satisfied ! You are *facile princeps.* I cannot imagine better accompanying: it was altogether delightful.

I am sorry I am very ill and too weak to write, myself, but Dorothy is writing at my dictation. I have not been outside the gates for months and months. I am too weak almost to speak, never tell of singing, so I treasure recollections of our happy singing days together. Great days, Gerald, and good work. But it's a far cry from those days. All good luck to you, and thank you for letting me know about this broadcast. I would not have missed it for worlds. I am proud to have been in it.

Stick to it, my dear Gerald.

Yours ever,
JOHN COATES

5

Solomon

A YEAR or so after the First World War a concert agent and impresario, E. A. Michell, inaugurated 'The Pianoforte Society'. About six Wigmore Hall recitals were given every season and the artists chosen by Michell were of the finest calibre; Moritz Rosenthal, Emil Sauer, Artur Rubinstein, Josef Hoffmann, Alfred Cortot, Youra Guller and a Londoner, still in his teens, by name Solomon. This young man's playing and personality made a deep impression on me, and I attended his London concerts whenever possible. Michell, noticing what a faithful follower I was, asked me one day if I would like to meet the pianist after the concert. The ice being broken, I made a habit of going round to the artists' room at all his appearances to shake hands with a most remarkable man. Thus was born a friendship which, begun nearly forty years ago, has ripened with age.

I must speak first of Solomon's pianism and artistry – for these are what originally attracted me.

Here was an artist, it seemed to me, who combined the magisterialism of Schnabel, the delicacy of Gieseking and the panache of Rubinstein. Of what is known in this day and age as showmanship there was no trace in his playing, nor did he seek to stamp the music with his own personality: there was no suggestion that 'This is *my* Bach or *my* Beethoven'. He was the medium between the composer and the listener. Hearing him play Beethoven's Waldstein, Appassionata, Hammerklavier sonatas, it seemed hardly credible that Mozart was performed by the same pianist, so entirely different was his approach. Exquisite in Scarlatti and Haydn, he was transformed when thundering the octave trills in Brahms's D minor Concerto. He put himself devotedly at the service of the music's creator; one heard the message without distortion, a message transmuted through the mind and heart and fingers of one who is a perfect-ly balanced artist and man.

In all my experience I have never encountered a man so free of mannerism or idiosyncrasy. His outlook on music was emin-ently sane. If you looked for the feverishness of Horowitz, thrilling though it sometimes could be, you would not find it in Solomon, it would have been out of character.

It was not without mature consideration that the distin-guished critic of *The Times* wrote:

It would be impossible to wish... for a more majestic and Jove-like exposition of the Olympian D minor concerto of Brahms. Mr Solo-mon presents it in a huge span which he effortlessly fills.... Interpre-tation as demonstrated at this level is seen as fundamentally the same art as composition – *the art of creating music*. [The italics are mine.]

That short paragraph epitomizes Solomon's art. He exempli-fied the affinity between architecture and music. His concep-tions had an air of authenticity, they bore the stamp of permanence and inevitability. Honesty is a virtue regarded with opprobrium in these days – for it seems when applied to an artist to signify stolidity, dullness, lack of imagination; very well then, I will not use the term, I will say that Solo-mon's playing was informed with truth and rightness. It was fresh, vigorous, transparent. His outlook on his music – and on life, as I was later to discover – was so clear and so decided that his fingers, obedient servants to his mind, conveyed to you exactly what was in that mind.

And what fingers. Technique, as I have said before, implies more than mere velocity – but there are few pianists in the world who could measure up to him in his command of the keyboard. There was an ease of execution in all he did. If – and this is merely a personal opinion – during his early twenties he, like a young giant exulting in his strength, was apt to take fast movements too fast – like a racehorse with the bit between his teeth – then this was only a phase that a young virtuoso passes through. Solomon soon settled down to be the mature and noble master that we now know him to be.

Many people in different parts of the world have given it as their opinion that he is the finest player of a pianoforte concerto they have ever heard. He had the art of blending his tone with the orchestra whether he was in heroic vein or wooing the softest *cantabile* out of a Mozart slow movement. It was the music that mattered. He listened to what went on around him and he became one with his conductor and his colleagues in the orchestra.

This is what made his chamber music playing such a delight. I know that Lionel Tertis has never experienced such joy as when he and Solomon collaborated, while those of us fortunate enough to have heard Solomon, Francescati and Fournier in their trio recitals at the Edinburgh Festival in 1955 will remember them as long as we live. These trios were played – and I add this for the benefit of any violinist or violoncellist who may read these lines – with the pianoforte lid wide open ; and the balance was perfect.

As artist and man Solomon is incapable of deception. He performed the piano concerto of Arthur Bliss on many occasions, but once, playing it at a Promenade Concert at the Royal Albert Hall in London, his memory played him false in the last movement ; he instinctively threw his hands up in the air and stopped playing. Many a pianist would have jogged along somehow, hoping to deceive the listener, waiting for some prompting from the orchestra : but not Solomon. Sir Adrian Boult, who was in charge, called out immediately to the players and with very little pause they went back to an earlier page and this time Solomon negotiated the hurdle.

I do not feel that I am detracting from my hero in recounting this episode, for every artist – sooner or later – has some sort of mishap and it is no disgrace. I know Solomon was most upset about it, though full of admiration and gratitude for Boult's quickness and presence of mind.

This is the artist I look upon as my ideal pianist. This is Solo – a delightful and apt abbreviation of his name – on whom I modelled myself as a pianist. And it should not be imagined that an accompanist's aspiration, no matter how hopeless, to take a great virtuoso as his paragon, is incongruous ; the ac-

companist still wants to play his instrument as beautifully as
he possibly can even though he falls far short of his beau
ideal.

The wisdom of Solomon is not an empty expression to me
for it seems during four decades I have run to Solo when I have
been in trouble, have even consulted him sometimes over
matters pertaining to fees and contracts. I believe one seeks
advice in order not to take it. I nearly always followed Solomon's counsel and found he was unerring in his judgement.
But what still astonishes me is his quickness of decision; he
gets immediately to the heart of a problem and makes up his
mind instantly. This is a miracle to one who is undecided and
vacillating. Let me give two examples of his quick ripost.

As a youngster he was rehearsing a concerto with the
Bournemouth Orchestra under the baton of Sir Dan Godfrey:
without warning the conductor addressed him very rudely
whereupon the pianist immediately – and in the middle of the
concerto – left the platform, leaving the orchestra high and
dry. After gazing blankly at his men for a moment or two Sir
Dan chased out to the artists' room and, true to his generous
nature, apologized profusely. He was only just in time – for
Solomon had donned hat and coat and was preparing to take
the next train back to London. After this episode the two became good friends and Sir Dan, who liked packed houses as
much as anybody, engaged Solomon at Bournemouth on every
possible occasion.

Out of the blue he was telephoned by a tuft-hunting lady in
Bayswater. (She was known as a 'Patroness of Music' though
what she did not know about music would have filled a book.)
At one of her parties she told her guests, 'In my youth I played
all the violin concertos of Beethoven.' A sensational remark
since Beethoven wrote but one violin concerto. Solomon was
unacquainted with the lady. His fee at this time was astrono-
mical compared with other English pianists – the conversation
went something like this:

'I am giving a dinner party on 1 May, will you come and
dine and play to us afterwards? I can offer you an expense fee
of ten guineas.'

'Madam, all my engagements go through my agent and he will tell you my fee and conditions.'

'But Mr Solomon, I do not want to talk to your agent – this is a private affair, everybody comes here and plays for this expense fee of ten guineas.'

'But really, Madam, my expenses will not be anything like ten guineas; they will consist of taxi fares from my house to yours and back to my house again, amounting in all to six shillings. I suggest you consider seriously three alternatives: whether you pay me six shillings, whether you pay me my proper fee, or whether you abandon the project. Good morning.'

Solomon would travel the length of the land to give his services for a hospital or for any deserving charity, but he would never reduce his fee by one penny unless the promoters were people he knew and liked. I think artists who are so frequently imposed upon could take a leaf out of his book when it comes to crushing an importunate bore.

To digress for a moment, I must admit that some of these Patronesses of Music puzzle me. Very often they are the kindest and most generous of people, but why do they make music their hobby and why do they like to surround themselves with distinguished musicians when they most obviously evince no understanding of music nor attempt to learn anything about it? Emerald, Lady Cunard seized Ida Haendel's Stradivarius by the strings – just as one picks up a parcel – and brandished it in the air wanting to know why it was so precious. And in the very same drawing-room, when a section of Sir Thomas Beecham's orchestra was performing for a large party, our hostess called, 'Sir Thomas, when are you going to play that lovely piece of Delius that you were rehearsing this afternoon?'

'We have just this very moment played it, my dear.'

During the last world war Solomon gave recitals for the fighting forces through India, Burma, North Africa, Egypt, Holland, Belgium, as well as in countless camps and hospitals in Great Britain and Northern Ireland. I was told that in North Africa, and most certainly wherever he went, Solomon was not content only to give his recital for the troops in the large hall at night; during the day he visited four or five hospitals and played with all his soul on the little, out-of-tune, ancient and battered upright resident piano – and the beds and invalid chairs would be wheeled in around him. As for the three guineas for his big evening recitals (whether you were Solomon, Sir Laurence Olivier, or a young woman singing in the back row of a musical comedy chorus, your fee was three guineas for these concerts), he invariably distributed them among deserving causes dear to him; they must have totalled several hundred pounds.

Instances of his affection and generosity to me are manifold, but never did he give me a warmer glow than when he met me in the United States. I was on my way back from Australia and at the San Francisco airport as I alighted from the plane, there he was – in the middle of an arduous tour of the United States – to meet me at seven in the morning. We were both feeling exhausted but had a hilarious day. I was installed in a spacious suite at the Clift Hotel and we ended up by having a Lucullan dinner at Trader Vic's. When I departed for New York in the early morning I called at the hotel desk to pay my bill – 'I am sorry, Mr Moore, but we have had strict instructions from Mr Solomon that we are on no account to accept your money.'

As young men we had lots of fun together with our early morning tennis – to be succeeded by our early morning golf. Early morning golf, with increasing responsibility and pressure of work, had to be abandoned. We would meet of an evening, periodically, for poker at which Solo is an adept. If there is a weakness in Solo's character, if indeed it is a weakness, it is his penchant for gambling. His numerous sallies at the roulette table at Cannes have been so successful that the management, more than once, must have heaved a sigh of relief when he decided to cash in his winning chips for the evening. Then there are the horses. The totalizator cannot work out the mathematical odds quicker or more accurately than Solo. But once his love of racing led him astray. I was the cause.

A personable young man asked to see me one afternoon. He was a stranger to me and had an unusual line of business – a confidence trickster. After a long preamble about Baroness This and Lady That – names unknown to me – he came to the main reason for his seeking an interview, which was to inform me that Lady Luck – name unknown to me (I must give more study to Debrett) – was a certainty for the three o'clock race at Kempton Park. I could not resist telephoning Solomon to ask if there really were a runner of that name and to tell him of my mysterious visitor. At a quarter-past three he telephoned me and said, 'Damn you.' He had been unable to resist the impulse to have a flutter on Lady Luck who came nowhere.

*

How strange it must seem to the layman that a master of the keyboard should be the slave of his instrument. This is nevertheless a fact that is proved again and again. A perfectionist, Solomon set such a terrific standard for himself that he was merciless whenever he felt he had not quite attained the level he strove for. His working hours – and by working I mean intense mental concentration and the physical effort that pianoforte practising involves – would have struck terror into the heart of a manual worker. An inveterate sufferer from insomnia, finding himself at four in the morning unable to sleep, he would practise until his maid brought him a cup of tea which constituted his breakfast. And, of course, during the day he would practise, eight or nine hours – rehearsals with orchestras and journeys permitting. His conscientiousness – or, as I said earlier, his attributes of truth and rightness – forbade him ever to slacken or take things easily : a concert in a small town in the Middle Western States or in Lancashire was every bit as important to him as an appearance in New York, Paris, Vienna or London, and caused him no less nervousness, no less arduous preparation. Like Paderewski he had, sometimes, to be coaxed on to the platform. No wonder then that his physique, splendid though it was, collapsed under the strain : he was stricken with a grave illness in 1956. Some years have passed since he was last able to play his beloved piano.

Solomon's countless admirers the world over will rejoice with me when I say that this great man is slowly emerging from under the heavy cloud overshadowing him for so long. Thanks for this are due to the indefatigable loving care that surrounds him in his home; and thanks to the unquenchable spirit of Solomon himself. Never was his greatness more evident than during this incapacitation; Enid and I visit him only to come away invigorated by his cheerfulness, his gentle courtesy, his absolute lack of bitterness. The tributes he has received from his dear friends and colleagues – Emmie Tillett, Sir Malcolm Sargent, Lady Wood, Otto Klemperer, Dame Myra Hess, Benno Moiseiwitsch, Lionel Tertis, Walter Legge and so many others – have been touching. And it was a moving experience to sit with him at a Philharmonia Concert in the Royal Festival Hall and see members of the orchestra – Manoug Parikian, the late Dennis Brain, Gareth Morris – waving to him as they took their places. Their eyes spoke eloquently of love and admiration.

From the first day I met him, Solomon's integrity, purity of spirit, exquisite manners and, last but not least, his superb artistry have been an ever-present example and inspiration to me.

6

Recording in the Brave Days of Old

THE express train from Paddington on the Great Western Railway passes huge buildings at Hayes, Middlesex, where the letters H.M.V. are largely displayed. In 1921, and carefully taking a stopping train, I alighted here to make my first record for His Master's Voice with Renée Chemet, the French violinist.

The recording studio was set in the uttermost interior of the building, completely shut off from daylight and outside noise. It was purely utilitarian : no soft lighting, no carpets or curtains brought warmth to the scene. The walls – or shall I say fences ? – were of unpolished deal, the floor of hardwood and, in the absence of any absorbent of sound, my footsteps thundered on the bare boards, my voice boomed as if my head were in the resounding womb of some giant double-bass. I ran my fingers over the keys of the pianoforte and was appalled at the metallic harshness of its tone ; it had the brazen splendour of a brass spittoon. This brittle sound was not to be attributed entirely to the acoustics of the chamber, for I found on examination that the piano, by the tuner's art, had been rendered as percussive as possible by the filing down of the felts on the hammers. The anti-upholstery campaign had extended even to my piano.

A huge horn or trumpet protruded into the room and tapered away into the wall ; it connected obviously with the machine-chamber, gathering the sounds and recording them on the soft wax disc. Next to this horn was a window just large enough to poke your head through, though it could not be opened from the studio. Artists were not permitted in those days to enter the machine-room for the process was very secret. Arthur Clark, the head recording engineer, explained the signals to the violinist and me ; there would be one buzz (it sounded like a dyspeptic motor horn) to warn us to prepare, two buzzes to command silence, and finally a red light to tell us to play.

In any recording session, the first record gives the most trouble because it is here that quality of sound and balance between the two instruments have to be settled. Many test records are made and played back to the studio before artists and engineers are satisfied. They had great trouble with me because I tried to play softly. Mme Chemet and I were dealing with a *Berceuse* but Arthur Clark, opening his kennel window, insisted on my playing *forte* all the time. I protested that it was impossible to bang out the notes of a lullaby; I should wake the baby. The result, in the test played back to us, was that I was unheard. I did not relish this. The piano could not be placed any nearer than it was; already the violinist had hardly enough room for her bowing arm between the trumpet and the piano. In the last reckoning I obeyed official recommendation and clattered my part of the lullaby like a charge of cavalry, to the approval of all.

With Peter Dawson, the baritone whom I next accompanied, the problem of balance was still more difficult. It must be remembered that the horn was the centre of our world, immovable, and of course the singer had to stand in front of it. Nay, more than this he would have his head halfway down the trumpet. Only the piano could be moved, now here, now there, and I would frequently find myself, by the time the balance was adjusted and we were ready to make master records, with a bird's-eye view of the singer; his buttocks were all I could see of him while my piano would be as far away as the length of a billiards-room. It is vital for the accompanist to hear what the singer is doing and my difficulties under these conditions can be imagined since his sounds were not emanating from the end of him nearest to me.

But the recording of duets provided me with the greatest fun. It often developed into a free-for-all between the tenor and bass, or the soprano and baritone protagonists. Each wanted to shine, each wanted to hog the trumpet, and the charging and pushing that went on made me marvel that they had any breath left for singing. Victory usually went to avoirdupois, a welter being no match for a heavyweight. The recording staff and I would exchange delighted winks while these tussles were under way but I had to hide my enjoyment from the singers for each would come separately to me and whisper, 'What am I to do with this fellow? He doesn't give me a chance.' I was strictly non-partisan and always gave the same advice to each – 'Shove him out of the way.'

Our séance, then as now, was supposed to last three hours but often two or more hours would be expended by the artists and the engineers solving tonal and balance problems, yet we would often set down four or five songs on record with only forty-five minutes remaining. The music we made was registered on a plate of soft wax, but the very act of digging a needle into this substance and playing the tests back to us ruined the wax. We could not hear our final effort, which we judged, guessed or hoped was the best, until a week or more later when the disc had been processed. How we ever succeeded in making records, and good records at that, remains a mystery to me to this day.

Only two sizes of records were issued under the wax process; the twelve inch running normally for four and a quarter minutes and the ten inch lasting three minutes and ten seconds. An extra half-minute could be squeezed on to the disc in extreme cases by narrowing the playing grooves. This was avoided as much as possible since the quality of tone deteriorated when the needle approached too near to the centre. A symphony or sonata movement would take up much more space than could be contained in one record side and the movement would perforce be halted midway – sometimes on an unresolved discord. This hiatus was altogether unbearable even to us primitives. Often, therefore, in the case of a shorter piece the pace would be quickened to a preposterous tempo in our efforts to complete it in record time. When the red light gleamed, not a second was lost, we were away. Runners in a hundred-yard sprint were not quicker off the mark than we. This, in fact, is how Selma Kurz – that wonderful soprano from the Vienna State Opera – and I endeavoured to record Beethoven's *Adelaide*, a lengthy song with an extremely slow first section. Long before we had finished this *larghetto* we were 'buzzed' by the engineer who put his head through the window to inform us that he had come to the end of the wax. We tried again and now I played my introduction at a speed that would have shocked Beethoven but Mme Kurz was standing so far from the piano, with her head in the trumpet, that not hearing me, and no blame to her, she became slower and slower. I am afraid we had to abandon poor *Adelaide*.

Already at the age of twenty-one or twenty-two I was becoming experienced as a recording artist; on my undampened piano my articulation was clear and incisive when reproduced. Any complacency I might have felt, however, was rudely shattered by the arrival of the terrible Melba on the scene and I should probably have lost my life at her hands had not the diminutive Fred Gaisberg, recording manager, been in control. He, charming and urbane, could be a lion-tamer and he leapt manfully into the cage when I was being mauled by Dame Nellie. She came to the studio, some time after her retirement, with a protégée, Elena Danielli, to listen to her recording and, deciding that I was young, inexperienced and frightened, enjoyed herself thoroughly by bullying the life out of me.

'Can't you find somebody', she screamed at last, 'who can get a good tone out of the piano? He' – transfixing me with a glare – 'plays so hard.'

But Fred was equal to her.

'Listen, Dame Nellie, you have been having a good time in the studio. You just leave this boy alone. Come and sit in the recording-room with me and you will find that he and Miss Danielli will make good records.'

The great woman looked him up and down – a process that did not take much time with Gaisberg – but Fred turned on his heel and sauntered out of the studio. She followed like a lamb.

None the less the Hayes days were enjoyable, there was a happy-go-lucky feeling about it all and a session usually ended with mutual congratulations and back-slapping: a red carpet was put down for the artists and I banged away merrily on my piano.

Albert Coates, with Florence Austral, Walter Widdop and a reduced orchestra, recorded the entire 'Ring' down there. The recording of an orchestra through the medium of one trumpet was extremely difficult. Players could not be seated as they would be in a concert hall, spread out across the room, for half of them would be unheard. It was necessary for them to crowd round the horn ; so fiddles, 'cellos, double-basses and wind instruments were piled one on top of the other. The scene resembled the 'Death-defying Ride' at a fair.

Feodor Chaliapin did all his wonderful recordings down there, attended by the ubiquitous Fred Gaisberg, the only man capable of keeping the unruly giant in order. Chaliapin, highly nervous and impatient, roared like a bull when things went wrong and intimidated the conductor or anyone near at hand. It was just a happy family.

The arrival of the microphone on the scene put an end to convivial jollity. To claim that I contributed to this scientific step forward would be an exaggeration, but at least I was 'there' for I went down for days on end to Hayes when the new electrical process was being tested. William Primrose, the violist – then a violinist – was with me and we played the same piece over and over again so that expert engineers could experiment and carefully compare each different 'take'.

My younger readers acquainted with modern tape recording with its expert cutting and editing (of which I shall have more to say later) may have little idea of the revolution created by the microphone. It was the cat among the pigeons. Whereas trumpet recording was accepted as giving an approximate reproduction at best and a distortion at worst (you could get away with murder), the microphone effected a faithful likeness of the sounds we made. It is still beyond our capacity to see ourselves as others see us – perhaps this is just as well for our peace of mind – but now it was possible to hear ourselves in very truth.

A newcomer to recording, hearing his voice for the first time, would ask with dismay, 'Is this really what I sound like ?'

It was a salutary cure for smugness. To think in terms of accuracy and vigour which had sufficed in the past was not enough, we now had to sing and play as musicians, with refinement, with light and shade, with delicacy of nuance. I even had to play very softly when necessary. The making of a good

record, it was quickly realized, demanded infinitely more concentration and care from the artists. The microphone picked
up everything.

Yes, but please to remember that for all its sensitivity it was
still committing its report on to the archaic, crumbling soft
wax. A test once heard, though it might send us into raptures,
was useless and had to be repeated. In fact, two 'masters' were
demanded in case an accident occurred in the processing of this
blighted wax. These repetitions could be a nightmare. At the
slightest mistake or inaccuracy one had to begin all over again.
A song might be sung twelve times or more: after each performance I would turn to the singer and ask hopefully how he
felt about that, but he would shake his head sadly – he had
been dissatisfied with one note or phrase – its intonation or
quality. After half a dozen attempts both artists would become
heartily sick of the tune and have to whip themselves up to
give a semblance of buoyancy and freshness to it. We have
been, let us say, over an hour on this one song but the eighth
or ninth record we feel sure was good. Our happy smiles slowly
evaporate as the recording manager enters the studio and tells
the singer that he sang a wrong word, or the accompaniment
was too heavy, or says, 'Sorry, you will have to repeat it. We
had an accident on our side of the fence with the wax.' At last,
for the twelfth time of asking, the singer sings his part beautifully and without a blemish but, alas, I have made a blob. I
have played this accompaniment with accuracy until this very
moment but now these difficult passages, encompassed so freely before, become complexities and I begin to go dry in the
mouth and feel butterflies in my stomach, my fingers are all
thumbs. I practise these proscribed passages over and over
again (simultaneously the singer is working with full voice at a
phrase which is worrying him – a phrase which bears no relation to my exercise – the two of us are making a cacophony)
and we are like greyhounds in the slips dying to get going to
re-record the song. But we cannot re-record, we cannot get
going until the engineers signify their readiness. What an eternity they seem to take ! At last comes the ritual of the prepara-
tory buzzes (I pass my fingers soundlessly over the keys), on

comes the red light, up goes my blood pressure and I start to play.

The microphone exposed – and continues to expose – so many shortcomings in my playing that I sometimes wonder why I am ever re-engaged. I can only assume it is because I have never been found out. It is a humiliation to record a piece of music one has performed in public for years and then to discover how poorly one has played it.

But at least the mike has taught me to listen to myself mighty critically. I owe much to it though still hating and fearing it. And, though I live to be as old as Methuselah, I shall continue to come all over of a tremble at the words, 'Now we will go for a master.'

7

Sammons and Beecham :

Nightingales and Crocodiles

DESPITE my experience of accompanying all and sundry on gramophone records, and the rich harvest I had reaped thanks to Coates, I still considered myself an apprentice. Most of my work, so far, had been with singers, but the complete accompanist is equally at home with the violinist's and violoncellist's repertoire. I started to practise on my own the piano parts of Beethoven's fiddle sonatas and the César Franck telling myself that one day I would play them with Albert Sammons. With my eye on Beatrice Harrison, though little did she know it, I set to work on the Beethoven and Brahms 'cello sonatas. Was it an altogether fortuitous circumstance that I eventually found myself associated with these distinguished artists from whom, again, I was to learn so much ?

I had the luck to be engaged to play for the violinist when he and Mark Hambourg embarked on a series of sonata recitals in the provinces. All I had to do was to accompany Sammons in his solo group of small pieces for which my fee was two guineas in addition to my hotel and travel expenses.

To give a more detailed picture at this juncture, I ought to explain that I ran to the other end of England for a few guineas and frequently found myself in three places at once. For instance, I sat up all night travelling third class from the north, recorded at Hayes with Peter Dawson after breakfast, rehearsed with Chaliapin at the Savoy Hotel after lunch, caught an early evening train to Birmingham by the skin of my teeth – donning my boiled shirt during the journey – and strolled with strategic slowness into the Town Hall just in time to play for Sammons as if I had had hours to spare.

On such days as these I was like a volcano, slumbering on the surface but fuming within and wondering how on earth I would manage to keep my appointments and anxious that the hectic race against time would not affect my playing. I had the good sense not to blab about my comings and goings, for the artists who engaged me would not feel inspired if I arrived on the scene tired out: each thought, and rightly, that my work with him was of prior importance.

I am ashamed to confess that on the Hambourg-Sammons tour I made more profit than my famous principals: Mark always alluded to me as the 'man who never loses' and while we would get fairish houses in some places the rental of the hall, the hiring of staff, cost of advertising, expenses for four people (the fourth was Cameron Stockwell, our manager from the office of L. G. Sharpe's Concert Agency) all added up to such a considerable sum that it took a large audience to cover it. In a bitterly cold and draughty hall at York, after every account had been paid – including my two guineas – Mark and Albert cleared three shillings and a penny, which was divided between them. They sniffed noticeably after this chilling experience, and I fear they must have contracted colds, but on the whole took everything with equanimity like the good troupers they were. Besides, an enjoyable time was had by all for after the concert we invariably played poker till all hours. Mark's axiom that I was the man who never lost was not necessarily water-tight during these séances.

Albert Sammons more or less taught himself to play the fiddle and had only turned twenty-two when he was leading the small band in the restaurant at the Waldorf Hotel. Sir Thomas Beecham was dining there one evening and Sammons for Sir Thomas's benefit played the finale of the Mendelssohn Concerto at a breathtaking speed. Beneath his imperturbable exterior the conductor was impressed but, true to his nature, sent a waiter to Sammons with a note – 'Splendid, but the tempo is *allegro molto vivace*, it is not *prestissimo*.' None the less he offered the boy a place in a new orchestra he was forming. Sammons accepted, and shortly after became first violinist. 'This gifted and resourceful youth', wrote Sir Thomas in his autobiography, *A Mingled Chime*, 'developed into the best all-round concert-master I have ever met anywhere, uniting in himself a technical faculty equal to any demand made upon it, a full warm tone, a faultless rhythmic sense, and a brain that remained cool in the face of any untoward happening.'

Albert's fiddle was a Matteo Goffriller with an enormous tone. He chose it for this property, for though he could elicit a warm rich quality from any violin, he preferred volume to sweetness. Being a man of considerable physical strength his tone was bigger than most violinists with this Goffriller under his chin.

His faultless rhythmic sense was a tonic which strengthened and steadied me. (L. G. Sharpe – Paderewski's concert manager – once told me that he gave a ticket for an orchestral concert to a ship's engineer : the man had never heard a full orchestra nor was he musical. Curious as to his reaction Sharpe asked him how he had enjoyed it – 'The rhythm reminded me of my ship's engines.' Mr Paderewski, told of this, said, 'The man is right. Rhythm is the soul of music.' I had learned this through Coates's mastery and I now learnt it again through Sammons's rock-like steadiness.) His playing was thoroughly masculine and if, in the final degree, it lacked the tenderness of Kreisler, the polish of Heifetz, it lacked nothing of boldness and straightforwardness. Elgar's Concerto with its *nobilmente* found in Sammons a worthy champion. His bold, slashing style suited the Brahms D minor Sonata or Beethoven's Kreutzer – works we often played together.

In all the years I was with Albert I never remember him making a musical error. As a quartet player or in pianoforte trios or sonatas he was impeccable ; his knowledge of chamber music immense. For me as a youngster it was an education to play Beethoven, Bach, Mozart, Brahms, Schubert, Fauré, César Franck, with this man ; my inexperience, tentativeness, nervousness, were offset by his strong attack and confident leadership. I must have graduated for eventually Sammons and Moore were featured as a 'pair' by the B.B.C. The partnership was heard in scores of different sonatas over the air.

*

My acquaintance with the violoncello repertoire at this time was confined to those war horses, the Boëllmann Variations,

Tchaikovsky's Rococo Variations, and dozens of small pieces which no self-respecting 'cellist could afford to play in an important recital. Beatrice Harrison widened my outlook considerably by introducing me to the Beethoven, Brahms and early Italian sonatas and to contemporary works as well. For a fledgling such as myself, it was of incalculable benefit to be associated with such a ripe artist.

We had many London recitals together and to rehearse for these I often visited the Harrison family's home near Oxted in Surrey. Here they kept a menagerie. There were precisely sixteen Aberdeen terriers, a very fierce airedale, and a huge wolf-hound. The airedale, kept on a running chain on the principle of an electric hare at a greyhound track, was intimidating; he barked unceasingly and menacingly at any sign or scent of human flesh. I left him alone. It was the wolf-hound who conceived a passion for me. Standing on his hind legs he was as tall as I and, with his forepaws on my shoulders, gazed soulfully into my eyes, panting passionately with bared fangs. These were the only dogs. Of budgerigars, canaries and parrots, chirruping and chattering, many abounded, and two baby crocodiles ruminated noiselessly in a tank in the dining-room.

It was here in this quiet retreat that Beatrice Harrison played in her garden of nights to induce the nightingales to broadcast. My presence, fortunately, was not required at these *al fresco* invocations. What was done to stifle the vocal efforts of the savage airedale I do not know but there were other dangers lurking in the dark woods as one of my friends found to his cost. He – as a beater on a tiger shoot – groping through the thickets to disturb the sleeping birds, suddenly shone his torch on the interrogating ears of a startled donkey and frightened out of his wits leapt in the air, dropped his torch and got a thorn in his eye. His groans of agony, until he was discovered and relieved, mingled with the nightingale's plaint.

These broadcasts were an undoubted advertisement for the 'cellist and thereafter the ubiquitous nightingale was depicted in the corner of her concert posters and embroidered on her concert frocks.

Beatrice with her mother and her sister Margaret, violinist, took me to stay with Frederick Delius at Grez-sur-Loing.

It was heartrending to see this man – his ardent love of nature so movingly expressed in his music – paralysed and blind. So emaciated was he that his attendant, a German monk, carried him about as if he were a child. Yet he talked in his Yorkshire accent with vigour and contentiousness. I dare not repeat his diatribe on other revered composers; he used the term murderers to describe conductors in general. It was with some trepidation that I contributed my share of his 'cello and violin sonatas and concertos with Beatrice and Margaret but he was most kind and told me I was a musical man.

At the foot of his garden flowed the river. It was a Corot scene, dear to the heart of Delius. Though it was winter when I saw it, I could well imagine it was this scene that had inspired *Summer Night on the River* and *On Hearing the First Cuckoo in Spring*.

But his house was not so warm as his music. He was put to bed early, and Mrs Delius, seeing me crouched over the stove, asked me if I would extinguish the oil-lamp by which I was reading when I was ready to go upstairs. Although it was but eight o'clock I decided to retire forthwith and read in bed. But it was too cold in my room to read and it was too early for me to get to sleep. I lay awake half the night struggling to get warm and hearing always the low voice of Mrs Delius from the next room as she patiently read to her husband. I wondered how I was to endure three more nights of it and envied the Harrisons who, I imagined, were in much better case. At least I thought they were at that moment, but I was wrong. The three of them had put up at the local hotel. Accommodation here was limited and the three ladies were shown into one room and they all had to get into one bed. Mrs Delius, in making the hotel reservation, had booked in the names of Mrs Harrison, Margaret, and Baba (as Beatrice was known to her friends) and in consequence the manageress assumed that the name Baba was the English equivalent of baby. A small infant's cot had been erected in the corner for Beatrice to sleep in. When I came down for coffee in the morning, Mrs Harrison – who had slept in her boots and overcoat because of the dampness of the sheets – was talking to Mrs Delius, and my heart leapt within me when I heard her say, '. . . So as the result of this surprising telegram we shall all have to leave for Paris this evening.'

Delius wrote his violoncello works with Beatrice Harrison in mind, and no wonder, for she had a poignant and luscious *cantabile* well suited to his music. Her playing of one heavenly phrase in the 'cello concerto still lingers in my memory though it is thirty years since I heard the work. She sang on her instrument and had an infallible instinct for feeling when the muscle of the music slackened, where it tightened again, where it accumulated tension till the climax was reached. No woman 'cellist I have ever heard had, at once, a tone so powerful and sweet.

*

I was anxious now to dig much deeper into the field of Lieder. John Coates had put me thoroughly through my paces in the *Müllerlieder* but there was much for me to do of Schumann, Brahms, Wolf and Strauss, not to mention hundreds of Schubert songs of which I knew practically nothing. I longed to play for Elena Gerhardt and Elisabeth Schumann, who made periodical visits for Queen's Hall recitals, but was not yet sufficiently developed to match up to them. That it is dangerous to run before you can walk was proved to me in the early twenties when a concert agent brought me before Frieda Hempel, then at the height of her fame, to go through a few songs with her at her hotel. She asked me to transpose Schubert's *Wohin* down one tone. Now this is a song which any good accompanist should be able to play easily in any key at a moment's notice. I made a complete mess of it. Ironically enough *Wohin* means 'Whither?' I stumbled blindly through the song, not having the slightest idea whither I was going until I was politely shown the door. When I did eventually play for Hempel in her sunset days and was transposing, as Peter Ustinov would say, in all directions, she had no recollection whatsoever of the gawky youth of earlier years who had wasted half an hour of her time foozling *Wohin*. I did not jog her memory.

At one of John Coates's recitals a very courtly man introduced himself to me and invited me to play for him. I jumped at the chance of playing for a man whose knowledge of Schubert, Brahms, Strauss, Wolf, was so profound. He was Reinhold von Warlich. In Paris and London he had a considerable reputation as a teacher ; John Goss, Pierre Bernac and – much later – that immaculate artist, Bruce Boyce, were all pupils of his.

As a performer Warlich would be akin, I imagine, to Dr Ludwig Wüllner of whom it was said that the aspect of vocalization, of *bel canto*, as a means towards an end made no special appeal – the approach of the trained singer, the display of a beautiful organ was foreign to his nature and background. Reading between the lines one is led to the conclusion that Wüllner was ill-equipped vocally. In point of fact I have always been told that he more or less recited the poem to the music. Not a good singer perhaps, but an undeniably superb artist. When he performed *Erlkönig* you felt the wind whistling through your hair. I have felt similar excitement and pleasure listening to Harry Plunket Greene. Von Warlich belonged to this category : he had the taste and style of a first-class musician. The poem meant as much to him as the music and I never knew him at a loss for a word in texts of Müller, Heine or Goethe. His care and feeling for the word invested his singing with great authority even though his tone was unbeautiful and his intonation insecure.

Many aspiring singers coming under the spell of Wüllner, Plunket Greene and Warlich might be persuaded that it was not necessary to have a good voice to be a good Lieder singer. Their misguided view can be explained perhaps by the fact that, in England at least, established singers with good voices confined themselves to the oratorio, the English song, and the ballad.

When I accompanied Warlich, he steered his course away from the buffetings of advertised public concerts into the more sheltered waters of the American Women's Club, and drawing-rooms in Mayfair or Kensington. Occasionally he would sing at the Chelsea Music Club, where his admirers were so musical that they could derive great pleasure from his artistry. The general public could understandably not 'tune in' to him.

He sang everything in so low a tonality that it was impossible to accompany him with my piano stool placed amidships and I shifted it six inches below dead centre of my keyboard for greater comfort. Nevertheless, much of my present intimacy with the Lied is due to Warlich. I acquired too the flexibility to adapt myself to a singer whose vocal handicap prevented him from giving the long *legato* line that *Litanei* and *Du bist die Ruh* demand. He had not the breath or support that was needed for their drawn-out phrases and was forced to take such songs quicker than was good for them. Even so he made them sound convincing because of his sincere love and reverence for them.

He was an extraordinary and most interesting man. His father had been chief musician at the court of Tsar Alexander in St Petersburg. Warlich was steeped in music from babyhood. I only mention this because in many ways he was typically Russian and might have been a character out of Dostoyevsky. He could be radiant, especially if he were the centre of an admiring circle of eager but silent listeners, but the morrow would find him in the depths of a black depression, his large blue eyes staring at you unseeing. He talked so much about doing away with himself that I never believed for a moment he would carry out this threat. I was wrong.

8

Chaliapin and the Egg

GREAT was my excitement when I was invited to play for
Chaliapin. My almost parenthetical allusion to him in an earlier
chapter gives no idea of the dread I felt at the prospect of
working with this man. I had seen him many times in opera,
glaring at the conductor and more or less leading the orchestra
himself by beating time with his hands if the tempo did not
please him. In recitals with pianoforte, his behaviour could be
much worse. Not content with thumping out the rhythm by
banging his hand on the piano, he had strode over to the accompanist in the middle of a song recital at the Royal Albert
Hall and beat time on the pianist's shoulder. What should I do
if this happened to me? I would certainly not submit to that
sort of treatment and pictured myself walking with sublime
dignity off the platform. Such an event would cause a sensation
in the newspapers, and the idea quite tickled me. Due reflection, fortunately, told me that such a misadventure would do
no good to my reputation, for the press and public invariably
range themselves on the side of the big battalions, and I should
be branded as utterly unworthy. Friends whistled in consternation when I informed them I was going to play for the Russian
bass. Their uneasiness on my behalf was not complimentary.

Not without relish I was told of the unrehearsed 'scene'
at a rehearsal of Rimsky-Korsakov's *Mozart et Salieri* when
the conductor, annoyed by Chaliapin's gestures and stampings
at the orchestra, laid down his baton saying, 'Kindly remember that I am the conductor.' To which came the instant reply:
'In a garden where there are no birds a croaking toad is a
nightingale.' This gratuitous insult terminated the rehearsal,
for the conductor left the building.

Charles B. Cochran who was promoting a lot of boxing
contests at this period was also sponsoring this heavyweight
performance and he must have felt in his element. In truth,

he had a worrying time prevailing upon the conductor and singer to get together again; he finally tracked down the former who promised to be on the rostrum for the opening performance the following evening. Next he had to pin down the Russian who was staying at the Savoy, but on calling there he was told that Mr Chaliapin was out. The impresario sat and waited for several hours, and at two in the morning, in strolled the giant with the blandest and most genial of smiles. Of course he would be ready for the performance 'tomorrow – or rather this evening. Dear Mr Cochran, you should not worry – *I* do not worry – I have been walking until this hour in the deserted streets of your so beautiful London!'

I resolved that there should be no such warfare when I played for Chaliapin and accordingly asked Fred Gaisberg to let me have his music to study. I expected to receive a couple of dozen songs and arias, an ample allowance for one recital. Instead I found I had two hundred to cope with and they were delivered in a portmanteau. It was a huge task to study them all.

Fred Gaisberg, the Lord Chamberlain, ushered me to the Chaliapin hotel suite for my first rehearsal and as the King was waking from his siesta in the next room I practised Mozart's *Madamina* at lightning speed. Above my noise I heard thunder in the distance.

'What's he say?' I asked Fred.

'He says – is good.'

Chaliapin came in clad in a pair of shorts and a kimono round his shoulders. His torso was bare and was so white, so vast, it reminded me of a wall on the Acropolis. In most amiable mood he expressed gratification during our rehearsal that I knew how to make a *rallentando*.

I was hardly ready, lacking self-confidence, to shoulder the responsibility of playing for such a mighty but wayward personality. Yet he never betrayed any impatience. Certainly he would criticize. I shall never forget as I played the long pianoforte introduction to Martini's *Plaisir d'amour* that he stopped me, saying, 'Not just the notes. Not just the notes.'

68

It can be so beautiful if played thoughtfully and expressively but my uninformed strumming made it sound commonplace. I took it home to think about it and ever since that episode I have devoted more time, more practice, more concentration to the music that looks easy. The average accompanist, I am afraid, only practises with diligence that which *looks* difficult.

At a Chaliapin concert booklets were sold instead of programmes. They contained translations of arias and songs, all numbered, of what might or might not be sung. Before each song Chaliapin boomed out, 'Numbaire forty-five. Numbaire forty-five' – then he would give the audience a moment to read the translation and this would give the accompanist time to find the music. All this gave the impression that the great man was obeying a whim. No indication was given to me in the artists' room as to his intentions and for my first two concerts I was on tenterhooks wondering what was coming next. But the realization soon dawned on me that he kept pretty much to the same programme on every occasion and always included *The Volga Boat Song*. Eighty-five per cent of the music I had sweated over was never performed.

It is easy for a small man to write derogatorily of a big man, but I hope I shall not be accused of doing so when, in the light of my experience now, I say that Chaliapin was not a first-class Lieder singer. A song by Schubert or Schumann would be distorted out of all recognition by his wayward rhythm and his own personal interpretation of the poem. In *Tod und das Mädchen*, death would become a sinister threatening spectre, instead of the sublime comforter that Claudius's words and Schubert's music indicate. The Grenadier in Schumann's music and Heine's words, expiring to the sound of the Marseillaise, became a conquering and resilient figure ; and when I played the pianoforte postlude – which depicts the dying soldier's gradual collapse, the music was unheard, engulfed by the storm of applause which Chaliapin deliberately evoked. He was bowing to all sides of the Hall while I played and was walking off the platform before I had finished.

The most discriminating devotee of Schubert and Schumann would be swept, temporarily at least, off his feet, against his better judgement, by the man's histrionic mastery and the power of his personal magnetism. The accompanist, on the other hand, far from being carried away had to keep the coolest head; his senses had to be alert as he tried to anticipate what the singer would be doing next: was he going to hurry a certain phrase, neglecting to take the breath in the middle of it as sometimes he did? – this next note, was he going to make a *firmata* on it or was it to be abandoned quickly? Was it going to be made the climax of the phrase or would it become a *subito pianissimo*? It was all a question of mood – not the mood of the music but of the singer and whether he considered himself in good voice or not.

Yet there is no doubt in my mind that I was playing for a great singer, who could lift the audience out of their seats and thrill them as few basses before or since have been able to thrill. Certainly I have never been associated with a more exciting artist.

At one concert while I was playing an introduction which in rehearsal he had asked me to play as softly as a whisper, I heard a deep rumble coming from the singer.

'What's he saying?' I whispered to Gaisberg who was turning the pages for me.

'He says – more sonorous,' came a hiss on my left.

Many years later when I was accompanying Ferruccio Tagliavini, *The Times* described me as the 'elastic Mr Moore' and I certainly merited this description when playing for Chaliapin.

Chaliapin was a large lovable baby and I believe that many of his displays of temper could be attributed to impishness. He was a spoiled child who expected to get his own way and he roared or adopted a tragic, majestic mien when he was thwarted.

Fred Gaisberg suggested to me in Glasgow that we visit the singer's bedroom at noon to see how our hero was faring. There he was sitting up in bed with the only solid food he allowed himself prior to a concert: a boiled egg and coffee. The egg standing in its cup looked exceedingly minute by contrast with the enormous torso behind it. Each mouthful, one felt, had a long way to travel: up, up, precariously balanced on its spoon between the waistline and the lips and then down, down a very long way before it reached its destination. It seemed to me like sending a boy on a man's errand.

'Well, Feodor Ivanovich, is everything all right?' And then I saw a tragic performance, Boris Godounov's death scene was enacted: a distant mumble like the growling of a double-bass came from the depths of his being, as with beetling brows and mouth drawn down in despair I heard these anguished words, 'M-m-m-m-they bring no salt with my egg.' Gaisberg immediately summoned the culprit and – 'Say, do you call yourself a waiter? Say, you are not up to your job – it is too difficult for you.' I almost felt sorry for the waiter under the lash of Gaisberg's tongue. I stole a glance at Chaliapin: he stole a glance at me – and immediately the expression of saintly martyred majesty slipped from his face like a mask and, like a naughty schoolboy, he gave me a large wink. He was thoroughly enjoying himself.

I believe I was Chaliapin's first English accompanist; previously he had brought a Russian pianist with him. I was very happy when Messrs Lionel Powell and Holt asked me to play again for him the following season when they engaged him on their 'Celebrity Tour'. And here I made a mistake for I told L. G. Sharpe, Chaliapin's personal representative in England, that the fee I had received before and was now offered, was inadequate. As far as I can remember I asked for an increase of five guineas per concert. Sharpe advised me to stick to my guns, that Chaliapin would have no other than me, that the firm of impresarios would have to pay it. But to some concert promoters in those days, and to Messrs Powell and Holt in particular, the accompanist was hardly considered a supporting artist: he was a cipher of little importance, contributing no more to the success of the concert than the cloakroom attendant at the other end of the hall. The star, I would be told, is the draw at the box office while the accompanist does not draw a bean. And the star would get the fees he demanded – in Chaliapin's case four hundred guineas a concert – while the promoters would do a smart stroke of business by refusing to augment the accompanist's stipend by a few guineas. It was a waste of time to point out that the accompanist must be worthy of the occasion, that the singer would scarcely give of his best if he received inadequate support from the piano. Perhaps it was not the moment for me to adopt such an attitude. Later in my journey I was able to establish much higher fees for the accompanist, but I was too young then and perhaps not sufficiently experienced as an artist to justify my stand. At all events, I lost Chaliapin – never to play for him again.

9

Hack-work and Auditions

IT is out of the question to accuse Anthony Trollope with his exquisite prose of modelling his literary style on mine, yet I must coyly confess that we have at least one idiosyncrasy in common. In *Barchester Towers*, for instance, the author hastens to assure the reader quite early in the proceedings that the amorous attentions towards the widow, Eleanor, of the unscrupulous and ambitious Mr Slope will most certainly not meet with success: after which we settle down with a sigh of relief and read on in smug content. The author and reader, says Trollope, should move along together in full confidence with each other. Let the personages of the drama undergo ever so complete a comedy of errors among themselves, but let the spectator never mistake the Syracusan for the Ephesian, otherwise he is one of the dupes, and the part of a dupe is never dignified.

I, on my part, also delight to take the reader into my confidence, to relieve his tension and assure him that I do eventually reach the broad and sunny uplands where fat sheep may safely graze, but I frankly give warning that I am not out of the wood yet.

My name in the late 1920s was fast becoming established in the English musical scene. Thanks, too, to my recording engagements I was meeting more and more artists from Germany, Austria, France and Italy. Yet, frequent though my concert engagements and gramophone sessions were, my fees were still small and only provided me with the most modest of stipends. To augment my earnings it had been necessary for me to turn, some years earlier, to hack-work. I could not yet afford to abandon this most disagreeable form of music chore.

Hack-work or coaching – not to be confused with the noble calling of teaching – means leasing yourself out by the hour to this singer and that, while they are learning operatic parts, oratorios or songs. It involves dodging to and fro from one part of town to another. Every young accompanist must undertake this work, it is his first step up the ladder. Nor is it always disagreeable. What could be more delightful and instructive for me than my hack-work with such accomplished artists as Roland Hayes and Astra Desmond? I heard with rapture the pure stream of sound, marked the refinement of his phrasing, as Roland Hayes studied Arie Antiche – *Amarilli mia bella* – *Come raggio di sol* – *O del mio dolce ardor* – Handel's *O sleep why dost thou leave me?* What an enviable young man I was to be able to learn from this consummate stylist and to be paid for doing so: with Astra Desmond, whose versatility was refreshing, I went through Grieg in Norwegian, Kilpinen and Sibelius in Finnish, and scores of Spanish, Portuguese, Greek songs. With these the minutes flew by.

But the hours were arid with unmusicianly singers and these far outnumbered the good ones. Today there is not a professional singer worth his salt who is not the equal of a pianist or violinist in musicianship, but in the 1920s many prominent singers could not read one note of music. Even some of the stars of the great Opera Houses would learn their notes parrot-fashion; the hack-pianist being required to hammer out the notes over and over again until they penetrated and stuck in the singer's brain. An aria or a song would be tackled phrase by phrase and you would remain on one passage interminably, perhaps repeating it twenty times. And perhaps that very passage which, by its endless repetition, had driven you crazy yesterday would today be erased from the singer's consciousness and you would start the same process all over again until you arrived at the haven of indelibility. It took time. The minute hand of your watch seemed motionless – you were consulting it surreptitiously as you played when that amateur baritone with his feet pointing at a quarter to three lisped, 'Isn't it marvellous the way I contrast those two songs? You would not think it was the same person singing them.' But I recognized only too miserably the same little pixie all the time.

I had to journey to the house of one singer, an amateur, and my experience with her was most distasteful. She was extremely wealthy, or at least her husband was, and my twice-weekly visits to her mansion paid the rent. I suppose the little knowledge she had was dangerous, for it persuaded her she knew everything. Backed by her wealth, overwhelmingly arrogant, she told me once how, after Coenraad V. Bos had played the pianoforte introduction to *Die Allmacht*, she ordered him to play it again and to play it properly. 'Are you teaching me to play Schubert?' asked the astounded Bos. 'I want you to play it as Schubert wanted it,' was the grandiose reply. For she carried, so she said, the torch of Schubert: there was no one else; and she laughed pityingly at such insignificant names as Elena Gerhardt or Elisabeth Schumann. A feeling of degradation came over me whenever I visited her. Her ostentation exceeded all bounds, however, when she went to Vienna and sang with the Vienna Philharmonic Orchestra under Bruno Walter. How did it come about that an ignorant amateur with an unremarkable voice should gain this distinction? Money opens many doors. And on her return – 'My poor Gerald, do you realize that in Vienna, England does not exist? It simply doesn't exist!' (Many subsequent visits to Vienna have proved to me that this statement is not so extravagant as it might appear, though it would have been more accurate to say that to *some* Viennese nothing exists outside Vienna. These are more insular than the English.) But when after some heated argument with me she declared it was impossible for anyone to play for her who was not in love with her, I felt this was the last straw. Was I supposed, I asked her, to fall in love with everyone for whom I played? If so, my studio would be known as an *Agapemone*.

*

The above seems to have degenerated into a Hymn of Hate, wherefore I beg the reader to look with indulgence on this glimpse I have given him of the spiteful side of my nature. His patience is craved, however, if without continuing in quite so bitter a strain, I use this chapter to unburden myself

75

still further and speak of that which is the reverse of dear to my soul. I refer to Auditions.

If you are hacking or coaching young singers, you must expect to play for them when they are auditioned by some impresario, conductor or opera house panel. In company with a dozen white-faced mutes, fellow-candidates of your colleague, you sit on a bench or stand leaning against the wall of some bare and dimly lighted entresol, waiting for the same to be called. This is what happens in an opera house or a cabaret audition.

Yes, I have had the experience of playing at a cabaret audition. Many years ago a Red Indian Princess [sic] was singing a small part in the Royal Choral Society's production of Coleridge Taylor's Hiawatha at the Royal Albert Hall. When this run was over she had the idea of a cabaret engagement and asked me to play for her audition. It was arranged I should call for her at her hotel and walk with her across Piccadilly Circus to the room on Shaftesbury Avenue where she was to be assessed. Little did I think what was awaiting me. She descended into the foyer of her hotel in full war paint; head-dress of feathers, strings of beads, fringed tunic and trousers, knives and a tomahawk in her belt (a Princess?), and greeted me with a war whoop, 'How!' The attention of one and all was riveted on her. Why should I have worried? The accompanist at an audition is the most insignificant of mortals, yet I could not for the life of me look forward to that walk across Piccadilly Circus with nonchalance. As we set out I tried to keep a couple of paces behind her but she would have none of it, talked to me with the loudest of voices and – calamity – dropped one of her scarlet blankets in the road and asked me to carry it. I have never prayed more ardently for one of London's fogs; a pea-souper would have been an answer from heaven. Whether her audition was successful or not I cannot say. The mists of antiquity have enveloped her though they came too late to throw their protective veil over me, while I, escorting her across Piccadilly, was her craven-hearted Brave.

Mrs Percy Pitt, whose husband was one-time Director of Music for the British Broadcasting Corporation, asked me to play for two of her pupils who were being given auditions for the Royal Opera House, Covent Garden. This I did after I had thorough rehearsals with each of them. I was very young and my charges were necessarily modest, but what happened when I sent in my little account? I received the most abusive letter from the outraged lady: I should consider myself lucky she had taken notice of me: accompanists were tumbling over one another to have the chance she had given me: what sort of a rustic youth was I to dare to presume, etc., etc. It seemed to me, as I wrote in response to this tirade, that if I were not to be given a fee for the time and work I had devoted to her pupils, I should at least be thanked for giving freely of my services instead of being insulted. To this the lady vouchsafed no reply.

With Stuart Robertson, a well-established bass singer with a most pleasant voice, I shared a humiliating experience.

He was anxious to sing for Sir Thomas Beecham and a meeting was arranged at the Aeolian Hall, New Bond Street. Stuart and I waited in the artists' room until an attendant informed us that Sir Thomas was ready. We walked on to the stage and there in the dim light we spotted him, a lone figure in the auditorium.

'What would you like me to sing, Sir Thomas?' asked Robertson.

A drawling, languid voice drifted up from the centre stalls – 'Sing something you *think* you can sing better than anyone else can sing it.'

Stuart's face went pink.

'Then I don't know what to sing, Sir Thomas.'

'Then sing something you *think* you sing well.'

Sir Thomas's attitude cannot be described as kindly or generous but then he had never been a candidate at an audition. And when Stuart Robertson and I did eventually get going on some aria from a Handel oratorio, I heard, whilst playing the introduction, the *seigneur* urging me to adopt a quicker tempo ; he clacked his fingers and thumbs at me. But since my singer had endured the Beecham superciliousness – I had to stick to my post and put up with whatever was meted out to me.

Later on I made a vow never to play at any more auditions. Great was my embarrassment when Elena Gerhardt begged me to accompany a pupil of hers whom Sir Adrian Boult had promised to hear. I told her how I hated doing it, that I found auditions humiliating and distasteful. But it is difficult to refuse a friend and I was cajoled into it. It was during a nightly season of Promenade Concerts that, at the end of a whole morning's orchestral rehearsal, the singer and I arrived at the Hall. The conductor was obviously tired and hot, and anxious to rest before his evening performance : it was equally obvious to me that he had forgotten the appointment. But true to his word he patiently heard the singer. The only outcome of this unfortunate affair, so far as I could see, was that Sir Adrian regarded me for some months after with some suspicion whenever we met. And who can blame him?

I gave up auditions.

*

Years after, I 'crossed the floor' and became a member of several boards of adjudicators. Here, seeing it all from a different angle I found that the man sitting in judgement is the kindliest of creatures, most patient and sympathetic. Take me, for example.

It is the easiest thing in the world to pass judgement on the very good and the extremely bad, but the halfway mark or border-line case threw me in my first days 'on the bench' into a huddle : it was difficult for me to harden my heart when a sweet and modest maiden presented herself shrinkingly before me. This indulgent attitude, however, was unfair to other and perhaps less comely candidates.

Auditions were held during the war under the auspices of the Arts Council of Great Britain – to provide concerts in munition factories, hospitals, etc. To perform under these auspices was rightly regarded as work of national importance and we, on the board, while seeking to differentiate between those who uplifted the spirit and those who cast us into gloom, dismissed any candidate who attempted to 'play down' in order to gain cheap success. The music had to be good music to please the discriminating trio of judges of whom I was one.

We sat and watched an endless procession – fifteen minutes per candidate – of young men and women bringing in their fiddles, their 'cellos, their clarinets, oboes, voices.

A pot-pourri of a bizarre nature was played at one of these séances. Sitting behind the green baize table were Ferruccio Bonavia, one of the severest critics and most benevolent of men, with Ivor James and me on each side of him and we heard a piano, violin and 'cello trio play us a selection of tunes. (This word 'selection' is one of my pet aversions but it is used advisedly in this instance. I place it in my little cupboard with 'vocalist' and 'artiste' spelt with an 'e'.) As I say, we heard an arrangement of tunes ranging from Suppé to Schubert's Serenade, thence to Guy d'Hardelot's *Because God made thee mine* ; from here we leapt to a Beethoven Minuet finishing up with a medley of Scottish tunes. It was a long and tedious journey and my thoughts were wandering. I was brought very quickly to my senses by feeling Bonavia's left hand – I was sitting on his right side – groping for my right hand ; his right hand was already grasping Ivor's left. Our trio had completed their tour and their grand finale was *Auld lang syne*. Below the level of the green baize cloth our arms rose and fell as we silently kept time to Bobbie Burns's invocation.

I am at the present time on the committee of the Kathleen Ferrier Scholarship ; the Guilhermina Suggia Gift Fund ; the Boise Award, etc., and have sat with the severest critics – John Barbirolli, Lionel Tertis, Martin Cooper, Richard Capell, Joan Cross, Astra Desmond, George Baker and others, and their kindness and patience have been exemplary. I remember particularly Barbirolli whispering to me of a young 'cellist, 'This girl, we have agreed, passes the test – extraordinarily talented. But since I heard her last year she has developed one or two unpleasant mannerisms : I shall ask her to come and see me and have a talk with her about this.' How typical of the generosity of this extremely busy man.

An attractive personality is an advantage in competitions of this type for the auditor must take into account, especially with a singer, the presence and deportment of the candidate. More than this, the singer no matter if the voice is good does not get a recommendation if his physiognomy is wooden. His facial expression must reflect the moods of the words and music, and a failure to do this only too clearly shows that he is not *living* in the song: he is not communicating anything. Again, gesticulations are suspect, a spurious indication of temperament.

It was while serving on the auditions panel of the British Broadcasting Corporation that one was able to listen with complete impartiality, for here the candidates are unseen, their names undisclosed: they are judged purely by what is transmitted to the jury sitting in a room far removed from the torture chamber. (Television was an unknown monster at this time.) Lionel Salter, Leonard Isaacs, Herbert Murrill were some of the excellent musicians listening with concentration on these occasions and, in the privacy of our chamber, we expressed unfeigned delight when we heard outstanding or promising talent. Each member of the jury would write his own report and at a subsequent meeting, where the unknown would be identified by the programme he had performed, each report would be read and a decision made.

More than once it has come to my ears that a failed competitor has complained, 'The B.B.C. has a grudge against me', but this is utter nonsense. Nothing can be fairer or more impersonal than these tests, for the panel is made up of men who are only human after all, and if the singer, violinist, pianist, has the melting beauty of a Venus and Aphrodite combined, we in our listening den are blissfully unconscious of what we are missing and remain *sans peur et sans reproche*.

The judge, umpire, referee should be strictly impartial. I like the story of the man at bat who on being given 'Out' by the umpire turned to him and growled, 'I wasn't out!'

'You look in tomorrow morning's paper and you will find you were most certainly out.'

I was reminded of this at one of our B.B.C. post-audition

meetings when the Chairman announced with a glum face, 'Well you have failed the daughter of the Chairman of the Board of Governors'. And that was the end of the matter.

10

Wigmore Hall – the Lieder Club

ALTHOUGH I took on all comers and filled my engagement book, I was concerned principally with getting my name in the paper; the fee was of secondary consideration. As to the musical standard of my partner – I asked no questions.

All these concerts would be advertised in *The Times*, the *Morning Post* and the *Daily Telegraph*. The last-named's Saturday edition was blazoned with announcements and I would see my name as many as twenty times on the very front page. Spacious days, literally. Deserving concerts would be reviewed at some length by such men as Frank Howes, Francis Toye and Richard Capell, their instructive criticisms being of the greatest help to a serious artist. On the other hand they felt they were wasting their time when they were imprisoned in a hall listening to some ghastly fiddler or singer; and it was Ernest Newman, after one such experience, who exploded in the *Sunday Times*, 'Miss So-and-so sang on Monday last in the Wigmore Hall. Why?' Similarly in a terse comment *The Times* critic at the foot of some damning indictment added, 'Mr Gerald Moore accompanied – inscrutably.'

Because of its somewhat flattering acoustics, the Wigmore Hall was, and is, most suitable for recitals or chamber music and it was not uncommon to find three concerts being given there in one day at three, five-thirty, and eight-thirty. The Grotrian Hall, now defunct, and the Aeolian Hall, now a warren of broadcasting studios, would get their fair quota too. But the Wigmore was my favourite, and began to see a great deal of me; I seemed to spend half my life in the place as Harold Craxton had before me. In earlier days Hamilton Harty was believed to have had his bed there.

For the ambitious probationer anxious to make one London appearance it was the mecca: only on the following morning did he read that it was the end of his pilgrimage, the last resting place of his hopes. I was in attendance at many of these obsequies, the sympathetic and decorous mute. But I had no conscience in those days, I could not afford such a luxury and was convinced that many of these misguided neophytes gave their recitals purely for the benefit of the accompanist.

An institution behind the scenes at the Wigmore Hall is Mr Lake who turns the pages, moves the piano, fixes the lighting and is the confidant of all those recitalists whom he deems worthy. One evening he came to me in the artists' room, hardly able to contain himself, to say I was wanted on the telephone (this is situated at the rear of the stage and connects with the Box Office). I was playing for a violinist – a beautiful violinist. Let me make myself clear: her instrument was the violin and she was beautiful, but this nymph had no aptitude for music. Our first offering was Max Bruch's Violin Concerto – my piano taking the place of the orchestral accompaniment – and it was at the conclusion of this that I went to the telephone to hear the husky voice of Mr Ferruccio Bonavia, one of the *Daily Telegraph* critics, saying, 'My dear fellow, before going home I feel I must thank you for the glorious relief of your *tuttis*.' He felt for me. His valedictory message was impelled by sheer humanity.

At a recital under Ibbs and Tillett's management, where the singer sang consistently flat, my friend John Tillett rang through to me demanding, 'Why can't you play in tune?' Mr Lake, hearing this, told me of Henry Bird, a well-known accompanist forty years ago, who, during the interval of the concert, said, 'Young lady, I have tried playing for you on the white notes, I have tried playing for you on the black notes, but I simply cannot play in the cracks.'

This back-stage telephone at the Wigmore Hall, however, is dangerous, it is an instrument which should invariably be used *con sordino*.

Richard Capell never imagined in his wildest dreams that he would be involved in the body-line controversy, but so it was. (In a series of cricket matches between England and

Australia – as important to us as the World Series games are to Americans – an extraordinarily fast and accurate bowler, Harold Larwood, was accused by the Australians of aiming intimidatingly at the batsman rather than at the stumps. The sporting world was agog, and even diplomatic circles vibrated.) He said of an Australian lady's recital that many years of study were necessary before she should allow herself to sing in public again. I must add in justice that it had been a disastrous recital – all the critics left the hall in disgust after her first group of songs – and Capell's was the only press notice she had. She was convinced that he was biased because she was an Australian. 'It's this body-line trouble in the Test Matches.' And this, I believe, consoled her though I assured her that, so far as I was aware, Capell did not know the difference between first base and a maiden over.

A Spanish tenor, a bleater incapable of counting three in a bar, received deservedly dismal notices. My pleasure on reading them turned sour when the management informed me that the singer attributed his failure to me; that probably he 'had been spoilt in other countries by having really good accompanists.' I wrote him in terms which even I, in my passion for understatement, can describe as vitriolic. It would be too much to hope, be it never so demurely, that my letter struck him to the heart, but he has not been seen since.

But I must cut short this casualty list. It would be unfair to the Wigmore were I to imply that it is only the graveyard of false hopes. Many of the past great, whom we recall with admiration, and many splendid artists of the present, whose names we hail with enthusiasm, made their initial London recitals in this dear little hall. For music of an intimate nature – Lieder for example – it is ideal.

The backbone of most song recitals is the group or groups of Lieder. In England and America these songs surpass all others in the esteem of music lovers and I cannot foresee a future when this state will not obtain. Its field flows so rich with milk and honey that the singer is ill-equipped who has not devoted many years of study to it.

We had at that time, to mention half a dozen outstanding

artists, Flora Neilsen, pupil of Elena Gerhardt, Astra Desmond whom I accompanied in so many Schubert songs which had rarely been heard before, the brilliant Joan Hammond from Australia, the two disciples of Warlich – Bruce Boyce and John Goss – Steuart Wilson who introduced me to the glorious *Magelone Lieder* – and last, but by no means least, Mark Raphael, star pupil of Raymond von zur Mühlen.

Thanks to my association and frequent appearances with this goodly company I began to be regarded as something of a Lieder expert. Singers from Germany and Austria began to consider the possibility of having me to accompany them.

And then the London Lieder Club came into being.

This Society, for several seasons, gave a series of recitals on Sundays in the ballroom at Dorchester House and later at the Hyde Park Hotel under the direction of Messrs Walter Legge and John Richardson. With Walter Legge in charge it can be taken for granted that the programmes and singers were of the highest standard, with Legge's beloved Hugo Wolf very much to the fore. I was asked to preside at the piano for all the concerts. The roster of artists – all from the continent – was formidable: the Greek soprano Alexandra Trianti, whom Legge placed on Parnassus principally because she sang Wolf songs that he loved but had not heard performed; Gota Ljunberg, Swedish and flaxen-haired; Hedda Kux, a vivacious Viennese; that accomplished musician, Julius Patzak; the gentle Herbert Janssen ('es ist so schwer' he would say of every song, though he was never in any difficulty whatsoever); Friedrich Schorr, Gerhard Hüsch, Alexander Kipnis and many others whose names I cannot recall.

Of all these, Kipnis made the deepest impression on me and I believe his was the inaugural recital. We met for the first time on the morning of the concert and rehearsed a splendid and comprehensive programme of lesser-known songs by Schubert, Schumann, Brahms and Wolf, which I had been at some pains to study. I acquitted myself fairly creditably, I believe, but received no answering glow from Kipnis who had a deep-seated prejudice against an Englishman playing Lieder. I managed eventually to overcome this distrust and on the many return visits he paid to England I always accompanied him and we became the best of friends. He was a superb musician with a deep bass, dark in colour, but velvety and capable of a wide range of dynamics. His *mezza voce* was magical though not insubstantial, for one sensed latent power behind it. It was a quality Chaliapin had and which we can hear today in Boris Christoff though the fame of both these artists rests on their operatic work. Kipnis easily eclipsed them as a recitalist and I would award him the palm as being the most consummate musician of all the basses I have partnered. (I am not forgetting the superb Hans Hotter, but he is more of a bass-baritone than a deep bass.) But Sacha Kipnis was not easy, he was mortally afraid of the piano tone being too heavy for him. All deep-voiced singers and 'cellists are haunted by this fear, and it must be admitted that their tone can easily be outweighted by an inconsiderate accompanist. Kipnis liked the accompaniment to be a shadowy background. In compliance to this foible of his my piano sounds as if I were playing in the next room in our record album of Brahms Lieder, greatly to the detriment of the songs, in my opinion. Sacha would have preferred giving his recitals *a capella* if he possibly could.

Gerhard Hüsch's Lieder Club programme was all Wolf and Kilpinen, the Finnish writer. Ernest Newman proclaimed Kilpinen as the greatest song writer since Wolf, but I think this is rating the composer too highly. Most certainly he has an intimate knowledge of the voice and the piano. His songs are distinguished by strength and clarity of vocal line and by the sparseness of his writing. Not diffuse or unnecessarily complicated as Medtner or Bax can be, Kilpinen achieves profound and moving results by the utmost economy of means. I had never played his songs before and was unable to procure copies of all that Hüsch proposed to sing, consequently, I was eager to meet the singer and get at the songs. But what happened? Hüsch did not arrive from Munich until the day of the concert; we met at his hotel and I saw these songs and him for the first time one hour before we were due to appear before the public.

Even then most of this precious hour was spent by him sitting at the piano vocalizing while I sat in an armchair trying to study the songs as Hüsch sang his exercises. I was itching to get to the keyboard.

I got through somehow at the concert and that is all that can be said. It was a nerve-wracking experience for me but I cannot blame Hüsch altogether. He did not know me from Adam and probably said to himself, 'Devil take the hindmost in this exigency so long as I am in good voice.' All the same, Gerhard Hüsch was a first-rate Lieder singer and his records of the two cycles *Die Winterreise* and *Die schöne Müllerin* with the fine partnership of Hans Udo Muller show the sensitivity of his art. And, not too parenthetically I may add, so do his recordings for the Hugo Wolf Society with the writer at the piano, though these recordings were made several years later.

Like Kipnis and Hüsch, Friedrich Schorr was a renowned opera singer. He was the finest Wotan of the time, the Hans Hotter of his day, and travelled the world singing this magnificent role. In recital he was not in his natural element. He held the music in front of his face, thus placing a barrier between himself and his hearers, for he never committed one single song to memory. Four or five fat volumes would be tucked under his arm when he walked on to the concert platform.

All in all I could not help feeling, what with their habit of one last-minute rehearsal and, in some cases, their use of the score at their appearances – due perhaps to their reliance on the prompter on the operatic stage – these experts, superb as was their art, did not take their work so seriously as their British counterparts. It may be they felt supremely sure of themselves: a London appearance could be taken without trouble, in their stride. Certainly, thirty years ago many musicians bred in the Teutonic tradition visiting England would portentously raise an index finger saying, 'It is like this —' and proceed to propound some monumental cliché which one had learned from one's cradle. Without bitterness – for most of the artists I have quoted became very good friends of mine – I imagine they forgot we had learned much from the frequent visits of Elena

Gerhardt, Elisabeth Schumann, Lotte Lehmann. As for an Englishman understanding and being able to accompany them in Lieder, they did not believe it possible.

Elena Gerhardt

THOSE of us who were ardent lovers of Schubert and his royal succession received impetus, as I have said, from the visits to our shores of many authoritative exponents of Lieder. But the first of these that I heard, and the name that consequently leaps to mind before all others, is that of Elena Gerhardt. No other singer in the first decade of this century made such an impact on the public.

As a student at Leipzig Conservatorium the young Fraülein Gerhardt was picked out by Artur Nikisch as a talent so exceptional that very soon the great conductor insisted on accompanying her on the piano. Lucky audiences attending those early recitals heard that unique Gerhardt-Nikisch combination.

No doubt the public was attracted at first by the name of the master-musician, for the singer would be unknown to them, but in next to no time she, in her own right, had London at her feet. Her first recital was at the Wigmore Hall. Thenceforth a bigger auditorium was needed to accommodate her admirers and she graduated to the Queen's Hall. There, as a callow youth sitting up in the gallery, I first heard and fell in love with her singing. Even up there with only a bird's eye view, her effect on me was terrific; with her splendid head, her hair brushed back straight and flat in the German style, and her eyes and lips shooting the song straight at her listeners.

Surely the legitimate aspiration, the ideal of any accompanist would be to partner Gerhardt. I envied her admirable partner, Paula Hegner, never believing the time would come when I would walk on to the platform with her. The most I hoped for in the dim future, perhaps, was to meet her. This opportunity came when her brother, Reinhold Gerhardt, gave a recital in the Aeolian Hall, New Bond Street. By a great stroke of luck I found myself sitting behind no less a person than Elena herself. She turned and smiled approvingly at the discriminating listener who evinced so much enthusiasm for Reinhold's *Winterreise*. It was years before I met her again and in the meantime she had had several English accompanists, Harold Craxton, George Reeves and Ivor Newton, and was naturally very happy with them.

In the thirties, without warning, I was telephoned by the concert agents some months in advance of the date and asked to book a recital with her. In due course I presented myself at her suite in Claridge's Hotel for our first rehearsal.

I have often been asked how, as a young man at a first rehearsal, I felt when I started working with an artist whom perhaps for years, I had held in deep respect and admiration. The answer to this question is very simple: I am always nervous at a first rehearsal whether it is with Gerhardt, Casals, Menuhin, or with the veriest débutante. I look forward to the first rehearsal with as much apprehension as I do the concert, for here the personality and the musical potential of each artist is assessed by the other. Madame Gerhardt will be listening intently to every note I play, hearing how I respond to this mood, how I reflect that colour, testing my sensitivity to the treatment of a phrase, my adaptability to a change of tempo. She will know in a moment if I am the sort of accompanist whose quintessential function is to be unobtrusive. Miss Jones, rehearsing with me for her début, is certain to ask herself, 'Can I possibly work with this man?' 'Will he give me confidence or rob me of what little confidence I have?' This is why the first rehearsal is so important. Whenever possible I prepare myself very thoroughly for it so that the singer immediately has complete faith in me. Recovery after a bad first rehearsal is slow and painful and sometimes never fully attained.

I found Elena charming and unpretentious as most great artists are, and in no time we were gossiping and laughing together in our pauses between songs. But chatting or not I took my work too seriously to take my eye off the ball. She was not the person to deliver a harangue (a violinist with whom I was preparing a programme preached me a forty-minute sermon before I had laid one finger on the keys), every suggestion was made *through* the music. Occasionally would she sense that I felt a song at a slower or quicker tempo than she and then she would explain why she differed from me. She hated tentative and unsubstantial support from her partner; like John Coates, she disliked the accompanist who was too retiring. 'Never', she said, 'be too discreet when playing for me; the voice and piano in these songs are of equal importance.' This one dictum – delivered almost as an aside – is one of the few she laid down and I never forgot it.

From that rehearsal at Claridge's till the day of her retirement Elena Gerhardt had no other accompanist than me.

Nervousness when appearing in public, far from being moderated by experience, increases as reputation and consequent responsibility grow. Gerhardt was one of the exceptions to this rule so far as I could tell. Rarely, if ever, do I remember her vocalizing. She would sit quietly before a concert, chatting about anything rather than the music. Did I like her frock? Was she getting stouter? ('Nikisch used to tell me one cannot have too much of a good thing.') During the course of the concert she was a model of dignity and composure, consulting unhurriedly her *aide-mémoire* between the songs.

Elena was such a mistress of tone-colour that Ernest Newman declared that were she to sing one single note unaccompanied, the listener would know whether she were in the major or minor mode. Her whole personality seemed to change as she lived through each song – for with never a movement except by lively facial expressions, she was able to bring us mood upon mood. In Brahms's *Immer leiser wird mein Schlummer* an ailing woman seemed to be singing, so pale and wan – without loss of line – was the voice. In the serene *Feldeinsamkeit* she had a curious and extraordinary way of dematerializing her tone at the end of each verse so that the world seemed to stand still; it remains a mystery to me how she spun out her tone in the song's long drawn phrases without apparent need of breath. But in *Die Allmacht* she was a diapason, and the organ-like accompaniment never threatened for a moment to submerge her ringing tone. Indeed, in the Hellenic songs of Schubert her voice shed its femininity, she positively attacked you in *Der Atlas*; and to the massive throb of *Dithyrambe* your body wanted to sway in concert with hers.

No woman has ever been able to sing the *Winterreise* cycle as she; one forgot she was a woman; yet one remembered the fact only too poignantly when moved by her *Frauen-Liebe und -Leben*. And has there ever been a singer who could project laughter and gaiety more realistically than she?

And yet, behind all this, Elena was in reality a simple person. All her subtle effects of colour, mastery of rhythm, structure of phrasing were not the results of probing analysis or cold-blooded calculation; she sang as she felt. She was an instinctive singer, born to sing.

Loving England, and greatly loved in return, Elena took up her residence with her husband, Dr Fritz Kohl, in a charming house in Hampstead. Here she accepted pupils from all over the world and thither I went to rehearse for our concerts. Years later when I married Enid, we went together for my rehearsals, for Elena and Fritz loved her dearly. After dinner we played bridge.

A concert which Elena and I anticipated with pleasure was at Colchester and this, though I am reluctant to speak derogatively of a Gerhardt appearance, must be written off as a failure. It was not that Elena was in bad voice or I below par; the audience too was as responsive as one could wish. It was – that there were no oysters! We shared a passion for oysters but, though it was the season for them, not an oyster could we find. Years later, after a lecture I gave in Colchester, a stranger came into my dressing-room, telling me he was an oyster grower and would I like him to send me some: I suggested that a couple of dozen would be most acceptable. My modest request was amply rewarded by my receiving a sackful of twelve dozen oysters a few days later. I hastily gave a few dozen away to various friends and took the rest to Hampstead where Elena and I regaled ourselves with four dozen each, watched by Enid who, glory be, is allergic to this exquisite *fruit de mer*.

Without emotion, without the air of one making an historic pronouncement she said to me quite quietly one March day in

1947, 'Gerry, this next concert at Liverpool is going to be my last.' I did not attempt to dissuade her for I held her judgement in too much respect. When an artist senses a declension of power she is wise to retire. But I had a feeling that we would be in a rather tearful mood in the Adelphi Hotel after our concert. To my relief Fritz announced he was coming and begged me to bring Enid. Only we four knew of Elena's decision, no trumpets were blown at the Liverpudlians and none of those present were aware that they were witnessing an historic event, seeing the curtain fall on a career ; a career not only brilliant for Elena personally, but a career that has been of inestimable value to music. How melting it would be – had I the power – to describe the scene afterwards ; the mutual tributes, the melancholy embraces, the silent tearful toasts. Nothing of the sort occurred, for we had the merriest of parties and said our 'Good nights' amidst gales of laughter.

*

Elena was a woman of great courage : I have indicated this in my account of her philosophical acceptance of her retirement. She showed this again when facing up to the loss of her husband, the wise counsellor and warm companion. Then, living alone but cheered by a coterie of affectionate pupils, by those admirers old enough to remember her singing when it was at its glorious best, by the proximity of her brother Reinhold and his wife whom she extricated from East Germany, she bore her last years with the same simplicity and dignity that had marked her singing of bygone days.

When in these present times a programme of German Lieder fills the large halls of London and New York we should remember Elena Gerhardt and be thankful, for it was her missionary work that did so much to convert the English-speaking world into worshippers of Schubert and his royal succession.

It is a tragedy that more effort was not made by those concerned to record this great artist when she was in her prime. The fact that so few of her records are available is a reproach to the gramophone companies.

12

1929–39. Yehudi Menuhin.
Feuermann and Suggia in a
Tea-fight

THE decade from 1929 till the outbreak of war was an extremely busy period for me with concerts good, bad and indifferent, with recordings, and all the necessary practising and rehearsing that these engagements involved. In addition I had singers to coach and several pianists to teach. The day was not long enough. What with the constant comings and goings of singers of all types and sizes, of instrumentalists of every description, my German maid who everybody told me was the double of Marlene Dietrich was occupied in letting people in and letting people out. My appointment book was as full as a fashionable dentist's. I had married a charming Canadian lady in 1929 but we separated by a mutual agreement five years later. Thus my bachelor way of life was resumed and I found it impossible after an exciting concert to come home alone, jump into bed and go off to sleep. I sought relaxation at a well-known bridge club where I played nightly till two or three in the morning, with a whisky and soda at my elbow. This is not to be recommended as a habit, though I liked to ease my conscience by recalling Ernest Hemingway's strategy that 'every good man drinks a little more than he ought'. (Jacques Thibaud when asked by an English admirer for the secret of his wonderful *vibrato* replied, 'It is your beautiful Scotch whisky'.) The hour after lunch was a particularly trying time for me and I indulged in many a nap when presiding at a lesson.

Of all the concerts – and they must have run into hundreds – I remember only the very very good ones and the downright shameful ones. 'Fancy forgetting me, you played for me before the war,' I am often told, but I ward this off perhaps rather clumsily by inferring that I should only have remembered if their recital had been bad.

My first appearance in Paris took place in 1931. I went to

play a Brahms programme for Reinhold von Warlich in the small Salle Chopin. (The recital included the *Vier ernste Gesänge* and I was told it was the first public performance of these songs in Paris. I find this hard to believe even allowing for the French indifference to Brahms.) In the audience was an old friend – the son of my professor in Toronto – Jan Hambourg the violinist who seemed very proud of me and introduced me to everyone as a Hambourg product. I had arranged to return to London the following day but he persuaded me to prolong my stay in Paris in order to hear Yehudi Menuhin. He and his wife Isobel were great friends of the Menuhin family. Already Yehudi was world-famous though but fourteen or fifteen years old, and Europe in particular was ready for him since the visits of Kreisler and Heifetz were rare. This *Wunder-Kind* had appeared several times in London creating a furore but I had never had the opportunity of hearing him. His programme, that memorable evening for me, had three works, the Bach E major concerto and Lalo's *Symphonie Espagnole* conducted by Georges Enesco with which he began and ended the concert – and in the middle, the Elgar Violin Concerto which Sir Edward himself conducted. I will only describe my reaction by saying I was transported. Since I keep no diaries, all my impressions herein recorded are dug up from the recesses of my memory ; it is an indication of the profound effect Yehudi's playing made on me that I remember every detail of this programme and concert.

To my great delight I was taken by Jan and Isobel out to Ville d'Avray the following day to have tea and supper with the family. Yehudi, on a new bicycle, careering round and round the garden at breakneck speed, I found to be as charming and simple as one could wish, completely unspoiled, modest and lovable.

I was told afterwards that Yalta, Yehudi's younger sister, conceived a 'crush' on me which was very pleasing to hear. Lest it should be imagined, however, that I am compromising a lady I would like to add that she was eight years of age at the time, while I was thirty. I have never met her from that day to this.

To be Yehudi's accompanist in his early days would not have been an unmixed pleasure for he came under the iron discipline of père Menuhin. 'After breakfast you will practise for two hours – that Mozart sonata needs much more work from you – and then you will rehearse with Yehudi until luncheon, then you can take a walk for an hour and afterwards you will rehearse with Yehudi again.' The same accompanist went everywhere with the family Menuhin – I should not have relished being in his shoes.

I would call Yehudi Menuhin the most interesting violinist at present before the public; interesting because he is human. He is not a machine, he has his ups and downs; at one moment inspired, the next lackadaisical and below par. He does not seek popularity the easy way by playing drawing-room pieces, his intellect loves grappling with and mastering a big work. Give him a Bach sonata or concerto and he is in paradise, likewise his listener. But partnering him I have quickly recognized when he was playing music that did not set him on fire. How can a man whom Bartok embraced as being his ideal interpreter show very much interest in a Paganini concerto? Sometimes, therefore, Yehudi gets a bad press. Whether or not he reads his critics I do not know, but he seems impervious. He smiled at me before some concert and said he had just been asked if he were nervous when playing in public and he had replied, 'Only the critics are nervous.'

Never will he lose an opportunity, between engagements, to play in a string quartet or a pianoforte trio at a friend's house, for he loves chamber music. At Elena Gerhardt's one night we played trios with Casals – Louis Kentner and I taking turns at the piano – till four in the morning.

Now a man in the forties, Yehudi still retains his hold on the affections of the public everywhere. His fabulous success as a youth, the abnormality of an infant prodigy's life, the adulation of the multitude, have left no scars.

It was not until Yehudi visited Europe in the war years that we worked together – yet I played for some superb violinists at this period, 1929–39. Mischa Elman, Nathan Milstein, Albert

Sammons, Max Rostal, Ida Haendel and, full of rich promise, Eda Kersey. Both Eda and a flaming boy from Israel, Josei Hassid, died before they matured. Hassid indeed, with the possible exception of Menuhin, was the most brilliant youngster I have ever heard. He was the Fischer-Dieskau of violinists – incandescent.

'Cellists would deny it emphatically were I to ask if their instrument is less arduous to master than the violin, yet, though outnumbered by violinists, it seems to me there are more good 'cellists than good fiddlers. At all events more violoncellists than fiddlers came my way: more good ones that is, for I naturally forget the second raters; there were Emanuel Feuermann, Gaspar Cassado, Guilhermina Suggia, Hans Kindler, Pierre Fournier, Raya Garbousova, Josef Schuster, and of course the mighty Casals, for whom I was destined to play much later.

Feuermann had a technical perfection akin to Jascha Heifetz on the fiddle; he was impeccable. His first appearances in London were made in trio concerts with, I believe, Schnabel and Carl Flesch. But for several years his own recitals were received so luke-warmly by the press that he thought of abandoning his English visits. After one recital with me he received a notice the following morning so devastating that he told me, 'If a pupil of mine received that notice I would tell him to give up the 'cello.' Artists from abroad find England a hard nut to crack; success is rarely, if ever, achieved overnight; they are in consequence jubilant when at last they are acclaimed by the critics. Feuermann's triumph in England came under the baton of Toscanini. The maestro insisted that Feuermann and none other should be his soloist in Richard Strauss's *Don Quixote*. It was a memorable performance and I telephoned him in the morning to tell him he had really 'unlocked the door'. Toscanini was overjoyed with him and the newspapers in raptures. Alas, this was his swan-song in England, or very nearly so. Shortly after he was touring in the United States and he remained there when war broke out in Europe. His home was Vienna and being Jewish it was impossible for him to return. He died of a deadly disease and of a broken heart when the news reached him that his father, also a musician, had been forced to his knees by the Nazis and made to scrub bare-handed the sidewalk outside his house with caustic soda.

Guilhermina Suggia had the greatest admiration for Feuermann. She, although a rival 'cellist, was the most generous of colleagues and, greatly excited by his playing, invited him to tea with her. The meeting was not a success. She had two instruments, a Stradivarius and a Montagnana. She played to him at his request first on one and then on the other but he only allowed her a few notes before seizing the 'cello from her hands and eliciting twice the volume she was able to procure. (Feuermann held the opinion that the 'cello was a man's instrument in that it requires physical strength to produce a big tone. The left hand of a 'cellist – and of a violinist – needs to be sinewy as well as supple, and the stretches it has to contain are huge. The bowing arm needs such an adjustment of weight that the player is able to get as big a tone at the tip of the bow as at the heel. Casals's wrist is like a cable.) Suggia felt deflated and secretly resentful of Feuermann's tepid appreciation of her, while he afterwards dismissed her to me as 'a drawing-room player'. But Suggia was very popular in London. Her striking appearance, caught and emphasized so superbly by Augustus John's portrait (John swore he would never paint a 'cello again), gave an impression of boldness, romance and colour. She persuaded you her playing was passionate and intense, but the reverse was the case: it was calculated, correct and classical and, like her nature, equable. She was far from being the fiery *prima donna* she appeared.

Perhaps Cassado's playing intrigued me more than anyone's. He was full of ideas, full of originality. He had some contraption on the bridge which amplified the tone so that when I played for him, even in *morceaux* such as Fauré's *Après un rêve*, he would sit in the bend of the piano and my piano lid would be opened on the long stick so that he could hear all my tone. Some purists, while admiring him as an artist, condemn him for this gadget, saying it takes away the character of the true 'cello timbre. But I must say I like it. Cassado is the only 'cellist when playing a concerto with orchestra whose every note of the solo instrument can be heard.

The concerts with these artists were highlights but there were shadows as well and many a Wigmore Hall recital makes me shudder to think of it.

My good nature was sorely taxed by the third-rate violinist who at our first rehearsal asked me who was the most popular violinist in England. After some thought I told him – not understanding the import of his question – that I supposed Kreisler was really most beloved by the English public. 'Good, then I will play here in the Kreisler style.' No doubt in Paris he had played in the Thibaud style.

13

1929–39 (continued)

Elisabeth Schumann and the Queen's Hall

ON the night of 10 May 1941, one single incendiary bomb destroyed the most beloved concert hall in the world, the Queen's Hall. It is now a car park. My concerts there with Elisabeth Rethberg, Dusolina Giannini, Frieda Hempel, Frieda Leider – the one and only recital she ever gave in England – Elisabeth Schumann, Ria Ginster, Jo Vincent from Holland and the two Greek singers Trianti and Nicolaidi, are warm to the memory.

These were all big occasions. The Rethberg recital was given when she was at the very zenith of her powers. Ezio Pinza was present at rehearsals with her and I recall with amusement how overcome with wonder he was when he discovered I was reading at sight some simple songs.

Frieda Hempel after a long absence from England now made a welcome come-back. She was a little difficult because she wanted me in several instances to cut out my piano postludes. Included in her programme were two Hugo Wolf songs, *Er ist's* and *Ich hab in Penna einen Liebsten wohnen*, each with brilliant and difficult piano parts and *Nachspiels* after the vocal line had finished. 'Just play a chord when the voice part ends – else my applause will be spoiled,' she insisted. But I would not give in to her. To do what she wanted would be an insult to the composer, I argued, and it was offensive to my *amour-propre* into the bargain: knowledgeable listeners would say that the difficulties were beyond me. I had to stand firm too over wearing fancy-dress. Her recitals of Jenny Lind programmes made it incumbent on her to change into the costume of the Jenny Lind period, no doubt, but I did not relish donning a green frock coat and climbing into the fawn trousers that had been handed on from accompanist to accompanist during the course of the Hempel tours. Besides I look bad enough already.

But of all this constellation my especial pet was Elisabeth

Schumann. An adorable person who, like her singing, was all sunshine.

She sang with a smile.

Before a concert she would sing her exercises and – full of trepidation on hearing a frog in her voice – would put words to her scales, 'Ja, my dear, that's a profession.' Then to the A major arpeggio, 'Why do we do it?' But on the stage all her nerves were cast aside in the sheer joy of singing.

She chose with wisdom songs which came naturally and easily to her. Just as in opera her choice fell on such roles as Susanna and Sophie rather than on Fidelio or Elektra – so in her recital programmes she preferred Mozart's *Das Veilchen*, Schubert's *Auf dem Wasser zu singen*, Schumann's *Aufträge*, Richard Strauss's *Ständchen*. These songs seemed to belong to her and I rarely hear them without thinking of her. This, however, gives a false impression of her art, suggesting that her repertoire consisted of a series of gay, quick-moving songs. True she avoided the dramatic *Die junge Nonne*, *Der Zwerg* and such, but no one could sing the *Frauen-Liebe und -Leben* more movingly, or sustain with deeper feeling or steadier line *Nacht und Träume* and *Ave Maria*; as for Strauss's *Morgen* it was incomparably lovely for the stillness and serenity she imparted.

Listening now to the record we made of the Schumann cycle, 'Woman's Love and Life', I marvel that it was made when Elisabeth was in her sixties. Her singing life was much longer than most women's because her voice was so perfectly produced. Naturally, as she aged her range became more restricted though the silver purity of her tone never suffered. No sooner did such and such a song become an effort to her than she crossed it off her list. Rehearsing with me for her last concert in London she confided that Wolf's *Frühling übers Jahr* was now beyond her, 'but it is down on the programme. What can I do?' We tried it half a tone lower. She looked anxiously at me. 'What do you think, my dear?' Without any hesitation I told her to delete it from her programme and instantly she was all smiles. 'Mein Schatz, now I shall enjoy the concert.'

She returned to England after the war and from a Sunday afternoon concert in Newcastle we travelled back to London.

Sunday rail travel in England is never enjoyable for the trains are crowded, are subject to delays and diversions due to repairs and maintenance on the line, and, to add to one's tedium, the restaurant cars are conspicuous by their absence for travellers are not expected to eat on the Sabbath. This was a tiring journey. Suddenly Elisabeth asked me what Messrs X and Company were doing. X and Company was our agent and it was our little play to infer that while we were travelling and singing, incurring all sorts of discomforts, our agent was sitting at home relaxing (I do not mention his name since he was a personal friend of Elisabeth's and mine). Answering her question I would say, 'Now he is sleeping.' Arrived back at the London terminus at midnight we found there were no taxis. Seizing Elisabeth's bag and mine I plunged down to the underground in the hope of catching the last train. At the bottom of the stairs I heard a voice behind me, 'Gerald, Gerald'. I looked up and spotted Elisabeth in a flock of people coming down and she called out, 'X and Company' – and inclined her head on her hand, pretending to be sleeping.

The dénouement to all this nonsense came a few days later when there was a Schumann recital at the Central Hall, Westminster. It was under the management of X and Company and the head of the firm was there personally to look after us. Just as we were stepping on to the platform to begin our concert, X pulled the curtains and said loudly and clearly, 'X and Company are *not* sleeping this evening.' There was not a second in which we could exchange a glance, though we longed to burst with laughter. It is still a mystery how our little joke reached the ears of X and Company.

Schumann was incapable of meanness and I never remember her saying an unkind word of anyone. Perhaps I can give some idea of her warmth and generosity by recounting the following history. During her sojourn in New York, conducting singing classes at the Curtis Institute, she invited my friend Lies Askonas to stay with her. 'Tomorrow,' said Elisabeth, 'a young singer from Vienna is making her début in the Town Hall. She is called the second Elisabeth Schumann, she wears her hair as I did with a white streak and I do not think I like all this, for I have a feeling she is imitating me. She starts her programme with Mozart, just as I did. We do not go.' But the next morning Elisabeth was singing and chirruping like a bird, 'Yes, my dear, we do go to hear Irmgard Seefried this afternoon.' Elisabeth, so Lies tells me, did not respond very enthusiastically to the Mozart songs, but when the Schubert group came and *Nacht und Träume* was sung – 'This is wonderful singing, I hope I sang it as well as that in my best days.' But when Seefried sang the Hindemith Sacred Motets – specially written for her – Schumann burst out enthusiastically, 'I could never at any time have sung those songs like that.' She hastened to the artists' room and folded Irmgard Seefried in her arms. One can imagine the joy of the young singer when the identity of the great lady was made known to her.

As she stepped before her audiences, Elisabeth Schumann warmed their hearts by her radiant smile, her charm and the simplicity of her manner. She at once communicated to them the pleasure that she herself derived from singing. She seemed to the man sitting in the back row of the gallery to be radiant with *joie de vivre* ; he was convinced that this radiance was not assumed just for the occasion ; put on as it were with her gown. He sensed that the sweet smiling aura surrounding her was the real woman and I can assure him he was right.

14

1929–39 (continued)

Maggie Teyte and some English Singers

QUITTING my seat in the auditorium at the end of a concert I found Fred Gaisberg standing in the foyer of the Wigmore Hall talking to a petite lady – the same height at himself – who looked at me with a mischievous twinkle in her eye as much as to say, 'You don't know me but I know you.' I was destined, I am happy to say, to see that impish expression very often. Apart from her Mélisande at His Majesty's Theatre I had never heard her sing since that far off day more than twenty years earlier when she sang Marguerite in Toronto, with a touring opera company. It was Maggie Teyte. Her faithful friend and superb accompanist, the late George Reeves, being domiciled in America, I began my long association with her.

My experience with French songs had been considerable: I had played often for Pierre Bernac (Francis Poulenc accompanied him in France but could not always get to England with him) and this had been of inestimable benefit to me in the study of Debussy, Fauré, Ravel, Duparc, Chausson, Poulenc and their forerunners. Today young singers flock the world over to Bernac's studio in Paris to learn the French repertoire. Yves Tinayre the tenor was a veritable archaeologist in unearthing lost treasures; at his concerts I played French music I had never heard before and have never heard since and I attended all Claire Croiza's recitals, though I did not work with her. In England we had our own Francophiles with that polished artist Anne Thursfield leading the way so that my experience with the French School had been considerable.

Maggie Teyte, however, was in a world apart. She had studied many of Debussy's songs as well as *Pelléas et Mélisande* with the composer himself and I was rightly anticipating that she would shed a new light on them. That the creator of guileless pianoforte pieces such as the Arabesques and *La fille aux cheveux de lin* was not the complete Debussy picture I knew by his Violoncello and Pianoforte Sonata, a passionate sardonic work with its occasional merging into more sensuous moods. (What an advantage to be *au fait* with the output for violin, violoncello, pianoforte, as well as the songs of each composer. This wide perspective is enjoyed by an accompanist.) True, Debussy was an impressionist but there were iron and vinegar in his make-up as well. Was it not he who described Grieg's music as a pink bon-bon stuffed with snow? Therefore, while it was incumbent for the accompanist to use plenty of sustaining pedal for washes of colour in some songs – *Clair de Lune* – *C'est l'extase langoureuse* – *Les Cloches* – to play with almost Mozartian clarity in *Green* where we see the dew sparkling on the freshly plucked flowers, it was essential in *Le Faune* for the piano part to be demoniacal. (The singer portrays the two frightened young lovers in the forest suddenly confronted by the effigy of an evil-looking satyr : the piano, in sinister vein, drums out the rhythm of an impious dance.)

Maggie Teyte confirmed all this. She described to me the character of this man – Debussy : his impatience, his cynicism, his gloom, gaiety, and his voracious sexual appetite. (It seems that no woman within a radius of six miles of Claude Debussy felt quite secure.) Knowing the vivacity of Maggie I ventured to ask her how she managed to resist the advances – surely inevitable – that her youthful comeliness must have inspired. 'I was not his type,' answered Maggie demurely.

Her knowledge of Debussy songs, through the composer's tutelage, was more profound perhaps than her intimacy with the works of other composers, but she was, of course, a mistress in this entire field. How extraordinary it is that a young girl from Wolverhampton should have been chosen by Debussy for his ideal Mélisande in preference to any French singer. Her training in Paris under Jean de Reszke was rigorous naturally, but she evidently had a flair for this vein. She sang French music with more authority than her own native songs. I am sure she will agree with me when I say that of all the numerous records we made together of Debussy, Fauré, Ravel, the ones which gave her the most trouble were the few Purcell songs sung in English.

In fact Maggie by temperament does not conform to one's conception of the typical English woman. Many singers could be found who in the last analysis might be described as theoretically superior musicians to her, but they lacked her magic. None of them gave you that spine-tingling thrill which was her especial attribute.

We became, and remain, very good friends. As a colleague Maggie was stimulating and amusing and, be it added, quite unpredictable. You never knew what she was going to do next. She telephoned me one day to say that Wednesday was the only possible day she could rehearse with me for our concert the following week : the Milhaud songs were new to us both and we must, simply must, get at them. Accordingly we booked a Wigmore Hall studio from midday for two hours. I arrived on the scene as Maggie was finishing a lesson with a soprano. Quite nonchalantly she greeted me with the information she had left Milhaud at home, 'so let us try for fun with Megan Foster these charming Schumann duets'. After a moment, 'You are playing a lot of wrong notes, Gerald dear.' I swivelled round from my keyboard and replied, 'No doubt, but I am a very surprised man. I go without my lunch in order to do some vital work on Milhaud and suddenly find myself playing – for the fun of it – Schumann duets.' This little *scena* was conducted *senza rancor*, I might add, for Maggie was not a sulker any more than I.

She was in America, where after the war she resumed her brilliant career, while I was preparing with an erstwhile pupil of hers for a London recital. This lady, a charming singer, had invited a dozen or more friends to hear her dress-rehearsal in the Wigmore Hall. We were approaching the end of the programme when, in the middle of a song and startling the daylights out of everybody, a voice boomed from the gallery at the far end of the Hall : 'In what language are you singing?' It was Teyte in person, returned unexpectedly. 'How delightful to see you again, Maggie. How are you?' I called, rather with a view to easing the tension than with any curiosity as to her health. But she disdained to answer me ; it would have spoiled her entry.

When Enid and I, after a long wait through many vicissitudes, were able to marry, one of the first persons I told was Maggie Teyte and her eyes filled with tears of joy. This is typical of Maggie.

Now by chance we find ourselves living almost next door to her in London. We never meet except by appointment – and when we do it is enormously amusing. If by any chance we run into one another at nine in the morning when we are busily going about our affairs, we avoid looking at one another. She is a perfect neighbour. And she is as vivacious, intriguing, lovable and, thank God, unpredictable as ever.

*

I cannot think of another English concert singer who had at that time an international reputation such as Maggie's. Eva Turner was world-famous, of course, and Joan Hammond was beginning to spread her wings but both of these thrilling voices were devoted principally to opera.

But we had very fine singers in our midst with whom it was a pleasure to work. In the specialized field of German Lieder, Flora Neilsen and Bruce Boyce were, in my opinion, head and shoulders above the rest, but the besotted idea held by our public that no British artist could possibly be an authoritative singer of Lieder told heavily against them though Boyce is recognized in Germany today as *echt deutsch* with his superb enunciation and his knowledge of the literature.

As for Flora, her own excessive modesty and sweetness of nature have been a handicap. Regrettable though it is, many of us in this profession have to be fighters – the writer included. Lionel Tertis, doyen of viola players, loved by all who know him, respected for his artistic integrity, was none the less a fighter with a mission, as witness his crusade victoriously waged for the viola. Flora Neilsen lacks perhaps this combative ingredient but she is held in the highest esteem by true lovers of the Lied.

Most of my engagements with British singers, however, were with Isobel Baillie (whose pure flute-like voice in the English tradition was more suited to oratorio than song recital), Astra Desmond, Heddle Nash, and Roy Henderson. Astra Desmond gave many London recitals, toured in Scandinavia and the Balkans and always, I am glad to say, wanted me to play for her. Her scope was wide, as I said earlier, and her industry prodigious. She was an adornment to the English musical scene. My heart warms towards her youngest son who, quitting the hall with his father after one of her recitals, addressed the taxi rank in Wigmore Street in ringing tones, 'My mother is the greatest singer in all space.' He was ten years old at the time and understandably partial.

Heddle Nash was our most prominent English tenor in these years: magnificent in opera, oratorio, and in concert. His egocentricity was bewildering but by no means provoking and one could repay him in his own coin without arousing his resentment. There are almost as many stories about Heddle as there are of Beecham. It was of him the legend is told that on a certain Good Friday when Handel's *Messiah* was being performed in a hundred different towns he, to his disgust, found himself disengaged, 'and me, the best b— Messiah in the country.'

On a first meeting with Roy Henderson one could hardly imagine that his quiet unobtrusive manner concealed a probing mind and an imagination that made every song he sang vital. On the platform he was packed with personality. He knew so exactly what he was going to do with a song that, once his mind was made up, he never deviated – would treat it with the same colour, mood, rhythm, a thousand times without robbing it of freshness or zest. Not for him the sudden inspiration or spur-of-the-moment whim: everything was carefully and methodically planned, considered from all angles, absorbed until it became a part of him, and finally presented as a finished picture.

Our enjoyable work together apart, I know of no colleague with a livelier humour and keener sense of fun.

One of Henderson's favourite songs was Thomas Arne's *Now*

Phoebus Sinketh in the West from Milton's *Comus*. The recitative refers to the sun who

> Shoots against the dusky Pole
> Pacing towards the other goal
> Of his chamber in the east.

Although he had sung this song many times, at a never-to-be-forgotten concert one word escaped his memory; it was the word 'pacing', and my accompanying chord had to synchronize with this word. At once his hesitation was apparent to me and I waited before striking my chord. It was then – as I told him later – that I saw, positively saw, his brain working at full pressure like a turbine engine as, searching for the word and knowing it began with a consonant, he tested various other consonants like a bather putting his toe in the water to find if it is too cold. I heard him emit these strange cabalistic sounds, 'Sss–Shh–Fff–Kkk–Ttt–Ppp–Pacing', and down came my chord on the vowel of the first syllable just as the doctor ordered. Having at last unearthed his treasure Roy was in no hurry to leave it and brandished it triumphantly before us. Of course I could have prompted him but this would have made his little lapse far more obvious to the audience. It was better he should track down the word for himself. Why should I have interfered with his sleuthing when the preliminaries before bagging his quarry were so intriguing?

*

I have dwelt perhaps at wearisome length on the 1929–39 decade, but it was a span of intense work and immense value to me in my development. All these superb artists and many more unnamed had enriched my experience and sharpened my perception. Yet one further treat was still in store; John McCormack insisted that 'Moore and none other' should play for him on his Farewell Tour of England.

15

1929–39 (continued)

John McCormack

A WELL-KNOWN society called the London Music Club, organized and run by James Forsythe, functioned in these years, meeting four or five times during the winter months on Sunday evenings at the Mayfair Hotel. Two hundred or more members would gather, drawn, so someone said, not by the music they were going to hear but for the opportunity to don their evening dress. A buffet supper where one could talk and be seen was another attraction. The artists invited to perform gave their services without fee; was not Forsythe a member of the Press? But they were urgently enjoined by him to play or sing something light. The truth was that the members of this music club were not really fond of music and the shorter the programme the more they liked it. This 'something light' attitude is a recurring theme; it is an unguent, easing the irritation or hurt of the listener who does not want to listen, it appeases the 'lover of music' who finds every moment of music an unmitigated bore: it is, too, an escape for the organizer himself who may be forced to remain within earshot, and it means that singers should confine themselves to popular operatic arias, fiddlers to Kreisler or Sarasate pieces and pianists to the E flat Nocturne and the A flat Ballade of Chopin and a Liszt Hungarian Rhapsody. Bach's Air on the G string is not taboo as it may be recognized. String quartets, however, or any form of chamber music are *persona non grata*.

The grim realities that followed this pre-war decade have put an end to these meaningless functions; we are living in an age that has no use for *chi-chi*. At least I hope so. I am far from insisting that the friends I make shall be fond of music, I only beg of them not to pretend to an appreciation of it when it means nothing to them.

I was delighted to accept Jimmy Forsythe's invitation to play for a violinist when I heard that the guest of honour on that particular evening was to be John McCormack the tenor, who would sing a group of songs with his faithful collaborator, Edwin Schneider, at the piano.

Never was there a man with less pretension than this famous Irishman. His amiability and complete naturalness charmed me. What could be more flattering to a young man than McCormack's greeting when we first met? 'Hallo, Gerald.' It implied that he knew my name, that we were fellow-artists. I fell under his spell from that moment.

He only sang four or five songs that evening, not enough to get his voice warmed up and was therefore far from being in his best form. I knew his voice and the wonderful things he could do with it quite intimately, having heard hundreds of his records, though this was my first experience of him in person. I next met him a few days later. Lady Ravensdale, a great friend of John's, wanted his opinion on a young soprano in whom she was interested and she asked me to play. True to type, John pushed his chair next to my piano-stool and turned the pages for me. The song was Szulc's *Clair de Lune*. Now, unfortunately for the singer, John McCormack was incapable of subterfuge; he had to say the first thing that came into his mind without inhibition, and instead of saying something about the singing he blurted, 'What a marvellous way Gerald played that accompaniment'. Before I said my adieux, he whispered to me, 'One of these days, me bhoy, when Teddy retires you'll be playing for me.'

In 1938 the Holt Office booked me for a huge tour throughout the British Isles; it was to be John McCormack's Farewell Tour. We met to run through the programme in his sitting room at the Dorchester, but after two or three songs he, with his eyes popping with Irish indignation, fairly exploded at me, 'What the hell are we rehearsing for?' I cannot recall ever having a rehearsal with him beyond this. Even at his Royal Albert Hall recital when he had to sing César Franck's *Panis Angelicus* with obbligato of violoncello and organ, he refused to go to the hall and rehearse; I was deputed to go in his stead and sing for the guidance of the other artists and for the delectation of the cleaning staff.

At the first concert of our tour in the North of England, I knocked on the door of his sitting room – McCormack having journeyed from London the day before – to let him know I had arrived. 'What the hell do you want?' was the whispered greeting I received. (I do not remember ever being greeted by him in any other way.) He never spoke above this whisper on the day of a concert, and this self-enforced discipline may, in his case, have been really necessary for he was a great talker.

McCormack has been accused from time to time of filling his programme with trivia such as *I hear you calling me*, *Mother Machree*, and so on. But his bon-bons always came at the end of the evening. Fritz Kreisler concluded his recitals with Kreisleriana but before this he had played Tartini, Mozart and Beethoven. McCormack's scheme followed the same lines. The Irish ballads condemned by the highbrows were preceded by Handel or by early English songs or early Italian; there would be a German group with at least one or more Wolf songs, while the third group was composed of such songs as Lidgey's *Earl Bristol's Farewell*, with Stanford, Parry and Rachmaninoff songs. And in this proscribed last group those charming folk tunes of Herbert Hughes would be found, and who can compare with him for his singing of these? In fact he gave to these Irish and sentimental ballads the same flawless technique and sincerity that he brought to bear on Mozart's *Il mio tesoro*. If he liked the tune of a song and believed in the words – he sang it. It was either the best song in the world – he described many a song in these terms – or else it was hateful, obnoxious, and he could not bear the mention of it.

The claim that very little music is performed in strict time with a slavish observance of bar lines is not an empty one, and John McCormack – and John Coates before him – were living exponents of this. Just as Coates refused to sing the phrase 'Come into the garden, Maud' with the equal, stilted one-two-three-four rhythm of Balfe's notation (if you were really speaking the words to Maud you would naturally stress

'Come' and 'Garden'. 'Into' and 'the' would be thrown away), so I found McCormack employing this natural speech rhythm in his songs. Examples of this can be heard in his records of *Fairy Story by the Fire* by Merikanto and in Herbert Hughes's *She moved through the Fair*. This speech rhythm kept me on the alert for sometimes McCormack would try to catch me napping, particularly in *The Star of the County Down* where he used every sort of elasticity of rhythm. This song had one line which was a real tongue-twister for him: 'No pipe I'll smoke and no horse I'll yoke till my plough is a rust-coloured brown'. I will swear I once heard him declaim 'No horse I'll smoke and no pipe I'll yoke till my rust –' and then the phrase dwindled to an indistinguishable mumble. A mishap like this was clearly noticeable when it overtook McCormack. Any other singer would have bluffed his way out of it, but John was not another singer, nor have I ever heard enunciation such as his. You could hear every syllable he uttered no matter how softly he sang and you could almost *see* his consonants.

This being so I was puzzled when I heard him sing the old English song by Thomas Ford, *Since first I saw your face I resolved to honour and renown you*. I played it for him many times and it seemed to me he substituted an 'l' for the 'n', thus 'to holour and renowl you', and later instead of 'shall we begin to wrangle' he seemed to sing 'shall we begil to wralgle'. I asked Robert Irwin, who never missed a note that McCormack sang if he could help it, if I were imagining things and he absolutely agreed with me. But all John would do was growl, when I referred it to him, that I was talking a lot of rot. I am content to leave it at that.

John loved arguing for argument's sake and you never knew on which side he was going to be – it depended on the day and the mood. One day he would be more Irish than the Irish and the next – to use his own words – more British than the British. 'I suppose like all Irishmen you are interested in politics?' his handsome neighbour at a dinner party said to him. Upon which she was given John's private opinion of several members of the Government. 'But what do you think of the Foreign Minister?' 'That pompous jackass!' His companion was convulsed with laughter. 'He is my father,' she told him. For some minutes John kept very quiet after this.

There was no compromise with him – he either loved or hated. He called a spade a spade. After a concert at Derby during the war when he gave concerts for the Red Cross, the Chief Constable came uninvited to his supper party and behaved objectionably. 'Go away and leave me with my friends,' said the uninhibited John, and, the *coup de grâce* having been delivered, the enemy routed, nothing more would be said about it.

The champagne flowed freely at these post-concert supper parties, no attention being paid to the clock. At the Midland Hotel, Manchester, we were joined in John's room by Fay Compton and Stephen Potter. After an hour or so Stephen quietly slid out of the room and telephoned me from the hall porter's desk down below to say as it was so terribly late and he had a broadcast the next day would I make his excuses to John. When next I saw Potter some years later, I reminded him of our pleasant party. 'And do you know', said he, 'that after telephoning John's room, I seized the script of my next day's broadcast and made off for my own hotel. Waking later than I intended the following morning I took up my script to study my radio talk and found I was reading, in their entirety, the call-sheets for the Midland Hotel. I wonder how many people missed their trains!'

When I toured with John there was nothing I could do about these late hours nor would he hear of my retiring before he was ready for bed himself. But in London when he telephoned and asked me to dine with him I had to find some excuse, for I had work to do the following morning. It was no good telling John that I wanted an early night so I found myself lying to him, saying I had a concert that evening or a previous engagement. He always believed me. John suspicious I would not have minded, but John deceived always made me feel ashamed of myself. He could not tell a falsehood himself, nor did he indulge in the luxury of self-deception. When I asked him, for instance, how he enjoyed singing in opera he said, 'Not at all. I was a rotten actor.' Again on his farewell tour, finding him in such splendid form, I expressed surprise that he should have determined never to sing in America again. Why was this? 'Because I lost my public.'

This shattering honesty sent shivers down my back. I wonder today how many tenors there are in the world who can measure up to this man.

Lily McCormack wrote a moving story of her husband's life entitled *I Hear You Calling Me*: a remarkable achievement for one turned author for the first time. My friend the late L. A. G. Strong's effort, *John McCormack, the Story of a Singer*, was not a success. As Leonard Strong confessed to me later, he knew John but slightly when he wrote it, and it makes the man seem to be milk and water. If John had found the energy to write his own autobiography – he wrote as he thought and spoke, vividly and passionately – the *real* John McCormack would have made himself known, and perhaps even more loved than he was already. For he, like any colourful personality, had lots of rough edges. He was not all smooth by any means. Had he not been intensely human he would not have been the great artist he was.

His ebullience was the expression of an extrovert nature. His ambitions were to own a Stradivarius, a Frans Hals and a Derby winner. He realized the first two.

If he felt he had given offence to someone he loved, his repentance was expressed humbly and frankly. 'Forgive me, I would not hurt your feelings for anything in the world.' He once addressed these very words to me, having followed me out of the room to say them. It takes a big man to do that.

When he chirruped at Richard Tauber's wife in the artists' room at his last London concert before an immense audience, 'Come to count the house?' she knew and he knew there was no sense of rivalry between him and Tauber for they worked in separate worlds: it was simply that here was a situation he must use to advantage. There was no jealousy in his make-up; he informed me that if I had never heard Enrico Caruso then I did not know the sound of a tenor voice. His admiration for Caruso was reciprocated.

On one occasion when John appeared at the Royal Opera

AM I TOO LOUD?

House, Covent Garden, Enrico Caruso resplendent in silk hat and evening cloak tapped on his dressing-room door.

'What are you doing here, Enrico?'

'Do you think I would allow you to walk on to the stage without coming to wish you well?'

'I take that as a great compliment coming from the world's greatest tenor.'

'Since when, Giovanni, did you become a baritone?'

John McCormack's historic farewell at the Royal Albert Hall will never be forgotten by the thousands who were there. He began with the old German folk-song, *All mein Gedanken die ich hab*, of which Ernest Newman in his tribute to this great artist said: 'Rather than McCormack singing it to us, *we* should have risen *en masse* and sung it to him.'

16

The War Years

My tours in 1938 with Astra Desmond in Scandinavia, and with her and Clifford Curzon in the Balkans in the spring of '39, were not particularly happy days. This is not a reflection on my distinguished fellow-travellers of whom I am very fond, but on Adolf Hitler. We had enjoyable times it is true in Athens, where we were guests at the British School of Archaeology, and at Buda Pesth, Zagreb and Sofia, but I was oppressed by the threat of war. In that miserable city, Belgrade, Clifford and I found ourselves deprived of Gwen Desmond's company and we wandered disconsolately on our first evening through the town searching for a good restaurant. We found a restaurant. It was in a sordid neighbourhood that reminded me, I told Clifford, of the least inspiring stretches of the Edgware Road or Sixth Avenue. He sagaciously remarked, however, that perhaps it was in truth the Edgware Road of Belgrade ; but he proved wrong, it was the Bond Street, the Fifth Avenue of Jugoslavia's capital. And in my bedroom I sat with my ear glued to the thin wall, trying to glean information from a German press correspondent as he telephoned his report to his paper in Berlin.

The outbreak of war found me living in a glass-roofed studio behind a block of offices in Marylebone High Street. (I could not quite boast of dwelling in Mayfair, being two hundred yards north of that delectable quarter.) When blacking out became the order of the day – or rather the night – it was found that my blinds were inadequate and the police informed me that my glass roof must be painted black : in other words I must live by day as well as night by artificial light. I felt this might have a dampening effect on my resilience, nor did I feel that a thin sheeting of glass afforded much protection from a well aimed bomb. I therefore beat a strategic and not unhurried retreat to the home of Enid and her parents in south-east London – Beckenham which soon became a centre of great attraction to the German Air Force.

For a time, when no one knew what was going to happen next, all places of entertainment were closed, there were no concerts, no theatres. This was the spell known by Americans as the 'phoney war' when our island for ten or more months, though frantically preparing for the inevitable, never heard the blast of an explosion or the roar of a gun. Running into the office of Ibbs and Tillett, the Concert Agents, I found my great friends John and Emmie Tillett both writing furiously as if their lives depended on it. They were cancelling all their contracts. Our relations were always warm and personal, and I think I must have walked in on them unannounced because I felt it might restore my sense of balance just to have a few words with them. After John died and Emmie took over the reins, I, like many artists before and after me, found in Mrs Tillett not only the most adroit and unruffled of managers but a friend of unimpeachable loyalty.

I joined the Home Guard. No deeds of derring-do came my way, alas, nor can I recall one stirring scene in which I played even the smallest part, but I had one – what I might call – military experience. After some weeks of marching and drilling, our section of the Home Guard was to be inspected by some General or other. I was detailed to mount guard in a pillbox with two men under me. I repeat under me. Nervously looking through the embrasure of my fortress I saw – up and down the street – a charming picture of children going to Sunday School and later elderly ladies and their spouses returning from their devotions. Unseen by them and naturally not telling my subordinates I aimed my rifle (unloaded) at them and told myself how lucky they were not to be enemy troops. Having done my turn of watch and becoming rather bored I told my second in command to take over and took a stroll outside. It was two hours since I had been out in the sunlight. Judge of my surprise, when I saw a group of my fellows, who no doubt had been doing yeoman service in other and equally important pillboxes, standing at the street corner smoking and chatting. 'When', I stammered, 'is the

General coming?' 'Bless you, he's been, come and gone this last hour, he's at home now having his lunch.' I was disgruntled. The iron discipline I had enforced on my men and my own conscientious vigilance had gone for nothing. But I had done my good deed for the day. Horatius may have kept the bridge in the brave days of old but I had, at least, *manned* the pillbox.

Fortunately for everyone's morale two organizations sprang quickly into being, E.N.S.A. (Entertainments National Service Association) catering for the fighting forces and munition factories, and C.E.M.A. (Council for the Encouragement of Music and the Arts) arranging concerts in hospitals, air-raid shelters and manufacturing centres. It was soon pointed out to me that I might be doing more useful service by playing under these auspices than by drilling and undertaking those protracted route marches which took so much longer on foot than by taxi. When I resigned from the Home Guard my colleagues took leave of me with some relief, telling me I would be less dangerous with a piano than with a gun.

We musicians enthusiastically threw in our lot with E.N.S.A. and C.E.M.A. When the former sent us abroad we had of necessity to wear a khaki uniform and this gave me some embarrassing moments. Soldiers seeing a portly uniformed figure passing them on the streets took it for granted that my ample great-coat concealed the person of a General beneath its folds: at least I must be a Colonel. They sprang smartly to attention and saluted me. What could I do? I could not rush up to every one of them and explain I was not a commissioned officer; I sheepishly returned their salute and hurried on before I was found out.

One of the great features of wartime London life was the daily lunch-time concert at the National Gallery in Trafalgar Square. The project needed not only a big name to launch it but a name that was held in universal esteem, not to say affection. Who other but Dame Myra Hess? It was she who conceived and, with the help of Ibbs and Tillett, organized what was to become an institution. She naturally gave the inaugural recital and to her relief, for she had no idea of the public's mood in the matter, found on her arrival at the main entrance that a queue had been formed stretching down the steps from the doors to the street.

These concerts continued until the end of the war, mostly in the spacious galleries but occasionally through enemy action in the large air-raid shelter in the basement. Myra herself appeared more frequently than any other artist; occasions that filled the place. My appearances there, though not to be mentioned in the same breath as hers, numbered over a hundred. At my seventy-fifth concert she presented me with a beautiful Georgian silver dish with an affectionate personal message engraved on it. A charming surprise.

In England the German language was taboo during the 1914–18 war (Lieder had to be sung to English translations) but at these National Gallery concerts we heard Mozart and Beethoven, Schubert and Brahms sung in the language in which they were written. Even so it was with some trepidation that Emmie Tillett, on Dame Myra's behalf, sounded Mme Gerhardt as to her willingness to sing. Elena Gerhardt was eager to respond. Elena had been living in England for years – was identified with London – she had already applied for her naturalization papers but had not yet been declared a British citizen. She was in very fact an enemy alien. How would the public receive her? Would there be a demonstration? Myra herself decided to accompany her.

In her taxi to Trafalgar Square, so she told me later, Myra Hess made up her mind exactly what she was going to do and say should there be any protest from some member of the public. Their entry on to the platform was one of the tensest moments Myra had ever experienced – but as for Elena, well, she never thought anything about it for Myra had not communicated to her her private fears. And, in truth there was a demonstration: a demonstration of such overwhelming enthusiasm and affection that both artists were too moved to be able to begin for some seconds.

I have related this event not only in tribute to two great ladies: it is a compliment to a loyal, sensible and discriminating public.

During this time the B.B.C. engaged me to do a series of talks on the air about some of the artists I had played for, with records of their playing or singing, and to give my views, in a general way, on the aspects of my work. Myra Hess happened to listen one evening and she came to me with the idea that I give a talk at the National Gallery. She told me that I had a delightful touch of humour (I do not claim this, I only repeat) and that my talk would be a change from the eternal round (her words) of pianoforte, violin or song recitals, chamber music, and would bring a smile to the lips of the war-weary. This was a very different proposition – addressing a visual audience, from reading a typewritten script over the air. I took the plunge and, assisted by Roy Henderson and his pupil Joan Taylor, gave my first illustrated talk in public. This opened up a new branch of activity for me – Lecture Recitals – of which I shall have more to say later.

These B.B.C. chats on my work which Dame Myra had heard gradually assumed wider proportions when Alec Robertson, in charge of music talks from Bedford, asked me to prepare, helped by records, a series of talks on Beethoven Symphonies and Chamber Music suitable for the man in the street. This was just my level. I composed conversations between a know-all (myself) and a nit-wit (Enid. What our poor wives have to suffer!) Of course the questions I put into her mouth were designedly simple or I could not have answered them: if I had allowed another to formulate the questions, I should have been floored. I see, in retrospect, that these broadcasts were important to me in one way: I met Alec Robertson.

I have been told I talk with naturalness on the air; if this is so, I owe it to Alec Robertson. I listened attentively to all he had to say :– 'Your talk must sound as an improvisation, not as a reading, it must, like music, have rhythm – elasticity – and not be iron bound. It must have light and shade, ups and downs.'

As an example of Alec's ideas on this matter, I had on my script the sentence, 'Now we would like to play to you Beethoven's Spring Sonata'. First of all 'we would like' was altered to 'we'd like'. Then it was found my voice dropped at the end of the sentence, as if I were not really interested, whereas the highest note, to use a musical term, the note which should ring out, was the word 'spring'. These improvements gave the utterance naturalness and life.

Behind all these little technical recommendations I sensed the mind of a musician of felicity and erudition. There is a deep spirituality in Alec which pervades all his writing and talking on music, and it had, and continues to have, a profound influence on me.

As a postscript to this chapter, it occurs to me that some of my younger readers may be surprised to learn that the broadcasts referred to above were from Bedford; the reason was that the B.B.C., as in Ariel's song, wanted their sounds dispersed. This was done as a precautionary measure. The broadcasting studios were scattered, some in Bedford, some in Bristol, others in Evesham in Worcestershire. A valuable music library was hidden away somewhere in the country with a special fire guard to watch over it, though the choice of fire guard proved to be an unfortunate one. He was a pyromaniac: after pouring petrol over his cache he put a lighted match to it.

17

The War Years (*continued*)

FOR many years the names of Frederick B. Kiddle and Samuel H. Liddle had been familiar to concert goers. It was delightful to read their names one above the other when they appeared on the same programme at the Chappell Ballad Concerts at the Queen's Hall, both for the rhyme and the friendly rhythmical approximation. The fact that they were both accompanists inspired the late Harry Graham in his *The World We Laugh In* to indulge in the following:

> **THE RIDDLE**
> With the cunningest collusion
> And a deep desire to diddle
> Mr Kiddle courts confusion
> With his colleague Mr Liddle.

These gentlemen were the best of friends and indeed it would be hard to find two artists more courteous and affable. If one were mistaken for the other, however, they were immediately transformed into snarling homicides.

The programmes of the Promenade Concerts were designed so as to include in the second half a group of songs with piano to give the conductor and orchestra a breather. For as far back as I can remember Freddy Kiddle was the official accompanist.

Eventually the B.B.C. took these wonderful Proms under their wing and Berkeley Mason was their accompanist but now in 1940 he had retired and I was invited to take his place. Thus was history repeated, for I had succeeded him as John Coates's partner in 1925.

It was not to be expected that Sir Henry Wood would call off a Promenade Season because of a mere war. At first all went merrily, the audience willingly resigned to a struggle home in the blackout. Then, one Saturday afternoon the enemy decided to give us our baptism of bombs. As I changed into evening dress at my club overlooking St James's Park I saw, a mile away to the eastward, huge columns of black smoke. But, nothing daunted, the gallant Sir Henry, carnation in button-hole as usual, strode jauntily through his orchestra at ten seconds before eight to start his concert. The Queen's Hall Promenades were going on, come what may.

As regularly as clockwork for the next twelve months the sirens were destined to sound at dusk, but it was during this concert that their nightly banshee wailings actually began. Everybody was advised, when the programme was over, that they would be safer to remain in their places. Half the audience preferred to return to their homes and how wise they were was to be proved later, but for those who did not budge something had to be done. Basil Cameron, Sir Henry's assistant conductor, some of the orchestra, and I at the piano, led the audience in community singing; this was alternated by solo pieces from members of the orchestra and even by some of the audience contributing solos until our dispersal, hours later, when the 'all clear' sounded. Obviously audience and players would soon have been exhausted maintaining this nightly vigil throughout an entire 'Prom' season; fortunately the end of the season was in sight, only a few more concerts remained. The problem did not arise again, for early one morning the following spring the Queen's Hall, hit by an incendiary bomb, was burned to the ground. Fortunately there was no loss of human life but the death of the Queen's Hall was a casualty, an irreparable loss ever-lamented by music lovers.

Plans were immediately made for the next season of Promenade Concerts to be held in the Royal Albert Hall. Once again that buoyant Sir Henry made his entry at ten seconds before eight, as if nothing had happened. To this day the 'Proms', under the guidance of Sir Malcolm Sargent, are still going strong.

The truth is that audiences for serious music, as evidenced by the Promenades, National Gallery concerts, visits to troops by our best orchestras and soloists, were bigger than they had ever been.

Full advantage of this demand was taken except by one impresario who, quite certain that he knew the public's taste, insisted that 'they want something light'. (This parrot cry had been his motto for ages and he uttered it with a grimace as who should say, 'There is no sugar in my coffee'.) His master-stroke was to send me with the brilliant artists, Joan Hammond soprano, Ida Haendel violinist, and the late Oscar Natzke bass, to give – in Cambridge of all places – an afternoon of light music. In blissful ignorance of what awaited them, since the programme had not been previously announced, Professor E. J. Dent, Professor Patrick Hadley, Dr Hubert Middleton, attended the concert. They were the *crème de la crème* of the University's musical life and, on buying their programmes, saw with surprise that they were going to hear *Un bel dí vedremo* from Madame Butterfly, *Si mi chiamano Mimi* from La Bohème, the Prologue from Pagliacci, the *Largo al Factotum*, and fiddle pieces by Kreisler and Sarasate. They withdrew before we started. As the concert proceeded so did our audience dwindle. Our reception was so lukewarm that Natzke supposed, so he said to me, that the programme was too good for them. I asked him, 'If we all had to appear on the pier at Blackpool on a Bank Holiday Monday, would you not choose a programme exactly the same as this?' Since he agreed I followed with a further question: 'Does it not occur to you that the audience on Blackpool Pier is not quite the same as an audience from the University Town of Cambridge?' But he looked at me as if I were quite mad. It was this very firm in the piping times of peace who had booked the Lener Quartet at this same Cambridge. The quartet had to withdraw from the engagement owing to the indisposition of their leader and Paul Robeson went in their stead. But the impresario boasted of this, saying that he made it a point never to disappoint the public – 'If accident or illness causes the cancellation of one programme I send a better or more expensive one to take its place.' In this instance the Cambridge audience buying tickets to hear Beethoven quartets heard *Old Man River* and spirituals instead.

*

Between wartime concerts, a little teaching, and spells of fire-watching I began to write a book. Walter Eastman, head of the music publishers Ascherberg, Hopwood and Crew, came to me with the proposition that I put down on paper my ideas on accompanying. I christened this effort *The Unashamed Accompanist*. I sketched it out on the backs of envelopes and odd bits of paper in my free time and during occasional – very occasional – weekends spent out of London to get a little respite from the noisy nights.

The term 'unashamed' was inspired by a question that was always being put to me: 'When are you going to become a soloist?' and it was meant as a compliment. This was the unvaried greeting – though put less kindly – of a dear old aunt of mine whenever I visited her, and for forty years until her untimely death at the age of ninety-three I tried in vain to explain why it was I preferred to be an accompanist.

One fine day my little book was completed and it was with mixed feelings, walking along the street with the manuscript under my arm, that I ran into my friend L. A. G. Strong, the writer, one of the directors of Methuen's, the book publishers. He said his firm would like to take it. Ascherberg's are a highly esteemed firm of music publishers but Eastman admitted at the time he was a learner where books were concerned. I was in honour bound, I told L.A.G., to give my 'Unashamed' to the man who had inspired me with the idea, nor have I ever regretted it. Its reception from the press was beyond all my hopes. That doyen of critics, Ernest Newman, devoting two witty and eulogistic articles to it in *The Sunday Times* was amused at my gibe of 'the music critics sleeping in the back row' and hit back, 'How mistaken to imagine we are sleeping! For years and years I have tried to get to sleep during concerts but failed miserably.'

It made its bow as a war baby and, due to paper shortage, appeared in a cheap paper-backed edition. L. A. G. Strong, however, never lost interest in it and thanks to him and to Alan White of Methuen and Company, and to the generous cooperation of Noel Johnson of Ascherberg's, the book in an enlarged and revised edition and with musical illustrations has now been issued by Methuen.

First published in 1943 the book is still selling in the English speaking world (Macmillan and Company took it up in America) and translations are now appearing in Germany, Japan and Russia.

Self-praise being no recommendation, I suggest that those readers who share my aunt's misgivings where I am concerned should purchase a copy of *The Unashamed Accompanist* forthwith.

But if my 'unashamed' efforts accomplished nothing else they gave me an inkling – and I claim no more than an inkling – of how to put pen to paper. This, with the lessons I was giving, taught me to bring ideas slumbering at the back of my mind to the surface, ideas which formed the basis for my lecture 'The Accompanist Speaks'. To my gratification my début as a lecturer at the National Gallery attracted a good deal of attention and I was approached by C.E.M.A. and E.N.S.A. to repeat these talks under their auspices.

In describing my talk as a lecture perhaps I am using too grandiloquent a term. It was, and is, an entertainment, for it was found that troops and war-workers laughed uproariously at some of my jokes and antics. Always I had one object in view, to arouse their interest for, or increase their appreciation of good music, and if I made them laugh in the process so much the better. Telling them how fatal it was if the accompanist drowned the singer by playing too loudly I instanced the famous conductor at the Royal Opera House, Covent Garden, who, visited by a friend in his dressing-room after the performance and complimented on the superb orchestral playing, was accused of having drowned his singers: here I would wait for several seconds before continuing, 'and Sir Thomas replied' (loud laughter), 'I know, I drowned them intentionally – in the public's interest.' I told them of the bass who, finding in Schubert's *Der Einsame* the key of F too high found it too low in the key of E, thereupon asking me if I had 'nothing in between'. But behind all this foolery which was the sugar round the pill, I was giving a lesson in musical appreciation; taking songs from Schubert's *Die Winterreise* or *Die schöne Müllerin* and showing the pictures the music painted, the meaning or moods beneath the notes of that dreadful bogy known as chamber music. I learned what a successful politician or music hall comedian knows (I give pride of place to the former as he is often the funnier of the two), how to seize the attention of the audience at once and hold it. My remarks were interlaced with many examples played on the piano. Now when all is said and done these excursions on the keyboard where I had to put into practice what I had been preaching were of supreme importance: it was vital that I should play these various excerpts and examples not only note perfectly but with meaning and as beautifully as I could. At a song or violin recital I can take my time before embarking on a piece of music – adjust the piano stool, push back my cuffs, get myself poised – but not at a lecture recital. When I say to my audience, 'Listen to the rustling of leaves in Schubert's accompaniment to *The Linden Tree*', I have to turn, drop on to my piano stool and start playing immediately, without a gap. This was made plain to me when I heard a violinist telling an audience of schoolchildren an Irish fairy story (one of Herbert Hughes's arrangements) and concluding with the words, 'And this is the lovely tune she sang –' And what happened? There was no lovely tune, for the violinist proceeded to tune her fiddle for a full minute. The children shuffled and some of them sniggered. The listener quickly loses interest if talk and music do not proceed in a continuous line.

It is not easy, I found, to throw myself into the music's mood and play it perfectly after five or ten minutes' talking. These illustrations on the piano needed great, but not too evident care. One can hesitate, hum and haw, make a slip and correct it in speech, and it only adds to the effect of extemporaneousness and naturalness. Can one do this in one's playing? Decidedly not. It is easier to talk than to play.

Sometimes I was asked to answer questions at the end of

my discourse: these could be pertinent or the reverse. I do not know if it was the nonplussed expression on my face or the cool insistence of my interrogator which caused the audience to laugh so loudly when I was asked 'Did you ever consider the idea when you were younger of becoming a pianist?'

A more naïve inquiry was to put me – though not during official question time I am glad to say – by two teenagers in La Junta, Colorado. They burned to know where and how I got 'that wonderful shoe-shine'. It was the first time they had ever set eyes on patent-leather shoes.

I considered at one stage the possibility of engaging a singer to perform the songs after I had talked about them but came to the conclusion it would undermine the *raison d'être* of my lecture for many of my listeners are hearing the accompaniments for the first time, literally the first time: they have heard most of the songs before it is true, but have only listened to – or taken in – the voice part. For their own good I direct their attention almost exclusively in my examples on the piano to what the accompaniment is saying and hardly touch the vocal line of a song at all.

If a soprano shares the platform with me she will steal my thunder, and what is supposed to be my lecture will soon develop into a song recital. Is she a dazzling beauty? If a blonde, the public will be unable to tear their eyes away from her: if a brunette, I in my turn will be distracted.

One more objection: be she dark or fair, slender or plump, she will walk away with half my fee.

Objection sustained.

18

Casals

I HAD paid a short visit to Canada to see my parents in 1929 and that was the last time I saw my mother, for on New Year's Day in 1944 a cable from my brother Trevor told me she had died. I owe much to her for it was her courage that launched the family across the Atlantic to make a fresh start in 1913 and it was through her determination that I became a musician and Trevor went to the University of Toronto. Trevor, let me say without any beating about the bush, is the star of the family, not only a highly successful man of affairs, but a man of authority and one, moreover, who has never lost his sense of balance. He is modest, generous and devotes much of his time and substance to the welfare of others. It was he who was the prop and mainstay, in every conceivable way, of my parents, while I, thousands of miles distant, was no help at all. In no way comparable to Trevor's, my career has been moderately successful I suppose, but poor Basil, the youngest of the three brothers, whose warm and affectionate nature made him popular with everybody, was the one who failed to settle down. He joined the Canadian Forces at the outbreak of war, was demobilized in England in 1944, married an English girl, and died a few years later after a brief illness.

Hardly had the last shot of the war been fired – in fact it was two months after the last V-2 bomb had exploded in London – when a cable from Toronto informed me that father was coming to stay with Enid and me in London and to visit Basil in the south of England. I sent a hurried reply begging my father to defer his visit as I felt certain he had no idea of conditions in Britain after five years of bombing, nor the austerity and strict rationing that were our lot. But it was too late, he had already embarked.

I had misgivings about his visit for several reasons: we were living at that time in a tiny flat in Bayswater with little room for a visitor, in circumstances that could hardly be described as affluent. The only engagements during the war where normal fees were paid were for gramophone sessions and broadcasting engagements. With the signing of the armistice I felt the day was now dawning when I could at last buckle down to some really hard work and think for a change of my playing and my progress as a musician. Father and I had always been on most affectionate terms but we were dissimilar in taste and temperament. He, like most men of business, excusably knew little about my profession and the fearful absorption it demands. He had no idea that his presence in my studio when I was practising disturbed my concentration; for though I had trained myself to practise in noisy halls to the accompaniment of the song of the vacuum cleaner, in my own studio it is vital for me to have solitude, quietude and unlimited time for my work to get anywhere. I believe it was Osbert Sitwell, wrestling with an essay or a book he was preparing, who overheard the conversation of two domestics outside his study: 'Is he busy?' 'No, only writing.'

There was another self-interested reason that my father's visit seemed ill-timed. It had been announced some weeks previously that Pablo Casals was coming to London and that he wanted me to partner him. It can be imagined what this meant to me. After six years of existing in a blackout came this blinding light, I was to play for the world's greatest living musician. It was the biggest assignment I had ever had.

On 2 July 1945 I had a National Gallery lunch-time recital with Robert Irwin and my appointment for my first meeting and first rehearsal with the Master was in the afternoon. This was the very day that my father, whom I had not seen for sixteen years, arrived in London: Enid met him and saw to his comfort while I, with a fluttering heart, proceeded to my work.

Casals greeted me warmly, lit his pipe, and we started to play. Now the crux of the programme so far as I was concerned was the Sonata in D major Op. 102, No. 2, third period Beethoven. It is a great piece of music with a fiery first movement, followed by an *Adagio con molto sentimento d'affetto* and finishing with a hair-raising Fugue. I do not think I had previously performed this work in public, but I can be certain of one thing, and that is that I had practised the work with devilish care for weeks, as soon as I knew it was down on Casals's programme. It is a hard nut to crack in that it demands perfect accord and sensitive reaction between the players. The second movement, whose notes are easy to play, has a slow noble theme with the most delicate dynamic inflexions rising and falling within the phrase which each player observes in like degree. If one player augments or decreases more than the other, the music is thrown out of proportion and becomes meaningless. It was with this movement that Casals elected to start our work together that afternoon. He sang on his 'cello and I crouched over my keyboard with every nerve alert and my very soul in my finger-tips. Thus we played away together without exchanging a word. Then, when we had covered two dozen measures Casals abruptly stopped playing, laid his 'cello gently on its side and looking very straight at me said, 'I am very happy.' I wish to emphasize that it was not the intricate windings of the fugue or the dramatic declamation of the first movement that Casals used as a testing ground to see if our chemistry blended but the slow, apparently simple tune of the chorale whose notes, at least for the first twenty bars, could have been read at sight by the veriest amateur: I shall have more to say in a subsequent chapter on this subject of slow-moving music, however.

With Casals, as with all great artists, it is the music that matters: the music is more important than the man. Now the musician always pretends to put the composer first and loves to be told how faithfully he delivers the creator's message, but in ninety-nine cases out of a hundred the player is thinking of himself all the time. Conceivably he is an egocentric who imposes his personality on the music, but that is not the entire answer. Many a good musician of modesty unconsciously thrusts himself between the composer and the listener through his concern over his fourth finger, through technical insecurity, or through fright. The fight to gain control over self, the struggle to keep the bowing arm steady, to hit the note dead centre, absorb all his faculties and the music itself suffers.

Casals has no such problems, he has made himself the complete master of his instrument. And he begins from this point. He begins where many musicians leave off. He is able from this point to become the composer's *alter ego*, absorbed into the composer's heart and brain. This absorption was made clear to me more than once in the artists' room before a concert when he would raise his voice and sing some passage out of the work we were just about to perform. Suddenly his singing would stop and obviously moved he would look at me and cry, 'Is beautiful. Is beautiful.'

Years later at Prades where I played *Die Winterreise* for Fischer-Dieskau in the ancient church, Pablo Casals sat in the front row and was overcome by the young man's singing. We sat with him in his study afterwards when he impressed on us the necessity to be humble, to remember always that we were Music's servants, that the singer's gifts were from God.

He spoke at such length in this strain that Fischer-Dieskau asked me later, 'Does he feel that I am conceited?' – but this unjustifiable reproach was far from Casals's mind. He was moved, deeply moved, by this extraordinary artist's singing and was inspired to preach the gospel according to Casals. It is a good gospel which every musician might take to his heart. And it is truth. Perhaps it supplies us with the key to the greatness of Casals himself.

In his first post-war visit his hotel suite was a second Spanish Embassy; such a constant stream of Spaniards came to see and talk to him that he declared he was no longer a musician but a statesman. I told him how Georges Clemenceau, on seeing the impressive figure of Ignaz Jan Paderewski at the Versailles Peace Conference, asked who he was. On being told he was the great pianist who had become Prime Minister of Poland, Clemenceau exclaimed, 'Quelle chute'. Certain it is that the daily interviews Casals had with his fellow-nationals prevented us from doing much rehearsing together and for one concert in Chelsea we had only one run through on the eve of the performance on a programme which we had never previously performed together.

It was his political beliefs and single-mindedness, his refusal to tolerate the Franco régime, that caused him to settle in Prades, near Perpignan. There and in Puerto Rico he holds his festivals. The world may go to him. It is good for one's soul to make a pilgrimage to this sage, and it is good that one should have to take time and trouble to do so.

Of the man's music it is fairly obvious that words fail me. Of the man himself and his warm-heartedness I have indelible memories; his signature on my tattered copy of Beethoven Violoncello Sonatas to which he added the words: 'What a pleasure!' And finally the message he sent me through my young friend, Eileen Croxford, who had been studying with him in Prades. It had been some years since I had seen him and Eileen was taking her leave and he said to her, 'Please remember me to so-and-so, and my regards to so-and-so, and my love, you understand, my love to Gerald Moore.'

*

History seemed to repeat itself with me for, as in the pre-war years, my violoncellists far outnumbered my violinists. As against Joseph Szigeti, Symon Goldberg, Max Rostal, Ida Haendel – all first-class violinists – I played, after Casals, with Fournier, Tortelier, Navarra, Schuster, Antoni Sala, Nelsova, Eisenberg, and the English 'cellists Antoni Pini and James Whitehead.

I was 'teamed' for sonata work by the B.B.C. with Sala, a Catalan from Barcelona; he lived in a huge studio full of old Spanish furniture and a cask of Tio Pepe. His 'cello playing, his wood-carving, his cooking were tackled with *brio* and we were warm friends. He worked himself to death in the war farming in Sussex, growing potatoes, as he said, 'for Victoria'.

Next I partnered Jimmy Whitehead, a first-class musician. After one broadcast with him of the Rachmaninoff piano and violoncello Sonata I had a most charming note from Benno Moiseiwitsch in which he said that the performance had given him one of the most pleasant half-hours he had had for a long time. Benno is one of my best friends but I know he would not have written in this strain unless he meant it sincerely. He does such incredibly dazzling things himself that I appreciated his compliments enormously. However, he is a notorious leg-puller and there was a sting in the tail for he added, 'By the way, there is a piano part to this sonata but I did not hear it.' I replied, thanking him for his generous letter, telling him I knew he had played the work frequently but 'perhaps you have never listened to somebody else performing it and are consequently hearing the 'cello part for the first time.'

I was now closely associated with Yehudi Menuhin (this was before he was surrounded by so many pianists in his family circle) and we had a great many appearances together. In the course of one provincial tour we hurried back to London between concerts for an unusual assignment when Gainsborough Pictures Limited decided to make a film on the life of Paganini with Yehudi supplying the music on the sound track. While accompanying him on these occasions I asked one of the directors who was to act the part of the demoniacal Paganini with his cavernous white face and long black hair, and was told quite frankly that the actor they wanted was the type of man that the girls of Woolworth's would fall in love with. They chose Stewart Granger.

The tedium of these sessions when the *Moses* variations and other bravura pieces were repeated time after time *ad nauseam* was as nothing compared to the boredom I experienced when witnessing the finished film.

Singers, I am thankful to say, I had always with me, but I made a new friend when the great Dane Aksel Schiotz came to London to record *Die schöne Müllerin*. Now I believe that Aksel Schiotz was one of the few modest tenors that I have ever met. He was not always talking about himself; he did not tell me where he had been or where he was going, he did not tell me about his success here and how they were clamouring for him there. He was quiet, he was modest and this is a miracle in a tenor. After having worked in Denmark during the German occupation in the underground movement his career was opening up with the richest promise. His press notices for his London recitals with me and for his recordings were excellent: he alternated with Peter Pears in Benjamin Britten's *The Rape of Lucretia* at Glyndebourne, singing in perfect English: he was a huge success at the first season of the Edinburgh Festival in

1947 and then with a crash his career fell to ruins. He contracted a tumour on the brain. After a fearful operation and a long convalescence he learned to walk again, he learned to talk again, he learned to sing again and at this moment he is one of the most sought after teachers of singing in North America.

19

Kathleen Ferrier

EVERYBODY knows the glorious splendour of Kathleen's development as a being and as an artist, and much has been written of her life and work. Hamish Hamilton, one of her most devoted friends, published two books on the Ferrier story; a biography by her sister Winifred, and *Kathleen Ferrier: A Memoir*, wherein tributes were paid by Bruno Walter, John Barbirolli, Roy Henderson and other intimates under Neville Cardus's editorship. I ask myself if it is possible to find anything new to say about her. And yet I am engaged in writing the story of my life. Unexciting and colourless though it may seem, it would have been immeasurably poorer without Kathleen Ferrier.

During the war, rumours had spread of a girl with an exceptionally lovely voice singing on some of C.E.M.A.'s factory tours. She had been heard by Malcolm Sargent who had urged her to come to London. My first engagement with her was in 1943.

She had heard me playing at some London recital before I knew her and, bless her heart, had been impressed by my playing. This first concert together was in Lewes, Sussex. But as she was a last minute substitute through indisposition of another singer, we had not even met one another, let alone rehearsed. So modest was she, so ingenuous and blissfully unconscious of her own worth that, seeing me enter the train, she shrank out of sight in the corner of another compartment, and at Lewes waited until I had quitted the station before she made her way to the Hall. Was I pleased with her singing, she asked me afterwards, and if so would I tell Mr Tillett? It would help her a great deal. I was not merely pleased with her, I was delighted, though I quickly recognized that her voice and her beauty were not making their full effect: she lacked poise. She did not know how to acknowledge applause – to walk on and off the stage. It was not to be expected that the bearing of an experienced artist could be acquired under the unhelpful conditions of the impromptu wartime concerts. Mr and Mrs Tillett advised her to go to Roy Henderson, the very man to help her find her own natural style and dignity.

After the Lewes concert Kathleen and I became friends, but I was a critical friend holding such high hopes for her that I began to worry her, all unknowingly. Full of enthusiasm for her, I was raving about her singing to Richard Capell in the autumn of 1948. To my delight he spoke with warmth about her Bach, Gluck, Handel, and Purcell, Mahler's *Kindertotenlieder* and the Bach B minor mass. 'But,' he added, 'judging her from the very highest standards, she is as yet only on the fringe of Lieder.' What possessed me to pass this remark on to Kathleen? It was unutterably stupid of me. I suppose I imagined it would be helpful but it had the reverse effect. It discouraged her and created a cloud between us. I realized this when, telephoning her one day, she answered, 'What have I done wrong now?'

When one considers the prodigies this girl had achieved, how could she possibly be expected to become high-priestess of Lieder in four or five years?

For some months, during which she toured America with John Newmark, we saw little of each other. After an interval that seemed very long to me we were together again. Her singing of Schubert and Brahms songs had matured in a miraculous way, thanks to the affectionate influence of Bruno Walter, and I was able to tell her so. Kathleen knew that I could not dissemble or flatter where music is concerned and we were better friends than ever.

Kathleen's voice was naturally beautiful, it had not to be cultivated and carefully nursed like a hot-house flower, it flowed out of her like a pure crystal stream. It was warm, fresh and vibrant. You were moved by its soul-stirring humanity. There was nothing of the traditional 'plumminess' which we sometimes associate with the English oratorio contralto. John Mc-Cormack used to tell me that Caruso was not a tenor, he was a man with a high voice; I think of Kathleen not as a contralto but as a woman with a deep voice. This is not to suggest that her range was restricted, I have heard her singing glorious top A's in Gerontius, but like Caruso's high notes there was a depth beneath them, giving them an added richness.

Incredulous eyebrows might be raised at my coupling the names of Caruso and Ferrier. I am conscious that with the tenor we had a miracle voice the like of which we have never since heard, a voice that has become legendary. Kathleen would have won fame merely by the sound of her voice for it was a superb instrument, expertly handled. However, it would be idle to say, as in the Caruso case, there has never been a voice like it and never will be, for there have been great contraltos in the past whose voices were as beautiful in quality as Kathleen's. Her voice would not have made the indelible impression it did had there not been a lively sensitive mind, a frank fresh spirit to inform it. Her message was simple, unspoiled and true, and it went straight to the heart. This was her glory, the reason why a kind of magic has clung to her name. The romance of her rise was a fairy story and seems now to those of us who were intimate with her to be a sweet dream. It appears to me now in retrospect that we who loved her must have been haunted subconsciously by the fear that her summer had all too short a lease.

Kathleen Ferrier became recognized the world over as one of the finest singers of her time, but to us in England she was something more, she was a phenomenon. Conductors and pianists we had of international repute but it is difficult if not impossible to think of any native concert singer contemporary with Kathleen who could be put in this category. The coming of Ferrier put an end to all this. The prophet 'not without honour' did not apply to her for we, in her own country, quickly recognized her stature nor did we have to protest on her behalf. Vienna, Milan, Paris, Amsterdam, New York, Copenhagen, all welcomed and hailed this English product, this rose of Lancaster.

How many of us, one cannot help speculating, could stand up to the adulation that came her way without it affecting our character? With her the test was made unimaginably more difficult by the very suddenness of it all. She sprang into fame like a flash. The one mighty bound with which she leapt to the front did not alter her nature, though she would sometimes marvel at the wonder of it and would laugh incredulously at the metamorphosis of the girl on the telephone exchange turned star. This simple unaffected outlook of hers turned aside any sense of rivalry from those who had been longer at the game, were older in experience, than Kathleen. Some of our finest contraltos – Gladys Ripley, Nancy Evans, Marjorie Thomas – were Kathleen's best friends and Astra Desmond, so long established in the public's esteem, wrote her the sweetest letter when Kathleen substituted for her in Manchester.

Indeed Kathleen generated goodwill and affection. She gathered friends around her as a light attracts the moth ; but she made no demands, nor was there any question of having to pay court. She was unspoiled. You went to see Kathleen because you wanted to be with her and laugh with her ; under her spell a bond was woven not only binding us to her but linking those of us in her circle one to the other.

Yes, unspoiled, always ready to laugh, she none the less knew her own value. At the first concert of our Holland tour – it was at Rotterdam – she complained of the draught on the stage. 'I am afraid of catching cold,' she told the local manager. He had the temerity to reply : 'You are in wonderful form for the concert and that is all that matters to me.' 'But the future does matter to me. This is the first and least important concert of my tour. Those windows must be closed otherwise I shall not sing another note.'

Kathleen did not regard the concert as unimportant but the man deserved to be treated roughly.

This awareness of one's own value is a regal quality attaching itself to the really great and bears no relation whatsoever to the vanity with which the mediocrity sometimes preens himself. I see it today in Victoria de los Angeles and Dietrich Fischer-Dieskau and it does not detract one jot from their humility as seekers after the truth or make them less human to their friends. It is an added dignity grafted on to the personality and acts as a protection. Kathleen being great herself naturally acquired this majestic pose. She would not dissipate her strength by appearing five or six times a week, though Emmie Tillett could easily have filled her engagement book. (Ben Davies scathingly alluded to singers who accepted every offer made them as commercial travellers, dashing daily from place to place.) Kathleen took her work far too seriously to follow such an undignified course and was able to put two or three days aside each week for rest and study. Thus she gave invariably of her best, thus did her every appearance become a notable event: it inevitably followed that her fee rose to realms undreamt of by any previous British singer. She anticipated an important appearance with the nervousness of a racehorse, but it was an eager nervousness unclouded by dread ; worry and anxiety suffered by so many artists – and fine artists too – were unknown to her. She was supremely sure of herself and of her vocal technique but such were her dignity and grace that this assurance was carried without arousing the slightest hint of self-satisfaction.

My feelings for Kathleen are expressed in a note I wrote her at the end of a three weeks' tour :

This visit with you to Holland has been undiluted pleasure: I have never felt so comfortable or happy in all my years with any other singer. On trips like this when two people are so constantly thrown together, it is easy for little nervous temperamental tiffs or moods to cause temporary clouds where personal relationships are concerned – but nothing like this has occurred with us. Certainly I have felt happy all the time – thanks entirely to your sweet nature, your unselfishness and un-prima-donna-ishness . . . I have said nothing of the enormous pleasure your thrilling triumph has given me. You have sung gloriously and it has been my fortune to be able to enjoy a share of this huge success. May I be associated with you for many years to come.

This was written in 1950. There were only three years left. The concerts that remained are precious to recall. She had European recitals with the admirable support of Phyllis Spurr, but America was too far away and had to be abandoned, to her sorrow. It was stirring to be with her in Germany and witness the enthusiastic reception her Lieder singing evoked ; thrilling in Paris where the audience was as sparkling as champagne. But perhaps the two most moving recitals were in the Norman Cathedral of Peterborough – she moved us to tears by her singing of Brahms's Alto Rhapsody with the choir, and her last appearance in recital with me in London at the Royal Festival Hall.

As I shall tell later, we had bought by now a house near Dorking up on Box Hill with an incomparable view over Surrey and Sussex and to our infinite joy Kathleen fell in love with it. With her sister, Winifred, and Bernie (Bernadine Hammond, her secretary-nurse-faithful-friend) she came down for frequent week-ends and said she was happier there than anywhere. She even made it her headquarters when we went off for concerts in the West Country and each time we returned would say to me as I drove through the gate, 'It's good to be home, luv.'

Her last visit was made before she started her Covent Garden rehearsals for *Orfeo*. Did she have some premonition she was seeing our place for the last time? I only know that she said to Enid and me before we drove her to town that she wanted to be alone for a few moments to drink in the view.

In the very house where I am writing these lines, in St John's Wood, Kathleen lived and it has a garden made beautiful for Kaff by her devoted friend, Ruth Draper. She called Brockham Warren 'home' and now we call this 'home'. We therefore have memories of Kaff all around us, and it would be but a poor tribute to her if they were sad memories. In her lifetime she was uplifting, she was inspiring, full of laughter, and that is how we remember her now.

She lived here no more than a few weeks before making her last visit to the nursing home – never to return. Enid and I visited her just before the end to be greeted by her with smiling affection. She tired quickly and gently sent us away by murmuring, 'Now I'll have eine kleine Pause'. Those were the last words we heard her utter.

*

After Kathleen's death the *Sunday Times* asked me to write a short tribute to my beloved friend and with their permission I now quote it.

KATHLEEN FERRIER

'She is irreplaceable.' With these words Bruno Walter expressed the feelings of all lovers of music, of truth, and of beauty over the loss to this world of Kathleen Ferrier. Her stay with us was so cruelly short, the love she kindled so great, that our grief is hard to bear. It was not yet time for her to go.

Within the space of one decade Kathleen emerged from the quiet shelter of her Lancashire home and conquered the world. We saw her grow from talent to greatness. We saw this with our very eyes. We heard that voice – a voice naturally warm and lovely – becoming more and more glorious with each succeeding year until it finally acquired a spiritual beauty, an unearthly nobility, an all-embracing humanity that seared our souls. Those of us who were blessed with her friendship know the measure of her greatness.

20

Canadian Classes

I LEARNED a great deal from the few private pupils who came to me for tuition during the war, but they did not teach me how to teach in class, and when the late Sir Reginald Thatcher, Principal of the Royal Academy of Music, invited me to hold a class for accompanists at that institution it was a new experience for me. Though I continued at the R.A.M. for several terms I soon realized the futility of trying to teach *en masse*. Where music is concerned each person needs individual treatment and does not get it when dealt with in a group. A convoy, they say, moves at the pace of its slowest vessel, and in class progress is slow : it is frustrating to the good ones and unnerving to those who are not keeping up.

I do not wish, however, to queer my pitch or to discourage schools of music from paying me nice fees to conduct masterclasses when I am free to do so ; therefore, in pursuance of this laudable point of view I accepted with alacrity the invitation of Ettore Mazzoleni, Principal of the Royal Conservatory of Music in Toronto, to hold a class for accompanying at their summer school in 1948.

Accordingly Enid and I flew the Atlantic – nor do I ever wish to cross that unpleasant ocean any other way – leaving London in the evening and lunching with friends at the Montreal Yacht Club the following day. Planes now accomplish this little hop in less than half the time we took then, but this flight was too quick for us : I had not been to Canada since 1929, nearly twenty years, and this was Enid's first visit. The transition was too sudden ; our Canadian friends found us dazed and tired. Having flown to the American continent every year since then I now find that I take this flight in my stride and feel no need for a gradual process of acclimatization.

My class in Toronto was held in the Concert Hall of the Conservatory with me on the stage, and the students and

The abnormality of an infant prodigy's life has left no scars on
Yehudi Menuhin

Solomon: No other pianist could compare with him in the playing of a concerto

Elisabeth Schwarzkopf: It seems to me quite unfair for anyone to look so ravishing and sing so beautifully

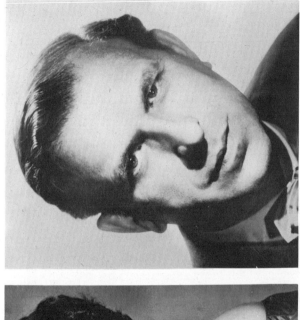

Victoria de los Angeles: She flooded the hall with a golden stream of sound as luxuriating as the sunshine of her native Spain

Hans Hotter, the outstanding Wotan of our time

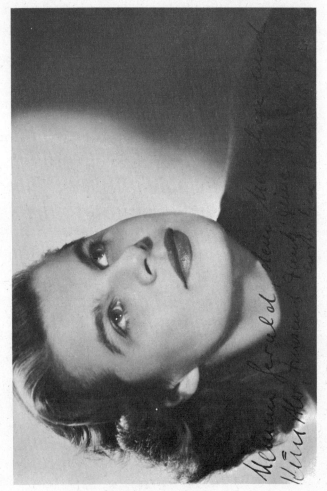

Irmgard Seefried's animation and zest delighted everyone

Pablo Casals: After a minute's playing he looked straight at me and said 'I am very happy'

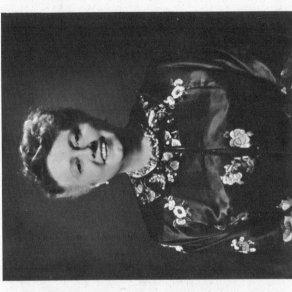

Elisabeth Schumann: An adorable person who, like her singing, was enchanting

Kathleen Ferrier: Her message was simple, unspoiled and true, and it went straight to the heart

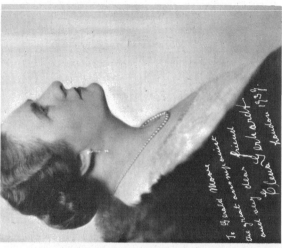

John McCormack: I wonder how many tenors there are in the world who can measure up to this man

Elena Gerhardt: No other Lieder singer in the first decade of this century made such an impact on the public of England and America

Dietrich Fischer-Dieskau: He had only to sing one phrase before
I knew I was in the presence of a master

several paying listeners sitting in the auditorium. The scene was designed in a way to throw the spotlight on the teacher who finds it is incumbent on him to hold the interest of all by putting on a show. I found myself doing just this, and it was difficult to be simple and sincere under these conditions. True, I listened intently to the work of my students and tried to help all I could, but I had to talk in a loud voice that all might hear; confidences became proclamations; gestures became extravagant. With a timid pupil I would try to find something encouraging to say when it was unjustified, but an extremely promising player I might criticize for the sake of effect and to show how high were my own standards.

The young men and women were a bright and stimulating bunch and there was hardly any hesitation when I invited them one at a time to come on to the stage to play, be stopped, and held up for criticism in front of the others.

Mazzoleni was present at my first séance when I gave an introductory lecture and he suggested it might be helpful if a singer were present whom my pupils might accompany. There was, he said, a girl who was brilliantly gifted. I was most grateful for this suggestion and I met her next day. As soon as she sang I was staggered by the beauty of her voice, by her knowledge and grasp of Schubert's songs. When she sang the time flew by, she inspired the lot of us. Her name was Lois Marshall, and today she is famous.

I found the standard of pianism fairly good but not that of ensemble or accompanying. None the less the class must have been considered a success for I returned in 1949 to repeat the dose, and this in spite of a discouraging paragraph in one of the Toronto papers which read, 'Gerald Moore is giving a series of twelve public lessons on the Art of Accompaniment to a class of students at the Conservatory, though what can be found in this particular line of country to learn or to talk about one cannot possibly imagine.' This music critic would most certainly have benefited had he enrolled in the class, though he would have slowed down the rate of progress considerably.

These invitations to Toronto were made the more attractive to me by providing me with the opportunity of staying with my brother Trevor and his family. My father had died two years earlier so I cannot but be thankful that he visited me in England when he did. It was a joy to be reunited with Trevor and to meet his children, David and Nancy, for the first time. We stayed as his guests during the classes and afterwards went to his summer home up in the Muskoka Lakes where we basked in the sun. Halfway up to Trevor's place you pass Lake Simcoe where in the dim future pilgrimages will be made to visit the house where Glenn Gould lived and worked.

The Muskoka country is a three-hour drive north of Toronto and it is well wooded and studded with lakes, rivers and islands. Good hotels can be found for the occasional visitor, but your *habitué* such as Trevor has his own island where summer after summer he stays with his family.

Enid and I had a heavenly time swimming, boating, golfing, playing croquet (at which we all became very angry with one another), bridge, and going on picnic expeditions. My passion for corn on the cob was indulged to the full for we would often of nights squat round a camp-fire and have roasted corn washed down by rye whisky. Could anything have pleased me more? Yes, only if the corn had been washed down by Scotch. There was no piano within two hundred miles, unless we except Gould's Chickering, which made Muskoka perfect bliss for us.

And yet in one respect the islands in Muskoka are not exceptional; they are, not to strain the reader's credulity, like any other islands the world over in that they are surrounded by water. For getting around, for your shopping, your fishing expeditions, you depend on boats. Trevor had a fleet of canoes, rowing boats and two motor launches. A brace of the latter, I suggested, was rather an exaggeration but Trevor countered by stating that one in reserve was essential. A friend of his indeed was shortsighted enough to possess but one: sure enough one Sunday afternoon when his five-year-old son swallowed a button large as a fifty-cent piece, the father could not get the engine of his boat to start. He was forced to row under the blazing sun two or three miles down the lake to the quay where his car was garaged and then drive his boy to the doctor another fifteen miles further. The doctor fortunately was in and with the aid of a stomach pump succeeded in unbuttoning the frightened little fellow. Thence back to the garage and once more the long pull home. Slowly the fatigued man, dripping with perspiration, pulled on his oars and was within sight of his house when he heard a whimpering and a wailing behind him; turning round he saw to his consternation that the resourceful boy had stuck his finger in the rowlocks hole and could not get it out. I never heard the dénouement to this intriguing situation; and therefore picture the youngster – now a young man – going around with a portion of gunwale decoratively adorning one hand.

*

After the peace and rest of our visit to my brother, Enid and I found the noise of our flat in Bayswater intolerable. It was situated on a busy corner with traffic lights; lorries laden with freight for Paddington, Euston, King's Cross, and St Pancras thundered past our door since we were on the direct route serving these termini. In warm weather with windows open one might have been sitting in Times Square or Piccadilly Circus. We resolved to find a retreat in the country. There was a charming old house with a walled-in garden near the Sussex Downs in a village named Ripe. Intoxicated by the charm of the scene and the situation of the house I resolved to buy it and paid down a handsome deposit. Then I took my old friend and solicitor, Mr T. E. Crocker, down and showed him around and complacently awaited his approval. He took one look at the old oak beams which ran through the house and said to me, 'Are you mad? Look.' He stretched up his hand towards a beam previously caressed so tenderly by us, roughly grasped it and brought away a handful of rotten wood. The place was riddled with dry rot. Crocker found a discrepancy in the house agent's measurements of the garden by crawling through the brambles and briars of this jungle with his measuring tape. He tore his trousers but saved my deposit. I felt it was well worth it.

Undeterred we still searched for a place in the country and eventually settled, as I said in my previous chapter, for Brockham, near Dorking. It had long wide lawns and trees, a rhododendron bush which would have filled Oxford Circus and, un-believable to relate, the house was centrally heated. On two successive summers Trevor and his wife, Kathleen, came from Canada to stay with us and nearly froze to death.

21

Elisabeth Schwarzkopf

INTERVIEWERS continually ask me who is my favourite of all the singers I accompany ; a silly question and I would not attempt to answer it since I have not retired from the active scene : again, how can one compare, for instance, Elisabeth Schumann with Alexander Kipnis ? Which of these two rates the higher ? Certainly at the present time three of my favourite singers – to name them, as theatre programmes say, 'in order of their appearance' in my life – are Elisabeth Schwarzkopf, Victoria de los Angeles and Dietrich Fischer-Dieskau. I play for these three more frequently at the time of writing these lines than I play for any other artists ; I love working with them and we have become close friends.

Neville Cardus considers I lead a charmed existence in that I follow some of the most beautiful women in the world on to the stage and I agree most enthusiastically with this highly qualified judge. A list of these Graces would be intriguing but it would have to be compiled in strict alphabetical order and here my difficulties begin. Does Victoria de los Angeles come under the letter D or L or A ? Is Lisa della Casa D or C ? But the S's – Elisabeth Schwarzkopf, Elaine Shaffer – are easily classified and would appear at the tail-end of the list and I could not bear that. Supposing too that I omitted, intentionally or unintentionally, some Jezebel, some Tell-me-mirror-on-the-wall-who--is-the-fairest-one-of-all type ? No, I must beg to be excused.

These ideas passed through my mind when recalling my first meeting with Elisabeth Schwarzkopf in the recording studios. It seems to me quite unfair for anyone to look so ravishing and sing so beautifully. But though her looks are a gift from the gods, the renown she has won with her artistry is due to application and industry.

In fact I can state with certainty that I have never met a singer who has Elisabeth's capacity for work. And by work I mean not only the mental processes – the silent study that must go into the creation of an operatic role, the concentrated thought required for the realization of Mignon's psychology in the Wolf settings of Goethe (for every serious artist must of necessity subject all she performs to this rigorous and deep reflection, after which the act of committing it all to memory naturally follows as the result of this disciplined procedure), no, she amazes me because she practises hour after hour with full voice. She necessarily has the physical strength and the vocal production to stand up to this.

Very frequently, accompanying a singer new to me, I have heard the full voice for the first time at the actual performance since all our rehearsals had been sung in *mezza voce*. Some singers hold back and save themselves in this way from fear of tiring the voice – even fine artists do this : lesser artists have good cause to do it if their voices are faultily produced, but with Schwarzkopf there is no holding back – no saving ; she has worked for two hours or more with me on the day of a concert and goodness knows how much more she has sung on this very day on her own without me. She has no room for technical imperfections and makes quite sure in advance exactly where every tone and every vowel must be placed ; there is a definite channel for each note. As a result of this she is the only singer in the world who can sing – to take but one example – the last phrase in the third Mignon song, *macht mich auf ewig wie der jung* (make me eternally young), as Wolf wrote it. The composer was merciless here : the phrase begins *forte*, high up with G flat—G natural—F, drops an octave with a *diminuendo* and then ascends a full octave again on a *piano*. It demands the technique of a virtuoso. True, I have heard singers sing the notes accurately, but they have been unable to obey the composer's demand for a gradual *diminuendo*, and have attacked the last note with a shrill and meaningless *forte*. Those who have faithfully tried to obey Wolf's dynamics have returned to this proscribed final soft high note with a strangled quality of tone that made the listener as uncomfortable as the singer. Schwarzkopf does it perfectly. The singer watches anxiously lest this self-imposed discipline involving repetition after repetition robs a song of its spontaneity ; the violinist, the pianist, working with like method and pertinacity are faced with the same problem. But it is the only way that Hugo Wolf can be mastered and that is why Schwarzkopf is the greatest interpreter of this composer among women singers.

I said earlier that Elisabeth was sure of herself, but perhaps it would be more accurate to say that I am always sure of Elisabeth. The more serious, the more idealistic the artist, the less sure of herself is she. If at rehearsal Elisabeth states quite positively that she is out of voice – 'Listen, I cannot sing this note at all, it will be quite impossible for me to sing tonight' – I regard these complaints as a good augury ; were she to lay claim to being in tip-top form I should refuse to believe my ears, should feel that something was wrong.

For she is the most cruelly self-critical person imaginable. Accuracy of intonation is a fetish with her. Time after time, at a gramophone session, she, her husband Walter Legge, and I will listen to a play-back and every other second she will mark her music with pencilled arrows, stabs, slashes and digs (her scores have to be seen to be believed, they appear to have been attacked by a drove of doodlers) muttering : 'That was sharp' – 'That was flat' – 'My God, how awful' – I sometimes despair of our ever making a record. Walter has a highly developed listening sense ; my ears are not bad ; but sometimes Elisabeth will confound us by accusing herself of singing out of tune when we cannot hear it. I have before now suggested that the most common-sense way for her to make good records is to prevent her at all costs from hearing her own play-backs, so ready is she to condemn them out of hand.

Her modesty and lack of faith in her own musical judgement are unusual in a singer of her experience and renown. As Svengali listened to Trilby – so does Walter Legge listen to Elisabeth and, being a Diaghileff where music is concerned, has contributed enormously to her brilliant career. His knowledge of music is vast. As I have already mentioned it was he who founded the London Lieder Club when a young man in the twenties and he has now become a powerful figure in English musical life, being artistic director of the Philharmonia Society.

Where music is concerned he is ruthless; the Philharmonia Orchestra built by him is a criterion of the standard he fights to maintain. His word is law when it comes to Schwarzkopf's singing and she follows his advice without question. Every recital programme of hers is of Legge's choosing and it may be taken for granted these programmes do not follow a humdrum pattern. Her memory and her capacity to learn and master a new work are so extraordinary that Walter Legge sets tasks for her which would be beyond any other singer.

My seniors were wont to tell me once upon a time that the opera singer could not possibly be a good concert artist and vice versa. They cited John McCormack and Feodor Chaliapin. The former was not at home in opera but was a superb recitalist while the other, in the trappings of opera a lion, was considerably less in recital with pianoforte accompaniment. But this ukase is not axiomatic and at the present time we know of several brilliant artists who are magnificent in both fields. Of course they are not all equally good, some are more equal than others, Elisabeth Schwarzkopf for instance.

In opera the singer has a large orchestra to sing with – or against – and any imperfection is far less noticeable than when only a pianoforte accompanies him. In opera he has make-up and costume, he can move about more and, we hope, can act. Standing in the bend of the piano he is restricted, for any movement is strictly taboo : in recital it is his voice that counts. Of course he is living in the song he is singing, and his facial expressions will naturally reflect the mood or moods of the poem. In Schubert's *Erlkönig* the frenzied child, the consoling father, the ghostly pursuer all have different voices and the singer's physiognomy changes for each of them ; but he makes no movement. Why, bless my soul, I remember one singer moving his body up and down to the galloping rhythm as if he himself were on horseback. It was extremely funny but it was not Schubert.

Nor is it Schumann when the singer gazes fondly at her left hand when singing *Du Ring an meinem Finger*. Why do not singing teachers or coaches watch and learn from Elisabeth Schwarzkopf? I ask this advisedly since I know many whose pupils seek to give verisimilitude by the waving of an arm or the turning of a head. Surely there is a lesson to be learned from this superb actress, an unrivalled Donna Elvira, Countess Almaviva, Marschallin on the operatic stage, who in recital never makes a movement. It is all voice, mastery of enunciation and liveliest facial expression.

I love partnering her because of her perfect musicianship and because her recognition of the importance of the piano part is most rewarding to the accompanist. She cannot be persuaded to acknowledge the applause without making me share it with her (as we stand to bow she calls to me, 'Was I in tune?' or some such question, but as I can never hear what she is saying above the hand clapping I invariably answer, 'Wonderful, Wonderful' – which is invariably true) and this generosity is extended to the opera house where her fellow-artists think the world of her.

At a recent performance in Salzburg of Don Giovanni all she could find to say to me afterwards was how marvellous Leontyne Price had been, and that she had never sung opposite such a Donna Anna before. I told the American girl of this praise from the finest Donna Elvira of our time but Leontyne said, 'Elisabeth made it so easy for me by her encouragement and friendliness.'

I have raved about Elisabeth's musicianship, her technique, her taste, but what of the voice itself? Perhaps by way of peroration I can do no better than quote another soprano singer who, as guest on Roy Plomley's radio programme 'Desert Island Discs', said: 'I shall always remember the first time I heard Elisabeth Schwarzkopf. It was at a performance of Fidelio in Salzburg. When she produced the first notes of *Mir ist so wunderbar* I thought I had never heard a lovelier sound coming from a human throat.'

The speaker was Kirsten Flagstad.

22

Victoria de los Angeles

THE year 1950 turned out to be a vintage one for me. Putting from the reader's point of view the least important event first, I presented myself in a Wigmore Hall Lecture Recital which later turned out to be a good investment.

So far as my accompanying is concerned the critics, across the ages, have given me encouraging reviews. If I refrain from quoting them it is not through lack of appreciation of these gentlemen's discernment, but rather out of deference to my innate modesty. I have no such scruples where my lecture or pantomime is concerned and can state unequivocally that I was remarkable and that the critics shared my enthusiasm. Apart from the wartime National Gallery concerts, this was my formal London introduction into a field which opened up new horizons for me.

Lest it be imagined that I am soaring too high on the wings of self-praise, let me admit at once that of far greater musical worth than my lecturing were my appearances with Irmgard Seefried, Hans Hotter, Bernard Sonnerstedt from Sweden, Boris Christoff and, reappearing after an absence of twelve years, Herbert Janssen. These recitals, the Wigmore Hall being considered too small, were held in the gloomy Kingsway Hall where more people could be accommodated. Elisabeth Schumann hovered between the Central Hall, Westminster, in which one had to have the hardihood of a Shetland pony to endure the draught – and the Royal Albert Hall where – in a joint recital she gave with Josef Szigeti – one heard two concerts for the price of one on account of the echo.

The Wigmore Hall, ever dear to me, was by no means neglected, however. It remains the ideal venue for intimate chamber music and for the ambitious Miss X, making her début and farewell on one and the self-same evening. None the less it has played its part in musical history, giants of the past – Ferruccio

Busoni, Eugene Ysaÿe, Vladimir de Pachmann – have graced its platform and it has witnessed the launching of many a distinguished career. And now on 4 March 1950 it was destined once more to be the scene of an occasion truly memorable, when Victoria de los Angeles, making her initial bow to London in recital, flooded the place with a golden stream of sound as warming and luxuriating to her listeners as the sunshine of her native Spain.

A few days before this recital for which I had been engaged by Wilfrid Van Wyck, I was passing through the foyer of the Wigmore Hall after a rehearsal with a violinist when I saw Astra Desmond at the box office buying tickets for the de los Angeles concert. Knowing Miss Desmond's discrimination I asked, 'Is she so good?' – for I knew nothing about her, not having yet rehearsed. 'Victoria de los Angeles', was the reply, 'is singing at Covent Garden tomorrow in *La Bohème*. You may be certain that after that performance this box office will be besieged and the hall sold out in an hour.'

And so it was. The little hall was jammed by a cheering, sobbing, stamping mass of people. Everyone knew that he or she was playing a part in a historic event. Mark Raphael, who knows as much about singing as anybody, must have expressed the feelings of all who heard her that night when he said that he wanted to fall on his knees and thank God for letting him hear such a voice.

She is unique as a prima donna in that she is not ambitious, is not a publicity seeker. Envy and uncharitableness are strangers to her since she does not compete with anybody nor wish to outshine her fellows. Sir David Webster and Mr Rudolph Bing, Administrators of the Royal Opera House, Covent Garden, and the Metropolitan Opera respectively, will say that in all their experience they have never handled an artist who made less demands or who fitted herself more smoothly into the scheme of things. For she is a quiet and modest lady whose happiest moments are spent in her own home, reading, studying, sewing, listening to records and the radio.

One has not necessarily to be a badly behaved person to have temperament and it must not be assumed because de los

Angeles is normally quiet and placid in her dealings with others
that fire and passion are not in her make-up. We hear these
in her singing and the revelation thrills us. She, like Eden
Phillpotts's farmer, could boast if she wished that 'a little
child can lead me but a regiment of soldiers cannot drive me'.
An instance of this was the first attempt to record *Carmen* in
Paris under Sir Thomas Beecham. All the soloists, chorus and
orchestra were assembled in the studio but there was no conductor. When Sir Thomas eventually arrived on the scene two
days late, they were so behind schedule that there was no time
left for de los Angeles to hear her arias played back to her. She
was dissatisfied with her singing of them and wished to repeat
them. 'No time, my dear,' blandly replied Sir Thomas. Whereupon she addressed the recording manager, Victor Olof, through
the microphone telling him he must inform the conductor that
she would either repeat her arias or not sing another note.
Beecham ignored all warnings, however, and went merrily on,
so the singer quietly closed her score and walked out of the
studio. Cries for help were sent to London; accordingly over
to Paris next day flew David Bicknell to straighten things out
and 'Where is my beloved Carmen?' cried T.B. 'I think at this
very moment', answered Bicknell in his matter-of-fact English
voice, 'that her plane will be touching down at Barcelona.'
'And she is quite right,' came Beecham's rejoinder, when he had
recovered from his astonishment. Record collectors well know
how triumphantly Beecham and de los Angeles subsequently
recorded *Carmen*, evidence in itself of the warm esteem in
which these two great artists held each other.

Back to Barcelona! How thrilled she is when she and her
husband, Enrique Magriña, are homeward bound. There and
there alone can she find the tranquillity for which her nature
craves.

How can this shy home-loving lady endure the restless life
of the prima donna with its travelling, packing, unpacking,
constantly changing hotels, telephone calls, interviews and
what not? She endures it because Enrique Magriña relieves
her of all responsibility and shoulders all the managerial side
of her career. Whenever Victoria walks into the wings from

operatic or concert performance – there is Enrique waiting with a glass of water and her cloak and, more important still, with words of encouragement and affection, for the truth is that the glorious career of Victoria de los Angeles is a partnership affair. Without Enrique, Victoria would have little urge to continue: persuasive when she is out of mood, soothing when she is ruffled, he is in every sense of the word a protector. Through him and his assumption of responsibility for all her affairs – correspondence, interviews, contracts, appointments – she is able to gain the seclusion so necessary for her study and her rest; precious hours wherein nothing is allowed to disturb her; even the ubiquitous telephone is ignored should Enrique be out on business.

In Spain she is a national idol and is mobbed if she visits a public restaurant and since she would not dream of being other than gracious to her admirers she finds it easier to remain in purdah.

Even when I am on tour with them in Italy or Germany I see very little of Victoria. Of course, we travel together – they love it when Enid comes too – and a happy party we are, but only on isolated occasions do we lunch or dine together.

True, I do see Victoria when we rehearse, but she is not the person to overdo this sort of thing. My great friend, Fritz Ganss, recording manager for Electrola (the German branch of E.M.I.) with his typical and admirable love of thoroughness, was surprised when de los Angeles and I did not meet to rehearse before the first concert of one of her tours in Germany. He had motored me from Berlin, where I had been recording with Fischer-Dieskau, to Bielefeld the day before the concert. Victoria and I had not met for six months nor did I clap eyes on her until, resplendent and dazzling in her evening gown, she entered her car with me to go to the concert. But as I explained to the slightly shocked Fritz, this was a great compliment that de los Angeles paid me: I was intimate with her programme and she knew without asking that I had studied and practised it anew, just as surely as she had been doing so in the privacy of her room.

Fritz, who had made the journey from Berlin specially to

hear her, confessed to me afterwards that never in his life had he heard such a voice as Victoria's.

The German audiences are so steeped in Schubert and in the Lieder tradition that it must be something of an ordeal for a foreigner to stand before them singing their own songs to them. I know Victoria anticipated her first few concerts in Germany with some trepidation but she need not have feared for her singing has the freshness and spontaneity that are the essence of Schubert. 'His music', as Capell wrote, 'suggests a rippling movement and by the side of the rippling a flowering: it has the variety and unsurprising naturalness of moving water and springing herb.' It is fascinating to me, used to playing for German and Austrian singers, to see how different from theirs was Victoria's approach to Schubert. Many of them hold him in such awe that they puzzle and worry the sparkle and sunshine right out of him. Not so Victoria, she opens her heart to him and sings. And Germany is at her feet.

When I first played Spanish songs for de los Angeles I felt just as apprehensive as she felt when singing German songs to her first Berlin and Munich audiences. True, I had a good knowledge of Spanish songs, Granados, Manuel de Falla, Joaquin Nin and the rest, but I played them for singers who were not of Victoria's stature.

We *Ausländer* are inclined to look on Spanish music as an enigma wrapped up in a mystery, and we make it the vehicle for a display of temperamental extravagance with angry splashes of vivid colour and exaggerated distortion of rhythm; all this to give it an air of authenticity. But this is wide of the mark. Victoria de los Angeles, Pablo Casals, Andrés Segovia, do not perform their national music with reckless abandon, their interpretations are refined, well-ordered and poetic with never a suggestion of inelegance. That I have won her confidence in the playing of these songs is due to a great extent to her guidance, and that I should have been all over Spain playing them for her I regard as a great compliment, for undeniably their rhythm and their colour must be in your bones.

The songs were born of the dance so that you hear when Victoria sings Granadina (assuming you notice the accompaniment) the stamping pride of the Zapateado, in Malagueña and Jota the flick and then the rattle of the castanets, and in all of them the nostalgic twang of the guitar. These suggestions are vital and are ever present in the mind of the performer, but they are not enough of themselves, for even in a single song or dance the mood is evanescent: a mood of languor – relaxed and sensuous – can turn suddenly to one of fierce energy that takes all your physical strength to give it the fire and virility it demands. The singer's and player's response to these moods should be as startling as the *sforzando* stamp of the dancer's heel, and yet, as I have said, should be accomplished without distortion, should never be thrown away with complete abandon.

After a lifetime of listening to hundreds upon hundreds of lovely voices I would say without hesitation that for the sheer quality of sound, Victoria's affects me more than any other. I cannot listen to her Mimi with a dry eye and was so overcome after a recent performance at Covent Garden that when I visited her in her dressing-room I could not trust myself to speak: this amused her so much that she embraced me, saying, 'Don't worry, my dee-ah boy,' (how I love it when she calls me her dee-ah boy) 'I was only pretending to die, you know.' When she sings *Adios Granada* to her guitar accompaniment in the Patio de los Arrayanes in the Alhambra, the jewels of her *Flamenco* – a perfectly matched and graduated rope of pearls – reduce me to tears even though I have heard her sing the song many times.

These emotions – I add this in self-defence – are aroused only when I am a listener, not when I am associated with her on the concert platform: there, living in the music, I am concentrating only on being one with her, dynamically, rhythmically, spiritually; trying in vain to make my pianoforte echo the gold in her voice. At performance I am not moved at all, I am too anxious to do justice to her. At performance, one brings nerves and sensibility to bear and devotion to one's work, but emotion has now become intellectual so that its outpouring is channelled purely into the singer's voice, into the pianist's fingers, and must be under control. As the actor who hopes to move his audience leaves his tears behind him in the rehearsal room, so does the musician. I have known a singer incapable of performing a certain song for the simple reason that she felt it too deeply – lost control.

At all events, the glory of Victoria's voice does not affect Miss de los Angeles for she is rarely satisfied with her singing. She has too much to think about, to study and memorize to have any inclination to sit back and look around her complacently. Her recital programmes indicate how catholic is her taste and as for opera, one can reel off one role after another: *Tannhäuser* at Bayreuth; *Pelléas et Mélisande*, *Manon* at Paris; *La vida breve* at Barcelona; *Butterfly*, *Bohème*, *Traviata* at La Scala; every imaginable role at Covent Garden and the Metropolitan. What versatility!

It is more than ten years since I first played for Victoria de los Angeles and each concert is still more thrilling to me than the last. And when after every song she turns her dark lustrous eyes appreciatively and – yes – affectionately in my direction I feel it is good to be alive, to be there with her, to bask in the radiance of her adorable personality.

Of course I love her, but who am I among so many?

23

Dietrich Fischer-Dieskau

WITH Kathleen Ferrier on 16 March 1951 I went to Cologne. I mention the specific date for it was after this very recital that my neighbour at supper asked me if I had heard of a young baritone – then in his early twenties – named Dietrich Fischer-Dieskau. I did not know the name but was promptly told, 'Then you soon will. He is one of the greatest interpretative artists Germany has ever produced and is already the world's finest Lieder singer.'

No more than six months later this young giant walked into the recording studio in London with his beautiful wife; we had been booked to record Schubert's *Die schöne Müllerin* together. He is big in every way: physically, intellectually and musically, with the commanding presence that was Chaliapin's though he comports himself with modesty; a modesty born of the subconscious awareness of the greatness of his capabilities, of the magnitude of the tasks that lie ahead of him, and of the burden of responsibility growing ever heavier with his increasing fame and lofty ideals. He had only to sing one phrase before I knew I was in the presence of a master.

How does it feel, it might be asked, when at my time of life, a quarter of a century Fischer-Dieskau's senior with my vast experience, to find myself playing for a man who is able, by his supreme artistry, to make startling revelations to me? Perhaps it is only fair to myself to say that I am too serious a musician to suffer any heart-burning on this account, and the everlasting joy of my profession is that one is always a learner. Age makes no difference and if anybody can open the door and shed a new light on things I gratefully accept the fresh air and the illumination. I found this with the boy violinist, Josef Hassid, and I find it now with Fischer-Dieskau.

When Frank Howes wrote of Solomon: 'Interpretation as demonstrated at this level is seen as fundamentally the same art as composition – the art of creating music', he might equally have applied the same words to the genius of this young Berliner.

Concerts with him are inspiring experiences, but to me the supreme thrill is rehearsing with him. At rehearsal he is as nervous and transported as an archaeologist bringing a long hidden treasure to light. His concentration is so intense that he is quite unaware that his hands are twitching with excitement. He greets me with his cherubic countenance wreathed in smiles, for despite the fierce effort our work requires, mentally and physically, it is anticipated by both of us with keenest pleasure.

This man, Fischer-Dieskau, has taken me deeper into the hearts of Schubert, Schumann, Wolf, Brahms than I have ever been before.

If this statement is to be taken at its face value it would surely imply that we have innumerable and marathon rehearsals, but this is not so. Before a recital in Berlin, London, Paris, Milan we may have two – at most three – rehearsals lasting no more than ninety minutes each; for programmes that we have previously performed together one rehearsal suffices. It goes without saying that we are musical intimates with a complete understanding, and in the course of our preparation each is vividly alive to the reactions of the other. It is a mutual affair. Grateful though I am to him for his inspiring influence, responding with electricity to his promptings, I should be doing this great singer less than justice if I gave the impression that he arrogates to himself alone the right to make suggestions. There are no conflicting personalities when we work together: we discuss, we test, we try this way and that way, and quite often Dieter will ask my advice and weigh it up; for he is an artist, not a prima donna.

What is the essence that illuminates his art? What is the magic formula that enables him to reveal to us with clearest understanding everything he touches?

It is not enough to say that his voice is wonderful, that he has an incredible technique which enables him to do what he will; it is not enough that his enunciation is flawless with perfect marriage of word and tone. Temperament? Abundance of it. Passionate love for music? Of course. But there are other great singers with these virtues.

If I had to put my finger on the key to Fischer-Dieskau's supremacy, setting him apart from every other singer, I would say, in one word, Rhythm. This is the life-blood of music and he is the master of it.

In my chapter on John McCormack I emphasized how the Irish tenor and John Coates tried as much as possible to use a natural speech rhythm, were not bound by the mechanical tick of the metronome or under any obligation to beatify the first beat of a measure. Fischer-Dieskau goes even deeper than these superb artists. His freedom and elasticity are not only influenced by the words he is singing but by a poignancy of feeling for the music itself. He understands what the composer felt, and is able to reveal and express it so piercingly that it goes to the heart. Let me put it plainly: I cannot think of one single song that Fischer-Dieskau sings where he would keep strict time throughout. In the pianoforte introduction to the first of the *Harfenspieler* songs by Wolf (*Wer sich der Einsamkeit ergibt*) the metronome and I would be at odds in the very first measure, for the third and fourth beats here take longer than the first two beats: the second bar is similarly shaped to the first; but the third bar – climbing in pitch to the fourth bar – is in a quicker tempo altogether; the fifth slow again. This is the shape as Fischer-Dieskau conceives it, a shape to be clothed by colour and feeling. The design, once set to one's satisfaction, dictates almost of itself the light and shade needed to give it meaning and eloquence, wanting here a thick stroke of the brush, there a thin. At least this is how it seems to me: colour, nuance, falling naturally on to the bare bones of the muscular and elastic structure.

Nor is this treatment confined to the slow moving or lyrical style of song, Fischer-Dieskau employs it in music of heroic or energetic vein. In Schubert's *An schwager Kronos* or *Abschied* it is tightened, as the muscle of Chopin's Military Polonaise is tightened by an almost imperceptible *rubato*. The series of re-iterated chords in Wolf's *Der Rattenfänger* are not played as printed – with the regular spattering of a machine gun nor with uniform *fortissimo* ; there is the sudden pause or comma, the drop in tone quantity and then the mighty rush forward with quickened speed and steep *crescendo*. Either it can be played with the soulless correctitude of a pianola or the human element of excitement can be imposed on it.

Rhythm, as Paderewski said, is the soul of music and no one recognizes its potency more than Fischer-Dieskau.

In his early twenties he was accused of being too serious : only in songs of a sombre nature, it was said, was he *par excellence* ; he lacked the light touch. It is possible that in those days he was particularly attracted by *Die Winterreise – Vier ernste Gesänge* – the *Michelangelo Lieder*, for these are gigantic challenges for a young artist which have to be met. But if there were any germ of truth in this criticism, it is most certainly not the case now. In his recorded album of Wolf's *Mörike*, *Zur Warnung*, *Storchenbotschaft*, *Abschied* are masterpieces of comedy. In *Zur Warnung* his portrayal of the man waking up with a fearful hangover after a night's drinking and attempting to sing is one of the funniest things I have ever heard. Is there a more pot-valiant Falstaff than he or a Count Almaviva giving point to Mozart's humour with greater delicacy ?

Perhaps the artist whose comedy is so superb in these roles, whose portrayal of Berg's Wozzeck or Busoni's Dr Faustus can be so pitiful or tragic, is a different person from the one whom I accompany in Lieder. He considers a song recital more of a strain mentally and physically than an operatic role : and I remember him so white of face, so full of apprehension, over what he called his shortcomings on the day of a Berlin concert we had together that his younger son aged eight declared, 'Daddy, I do not want to be famous like you because it makes you so worried.' True it is that his demeanour as he stands at the piano acknowledging his audience's greeting is unsmiling and grave : can this be the same easy and relaxed individual, one asks, who is such a consummate actor in opera ? It would not be in character for Fischer-Dieskau to present a smiling and confident countenance, nor, I might add parenthetically, do Heifetz or Casals exude an air of geniality when they appear before us : one expects an Elisabeth Schumann or a

Frieda Hempel to emerge smiling at their public for that is part of the picture, but a man does not of necessity have to do this, nor need he appear other than serious.

Fischer-Dieskau's personality has forced itself so strongly on all who see and hear him that curiosity is continually being expressed as to what manner of man this phenomenon is.

Were I to say he lives music, thinks music, talks music, I should be telling the truth and yet the statement gives an impression that, utterly dedicated to his art, he has no room for any other thought in his life ; this would be wrong. This would be to suffer from a complaint which is called in my profession 'being music simple', an affliction particularly trying and tedious to fellow-musicians of the delinquent.

I do not know a more stimulating companion than Dieter, for his mind and imagination range widely. He speaks English without the semblance of a German accent and his taste in reading embraces anything from Shakespeare to Somerset Maugham. This, with all the travelling he does in England, America and Italy, gives him a broad culture (he makes the word 'broad' rhyme with 'road', the only mispronunciation of which he is guilty) and as a result his humour is not Teutonic – his wit is quick and keen, he laughs frequently – but always quietly – with a long low gurgle which rapidly rises to the surface. I heard this delightful gurgle and joined in after putting a question to him in the early days of our friendship. 'Are you a Roman Catholic ?' 'No, I am a Lutheran,' he said, 'and my father was a Pastor in the Lutheran Church.' 'But,' interrupted his wife Irmgard, with great seriousness and vehemence, 'you must understand, Gerald, that his father was not a Priest in the Roman Catholic Church for in this case Dieter would not have been here.'

Had he his time over again he would either be an actor (no one who has seen him in opera could wonder at this) or a painter. For his holidays he forgets music, sits in his garden in the Lindenallee, paints and reads of painting. He delights in beautiful things and has a fine collection of glass, china, and old furniture. The reconstruction of his handsome house was planned by him and it would be unthinkable to plant a new tree in his garden without his anxious consideration. In his wife's clothes and jewellery he takes great pride for she is a sweet and lovely girl; when I expressed to her my admiration for an unusual bracelet she was wearing, she told me, 'It was designed by Dieter.'

Music, naturally, is the mainspring of his existence. His library of books on the subject and of gramophone records is vast. Do you wish to compare a Schlusnus with a Slezak performance of a Wolf song? The records are found in a moment – for they are all carefully indexed and have each their particular niche on his capacious shelves – and the performances discussed. Unlike many singers, interested only in songs or opera, Fischer-Dieskau wants to hear everything – having a passion for chamber music and orchestral music. The catalogue of his records compiled in his own scholarly hand is an encyclopedia in itself; for there beside the list of a composer's records is a picture of the composer with a short biography of his career; possibly there will be a picture of the singer, conductor or pianist.

Every so often his relatives and friends will be invited for an evening's music. Dieter will choose one composer and will give in his own words this man's biography. He will have registered this talk previously on his tape recorder so that his full attention can be given to the various pictures he flashes on the screen, synchronizing with his words. After the little lecture, informative, witty and sometimes moving, the audience settles back to a carefully selected programme of this composer's recorded works.

His thirst for music is insatiable. Finding ourselves sentenced to spend a week in Iceland, his wife, a very fine violoncellist, and I gave a sonata programme purely for his pleasure; a command performance.

Irmgard indeed is a remarkable young woman, for besides running the household with its staff of servants and looking after their two young boys, she and Dieter's secretary are responsible for all the business connected with the singer's career. For, according to him, when he is not working at his singing he is resting: 'There are only two positions for a singer; on his feet or on his back.' He has an uncanny assessment of his own physical strength and knows exactly when to cry a halt. For instance, my engagement book for our next recording dates in Berlin reads as follows: Monday – rehearse: Tuesday – rehearse: Wednesday – rest: Thursday – record: Friday – record: Saturday – rest: Sunday – rehearse: Monday – record: Tuesday – rest: Wednesday – record. Is he studying most of the time he is resting? Most possibly, but at least he is saving his voice and his strength. When he stepped on to the stage at Schwetzingen for his first rehearsal in Hans Werner Henze's *Elegy for Young Lovers* he had never previously heard one single note of the score though everyone else in the cast already had had several orchestral rehearsals. Yet he was note-perfect and word-perfect. He had learned and memorized the big role of Mittenhofer when ill in bed. I know at gramophone sessions that immediately he feels the slightest fatigue he stops and announces he can sing no more and no amount of persuasion will make him budge. Nor is he obeying the whim of a prima donna, he is simply doing what he knows is wisest.

This wisdom, this detached self-critical faculty of his, gives the answer to a question with which he has been pestered for years; namely, when will he sing Hans Sachs? This mighty part could be his for the taking whenever he wished and no one doubts that he would be the supreme Master-singer of his time. After all, a great operatic baritone in the German tradition must have the ambition to play Sachs, as a violinist aspires to the Bach Chaconne or as a pianist to play the Hammerklavier. His reply to all entreaties is inexorable. 'I shall not play Sachs until I am forty years old.' Impatient though I am to hear it, I cannot withhold my admiration for the wisdom of this young man, this refusal to be tempted by glory.

For the enthusiasm and appreciation shown by the public he is naturally grateful since he is only human, and being human he is pleased by a good press and disappointed when it is adverse, but the glory and glamour attached to him through his unique position in the world of music leave him unmoved. He guards his privacy very carefully. Not for him crowds of strangers and autograph hunters invading his sanctum the artists' room at the end of a recital; he will have none of it. His sense of dignity rebels when, tired and perspiring after an arduous evening's singing, it is taken for granted that he should be at the disposal of all and sundry who want his signature: the concert over, he wants to be out of sight and he slips away as unobtrusively as possible.

This disappearing act of his is not without its funny side. At his Munich hotel the receptionist and the hall porter never see him for the simple reason that he never comes into the foyer; he steals down a back staircase and leaves by the rear door where his car awaits him – he tells me all this with a twinkle in his eye. And he is vastly amused when I mention to him that on asking the porter on my arrival for the number of Mr and Mrs Fischer-Dieskau's suite, the porter's eyes clearly say, 'I do not believe in the existence of this man.'

This readiness to laugh even when the laugh is at his expense is one of his most endearing qualities; it is a manifestation of his warm personality and of his modesty.

I have learned so much from this great musician, this young man hardly born when I was playing for John Coates; he has come along in the autumn of my career and so stimulated and inspired me by his marvellous artistry that I cannot but say – for what I have received I am truly grateful.

24

Entracte

I READ every word of *Moby Dick* and it nearly killed me. The preparations for the sailing and the protracted voyage take an eternity but at last the reader's pulse is quickened by the sight of a whale's silvery jet. 'There she blows,' calls the lookout. This is the moment that Herman Melville corks up the fountain of the whale and of your excitement and gives you a long chapter beginning, 'It is some systematized exhibition of the whale in his broad genera, that I would now fain put before you.'

Again and again the author does this. No sooner is something exciting to be seen on deck, than you are taken below to be lectured on the monstrous pictures of whales, and on the less erroneous pictures of whales. I confess I lost my boyish enthusiasm, found myself inhaling the sultry atmosphere of the museum or laboratory instead of the salty tang of the sea.

They all tell me that *Moby Dick* is a great book, for Melville is an honourable man. Why, therefore, should I not follow his example? I have led the reader through the struggles of my early youth, he has seen me launched into my profession, has emerged with me safely through war's vicissitudes to witness the resumption of my career by association with Pablo Casals – and now I am about to embark on my first – and so far my one and only – tour of Australia. It seems the moment, therefore, for me to pause in this chronology of my breathless achievements, and to take a look around me.

Let me ease the reader's mounting excitement by taking him on one side to consider matters 'almost indispensable to a thorough appreciative understanding of the more special ... revelations and illusions of all sorts which are to follow'.

25

What are Brahms?

ONE summer evening my wife emerged into the mews from the Wigmore Hall artists' entrance whence I had preceded her by a few seconds, to find me red in the face yelling after the retreating figure of a man, '. . . at Merthyr Tydfil'. She asked me, naturally, what in the world I was shouting about and what was the excitement? I had been playing for the highly successful Welsh-American baritone Thomas L. Thomas; many of his compatriots from the principality had travelled to London to hear him and it was well worth the journey. Although my mother was Welsh and the Wigmore Hall at one time my spiritual home, I felt as I gazed around the sea of faces from Ebbw Vale, Llanfairfechan, Llangollen, and Dolgelly that I was, for the moment, in some corner of a foreign field. Escaping as is my wont at the earliest opportunity from the scene of action I was accosted by a stranger at the stage door who said, 'Excuse me, but do you belong to the singer or do you belong to the Hall?'

'Sir,' I thundered in Johnsonian style, 'I belong to myself. I play in America, Europe, Australia and Asia.'

As he retreated in a bemused condition along the mews I raised my voice. 'Last week I played in Moscow and next week I am at Merthyr Tydfil.' (I had certainly played in Moscow a week earlier but it was inaccurate to state I was Merthyr-bound in the next, for I was actually going to play in Swansea, but in the heat of my oratorical flood I preferred the alliterative Merthyr. I hope the poetic licence will be condoned.)

But why should this innocent fellow have had to suffer the vials of my wrath when those who ought to know better are more culpable? Even some of my fellow-professionals regard the accompanist's work with a jaundiced eye.

When the bluff good-natured Peter Dawson in his *Fifty Years of Song* suggests that the ideal arrangement at performance is for the accompanist and his piano to be hidden from view in order that the public may be able to feast their eyes on the singer alone and not witness the apologetic entry and exit of the accompanist, the fussy turning of the pages: when I recall the greatest compliment I ever had from him was that I was the only accompanist in his experience who did not *bother* him, I feel less indulgent, even though his world was the variety theatre rather than the concert hall.

But a more uncomfortable situation arises when a superb musician, Josef Szigeti, regards his colleagues at the piano – even when performing sonata duets – as an employee. I found it was a waste of time donning evening dress at a Szigeti concert, for he stood at the end of my keyboard between me and the audience rendering me invisible; and our sonata finished, Szigeti with an unsmiling nod in my direction – as if summoning a waiter – signified his permission for me to stand up and acknowledge the applause. Although I would not dream of awaiting his nod and would stand up and bow under any circumstances after a duet, his treatment was chilling after the warm handclasp and whispered congratulations of other colleagues. I would not minimize for a moment the pleasure and benefit it was to rehearse with Szigeti; only at concerts was his lack of humanity revealed. In his autobiography, *With Strings Attached*, he makes no mention whatsoever of Nikita Magaloff, his faithful friend and magnificent partner for so many years.

That Szigeti's bearing towards the accompanist is old-fashioned is endorsed by Coenraad V. Bos in his *The Well-tempered Accompanist* (published by the Theodor Presser Company) in which the doyen of accompanists of his time commits sabotage or at least does very little to promote the status of his brethren. Again and again he preaches 'self-abnegation', 'unobtrusive support', 'self-effacement', 'the presumption of self-obtrusion'. Any startling or arresting variety of tone in the accompanist's playing is described in this little book as 'an impropriety'. And then, should the modest little man at the piano be suffered for a moment to come from behind the green baize door, Bos caps it all with, 'if the accompanist is afforded an opportunity to play solos they should not be too elaborate or too long; nor should an encore be given without deferring to the soloist' and 'the singer's generosity in granting permission to play an encore should not be abused'.

The prima donna of a bygone age must have adored Bos if this were truly his attitude.

For me to quote an old colleague whose playing I much admired is unkind; it would be fairer if I were to assume that when Bos dictated these words to his amanuensis he had little idea how sickeningly obsequious they would appear in cold print.

There is no doubt at all that in 'the good old days' the accompanist was of a lower caste than the soloist. It was not without reason that Max Beerbohm in *Zuleika Dobson* described the delightful picture of the stout soprano dragging on, as an afterthought and with gracious condescension, the reluctant figure of her pianist of whose existence she had previously seemed unaware, to take a little bow.

The less cultured players and singers I occasionally partnered in my young days meted out the most arbitrary treatment to me, they wanted an accompanist to be a mouse; the thought of partnership, had it ever occurred to them, would have been obnoxious. And when my name appeared for the first time on a gramophone record, the singer for whom I was playing raised Cain. In fact George Reeves once complained bitterly to me that a certain accompanist had a vogue, was getting much more work than either of us, chiefly because he received such very bad press notices and that this was pleasing to the singers.

There are very few artists today of this nature, I am glad to say, so perhaps some progress has been made. If the first-class accompanist does not receive the recognition that is his undoubted due it is the impresario or concert promoter and the undiscerning journalist who should be indicted.

Even at charity concerts where my services were given without fee I have played without receiving a word of thanks. Worse than that, the organizing committee, having assembled a glittering array of stars, seem to conspire to upset the accompanist. If the concert is in some private salon, the committee will hide the pianoforte behind a pillar. Should there be no pillar then they fix the accompanist by arranging the floral decorations in a massive formation in front of him. This actually happened to me when my instrument, and I with it, were shrouded beneath and amid huge sheltering palms; through their fronds I was dimly discerned crouching and gibbering over my keyboard, looking, with the tail of my dress-coat brushing the floor, exactly like a monkey. After the concert a friend greeted me with, 'Hello, Tarzan,' and was surprised I did not join in his hearty laughter.

But one of the best of all tricks is to omit one's name from the billing, a master stroke this, and calculated to upset the artist more than anything else.

During the war I was asked to give my services at a big concert in the Royal Albert Hall in aid of some charity in connexion with the London Fire Brigade. I was glad to do this. I lived at this time in Bayswater, and Enid and I frequently walked of a summer evening in Kensington Gardens. Finding ourselves opposite the Royal Albert Hall we looked across the road at the posters advertising the different attractions. There it was, the Fire Brigade one, at which I was playing. I read the names of all the singers, actors, comedians, who were generously giving their services. I saw the artists for whom I was playing, John McCormack, Robert Irwin the baritone, Harold Fielding, violinist, but I saw no mention of the accompanist. The fact that I had to make more appearances at this concert than anyone and had to rehearse with three different artists, made no difference, my name was not mentioned. I wrote a letter of protest at this disgraceful slight to the accompanist to the organizer of the concert. Perhaps my letter was strongly worded, at all events they never asked me to play for them again. But I noticed with some satisfaction that on the next occasion a concert was given under the same auspices that the accompanist's name – I believe it was my colleague Ivor Newton – was treated with the dignity and prominence that any artist giving his services is entitled to expect.

Such a slight – not only to me personally, but, which is much more important, to my calling – can perhaps be condoned on the grounds of ignorance. But what is one to say when it happens at one of the great London colleges or academies of music?

At an informal concert on a hot Saturday afternoon, a rare day with the sun shining from a cloudless sky and cricket in full swing at Lord's, I went to the Duke's Hall where a presentation was to be made to Frank Eames on his retirement as secretary to the Incorporated Society of Musicians. A little music, it was thought, might grace the proceedings. Astra Desmond sang with me, May Mukle played some 'cello pieces with me, and in between these items Harold Craxton gave us some early English piano music. Presiding over the affair was the Principal, now retired, of one of our London Conservatories of Music. He thanked the singer, he thanked the 'cellist, and he thanked the solo pianist for their kindness in coming to pay this tribute through their music to the guest of honour, but he never mentioned the poor accompanist. I wrote *him* a letter too. He was most apologetic but the damage was done. That I was hurt personally does not matter very much, it is the contumelious attitude towards the accompanist's art which matters. For this I am jealous. And for this to have happened in the precincts of an establishment where I had given several lectures and held classes in accompaniment and where I was now playing without fee (and longing to be at Lord's) did not lessen the sting.

Happily the events I am relating are in the past, but in America to this day the accompanist is a nonentity, not indeed to the music critics who recognize the value of his work, but to the all powerful impresario.

I examined in Chicago with utmost care the posters of Renata Tebaldi's recital; I read her name, the name of the hall, the name of her impresario, the time and date, the ticket prices: I read the programme which was given in detail, but there was no mention of the artist who was to partner her through a recital in which the pianoforte played a vital part. I happened to know that Giorgio Favoretto was going to play; one of Italy's foremost accompanists.

I go to America annually for a lecture tour and I enjoy every moment of it not only for the friendliness and warmth of the people I meet but for the stimulation I get from my audiences – but nothing would persuade me to accompany any singer in America for I lack the meekness and lowliness of heart to swallow the anonymity which would be my lot.

Supposing that some conductor or solo pianist had intimated that he would like to be an accompanist on the occasion of the Tebaldi recital in Chicago, would the concert announcements omit his name? On the contrary. Moreover his name would be accorded equal prominence with Miss Tebaldi. So far as I know Tebaldi is always accompanied by Favoretto but there are some singers who, without compunction, will dispense with the services of a man well practised in this difficult and exacting art and put up with the discomfort of having a famous virtuoso pianist or conductor to play for them.

There are, perhaps, extenuating circumstances. One can understand the advantage it was to the young Elena Gerhardt on her début in England to have the renowned conductor Artur Nikisch at the piano, for huge audiences would be attracted at first, purely by the curiosity of hearing a great musician playing an unfamiliar role.

When Kathleen Ferrier told me that Bruno Walter had offered to play for an Edinburgh Festival recital of hers, I applauded the idea, realizing that association with him would reflect lustre on the young English artist.

Conceivably a young singer feels her career is given a tremendous impetus when she shares the platform with a world-famous man. But the accompanist finds it difficult to understand why a singer will dispense with his services in favour of a non-practitioner when that singer is well and truly established.

Alec Robertson, reviewing a record of Hilda Gueden accompanied by the solo pianist Friedrich Gulda, hit the nail on the head when he wrote:

It is surprising that in these days of demarcation in trade unions solo pianists or conductors have not been forbidden to become, on occasion, accompanists: a task, in which, very naturally, they rarely succeed. Gulda of course plays beautifully on this disc but *accompanies* less well, using too much pedal and missing the subtleties of the skilled accompanist.

Was Hilda Gueden's considerable reputation enhanced by reason of her association with a virtuoso soloist? I think not.

Naturally everybody who can put a finger on a keyboard has the ambition to accompany Elisabeth Schwarzkopf; her name is a household word and it is a delight to work with her but I wonder if it occurred to Edwin Fischer and Walter Gieseking when they recorded Lieder with her or Wilhelm Furtwängler when he played a Salzburg recital for her (with the pianoforte lid wide open overpowering the superb singing) that they were not giving this artist the support she would have had from a man dedicated to this type of music making?

The accompanist is not supposed to have any feelings in this matter, in fact I sometimes wonder if he is considered as an artist at all. Even the critics will allude to his craft rather than to his art, as if he were a carpenter or a weaver. In Bernard Shaw's *Saint Joan* the man who alludes proudly to his Mastercraftsmanship is none other than the Chief Executioner, though I concede the analogy so far as I am concerned is not a happy one.

An article appeared recently in *Time*, the American weekly magazine with a world-wide circulation, bearing a picture of me and discussing the accompanist's career: in fact it was entitled out of compliment to me *Unashamed Accompanists*. I was interviewed and was asked many questions. I supplied the names of some of the finest artists in my field, Erik Werba, Ulanowsky, Rupp, Lush, Favoretto, Klust, two young men Geoffrey Parsons and Martin Isepp, and one revered artist Harold Craxton who has retired from the concert world. After saying that I 'cut with Savile Row perfection' my rhythms and colours to suit my singer (a comment which did not altogether please me since it implies that slickness, suavity are on tap) the article ended with a *bon mot* from my friend Harold Craxton which undermined all that I had fought for. He said: 'When all is said and done the utmost the accompanist can expect in the way of gratitude from the singer after a concert, is when he says, "You must have been good tonight, I did not notice you were there!"' Now this was, no doubt, a high note on which to finish the article from a journalistic point of view, but from the accompanists' angle it was a very low note indeed and destroyed any good the article might have done and was the same old saw that Raymond von zur Mühlen used to Coenraad V. Bos seventy years ago.

Has the art of accompaniment made no advance since that time? Am I deceiving myself by claiming that this attitude towards my work is old-fashioned? Have I failed in my mission?

The answer comes from on high. It comes from Dietrich Fischer-Dieskau who wrote a glowing introduction to the German edition of my *Unashamed Accompanist*. After saying 'there is no more of that pale shadow at the keyboard, he is always an equal with his partner', he adds this trenchant sentence: 'It is quite apparent how new and unique the type of accompanist is which he represents.'

So the Philistines are routed, they are, after all, old-fashioned. Hope is restored.

26

My Work

PERHAPS after all there must be one other reason that gives birth to my complaints in the last chapter. Is the accompanist himself to blame? I am afraid the answer, generally speaking, is yes, for so often he seems to be deaf to the significance of that which lies under his fingers, comes nowhere near realizing its infinite possibilities and does not allow himself time to think, study, practise, in order to digest and master it.

I would like to get hold of many an average not to say mediocre accompanist (some of them are well known and are what is called successful) and make them write a hundred times daily the words 'It is not easy'. To the Toscaninis, Solomons, Fischer-Dieskaus, nothing is easy; and the further they progress, the deeper they probe, the more experience they imbibe – the harder they find the going and the less easily are they satisfied.

Let me rouse the incredulity of many accompanists by stating categorically that I do not know of one single Schubert song that is easy to play. I can anticipate a chorus of protests. It would be said that *Wanderers Nachtlied*, *Nacht und Träume*, *Thränenregen*, *Litanei*, *Du bist die Ruh*, *Der Neugierige*, to name half a dozen famous songs at random, can be read at sight with ease. But I insist that the accompanist's reputation is made by the playing of these songs, they need far more thought and jealous care than *Erlkönig*. Undoubtedly *Erlkönig* is a great creation and presents a formidable challenge to any pianist but, without being disrespectful, once you have mastered it you have mastered it, it is like riding a bicycle; and provided you are in good practice and physically fit it will be tackled without fear. Its difficulties are obvious, and the accompanist will work away diligently to overcome them just as he will peg away at the arduous passages in the Kreutzer Sonata, but for the life of him he will not or cannot see that *Wanderers*

Nachtlied needs any time spent on it at all. 'Practise *Wanderers Nachtlied?*' he will ask. 'Why, I can read it at sight.'

I am not one of those people who believe that the mechanical ability to read at sight is the chief requirement of an accompanist. One can easily read at sight most of the songs in *Die Winterreise* but it would be monstrous to suppose one could grasp all that is in Schubert's mind on first glance at his score. At least I, personally, am not so patronizing and I know I have not sufficient genius to be 'at one' with Schubert thus easily. You may read music as fluently as you read a newspaper but it does not make an artist of you and I count it just as clever to be a good stenographer.

Let me attempt to explain then, why I feel that *Wanderers Nachtlied* requires much thought and preparation.

It is a slow-moving song of religious tranquillity, with the accompaniment in block harmony. Goethe's words describe the night scene, the hush on the mountain top, 'even the birds are mute', all is peace. And then 'Only wait, my soul, only wait and you too will know such peace'. The introduction to this song consists of eight or nine chords which take a few seconds to play.

Dynamically this little *Vorspiel* is all *pianissimo* but within the bounds of that *pianissimo* there must be a slight increase or swelling of tone and a subsequent reduction of tone. It is a curve – rising then falling; the smoothest of curves with one chord joined to the next. So restricted in range is it, so narrow the margin between your softest chord and your least soft chord that if you go one fraction over the limit at the top of your curve all is ruined. Each chord though related and joined to its neighbour is a different weight, differing by no more than a feather. You listen self-critically as you practise it. You experiment. You play it giving each chord a uniform and gentle pressure so that there is no rise and fall of tone – all *pianissimo*. You then try to give it that infinitesimal *crescendo* and *diminuendo* that is really wanted to give shape and meaning to the phrase: but it is out of proportion – you have overdone it – so you start again. Now you find that your chords are muddy, your pedalling is faulty, one chord trespasses on another's pre-

179

serves instead of gently merging into it without blurring. You work at this. But despite the *pianissimo* you are achieving, you begin to realize that your chords are without character – they are leaden, and the whole phrase is lifeless. So now very delicately you experiment by giving a fraction more weight to the top finger of your right hand. Now the top note is predominating, is singing clear above the lower notes. This is too much and you try again, taking care that all the inner harmonies and your bass octaves are clearly heard, be it never so softly, and that the soprano tune for which that top finger bears responsibility – it may be the third, fourth, or fifth finger according to the shape of the chord – is wafted out so delicately that no listener could be aware that you are giving it more pressure. This is your secret.

All this is the most fascinating pursuit imaginable. In your search for the light and the shade you are as happy and as absorbed as the painter mixing the colours on his palette, and the satisfaction to the player when he does succeed in producing that perfect undulation, that clean line, when he feels at last that the whole design is shapely and fine, is immense. But this satisfaction or self-satisfaction is experienced but rarely. Just as surely as you are aware you *have* brought it off, so surely does your ever sharpening sensibility tell you how elusive is the prize and how many times you fail to attain it.

It may be argued that by working and experimenting in the repetitive way I advocate, the spirit, inspiration, freshness of the music may be lost. Indeed this is the greatest danger. Your playing must, simply must, be spontaneous and fresh. The serious artist, be he singer or player, practises in this way and it is only experience that tells him, no matter how ardent and persistent his search, when the time has come to give pause.

How inspiring for the singer when rehearsing to feel that his partner at the piano has given the song as much study as he, knows the poem, is aware of that awkward corner just approaching, anticipates with him – not responding after – to this inflexion and that. There is no argument over the *tempo* for it must be sung as slowly as it is possible for the singer to contain a phrase in one breath. Here the accompanist finds new material for thought arising with each different artist who sings this song, for some singers have a lesser breath capacity than others. A more flowing *tempo* must be adopted and now you find that the infinite repose, which is this song's essence, is threatened. How to counteract this? You look for a point of rest. After the phrase 'Über allen Gipfeln ist Ruh' – your singer breathes and here you rest. It is a punctuation mark in the text and in the music, and you make full use of it, stretching this point of rest a little more than strictness of time would allow. (I must make it quite clear that this point of rest is not an aching void, for the pianist sustains his chord, he does not 'breathe' with the singer.) I cite only this one point of suspension but several others can easily be found.

Little music, with the exception of dance-band music, is ever performed in strict time. A slavish adherence to the metronomical beat is inhuman; it cramps the muscle of heroic or noble music, starches out the elasticity of that which ought to be lyrical, and deprives of feeling or eloquence that which ought to affect the listener.

Some of my friends may have raised a supercilious eye-brow when I referred in an earlier chapter to my attributing my technique to John Coates. They would have questioned my possessing a technique at all had they regarded the term in a superficial way. Were technique to imply merely the wherewithal to perform prodigious feats of keyboard dexterity and velocity, then there are thousands of young men and women in the world today with a better technique than Schnabel ever boasted. On this gymnastic conception I could be described as mediocre: I could not get beyond the first two or three measures of Anton Rubinstein's *Staccato Study* and as for Balakirev's *Islamey*, I would not dream of attempting it.

But technique means more than that. It embraces production of tone in the same way that a singer's or a violinist's technique does, not only the production of a beautiful tone but a variety of tone colours; technique is called on when effecting a well-modulated *crescendo* or *diminuendo*, for controlling a *rallentando* or *accelerando*. The shaping of a phrase, a sure test of a pianist's musical grammar or musical good manners, is founded largely on technique. Obviously under the same heading comes pedalling; the pedal is the pianist's best friend.

Surely it is impossible for us on our percussive instrument to obtain a perfect *legato*? Our all absorbing problem is to give the impression that we can. But if I sit at my piano and with all my weight strike the chord of C major with both hands, and depress the sustaining pedal, what happens? Immediately the tone starts to decrease. True it is a gradual diminution but the process begins immediately all the same. The first tones to go will be your treble tones and if you stand on your head you can do nothing about it. The bass tones – with their longer, stouter strings – outlast the treble, but even they are reduced in a short time to silence. How is it possible to do justice to the noble theme of the Appassionata slow movement, making a long steady *legato* line, when each chord decreases as you play it?

That we are persuaded it is possible is the wonder of a great pianist's touch. Our ears, most fortunately for us, are deceived and are not so hypersensitive as the microphone whose vibrations are shown in the recording studio on the level indicator, where we can see plainly that the tone, after the initial striking of the chord or note, is most certainly decreasing. A few years ago a prominent scientist emphasized that the hammer strikes the string smartly and bounces back whether you drop your elbow or your foot on the keyboard; this so called 'touch' was an elementary compound of weight and velocity; therefore a pianist who attaches importance to the idea of 'touch' is talking poppycock; in other words the love or care or thought or sensitiveness with which you depress your note go for nothing: you can play loudly or softly, with a progressive scale of dynamics from the one to the other, but the quality of tone can in no way be influenced by the player, the quality having already been installed by the maker of the instrument. This was the scientific argument and it all looks very logical. But in point of fact these conclusions are quite wrong for one pianist can draw a beautiful tone and variety of tonal colour from his piano while another on the identical instrument will fail to do so. Who can say where technique begins and ends? Under the wider meaning of the word I would say my technique is by no means a bad one: this is entirely due to John Coates. And the point I am striving to make is this: that the homily on *Wanderers Nachtlied* the long-suffering reader has had to endure is purely and simply a matter of technique – the mechanical ability to produce a beautiful stream of sound and gradations of that sound. From this point onwards the human elements of love and feeling are added: but technique is the foundation without which love and feeling will go for nought.

If by my reckoning, then, the simple-looking *Wanderers Nachtlied* deserves so much thought it stands to reason that the accompanist's field of study and experimentation is unending.

I guarantee that I will find a hundred pianists and more who can dazzle us in the presto of the Beethoven Sonata to one pianist who will transport us in the Schubert song.

It is not easy.

*

Perhaps one of the most vexed problems the accompanist has to face is that of balance, the balance of tone between voice or violin and piano. The accompanist cannot set down his own standards of tone values; he cannot say, 'This is my *fortissimo*, this my *forte*; this is my *piano* and this my *pianissimo*.' These standards vary with every type of music (a Brahms *piano* is weightier and thicker than a Debussy *piano*) and with each singer: they are dependent also on the acoustic properties of the concert hall and again on the quality of instrument under the pianist's fingers. He listens sensitively to his singer's voice until he knows its potentialities as well as he knows those of his own pianoforte, giving his partner as much support as he possibly can but at the same time taking care not to overpower or cover the voice. It is a nice point. The vocal tone and pianoforte tone reach the listener in equal quantity. Nor is the issue simplified when it is remembered that at a concert, the one person in the hall who hears the voice less perfectly than the audience is the accompanist himself since the singer's face is turned away from him and directed into the auditorium. On the platform we have a false balance; at least it will be false if the listeners are to hear a just balance. Giving the singer the great body of tone he needs in a mighty song such as Schubert's *Die Allmacht* I can hear under my organ-like chords only the merest whisper from my partner even though he is using full voice.

All the same the accompanist has to exert some discretion; he dare not obey implicitly the markings of the composer. Even the biggest voices require, on occasion, a little clemency from the pianoforte. Playing, for example, Brahms's *Der Schmied* for Kirsten Flagstad, and Richard Strauss's *Cäcilie* for Lauritz Melchior, I could safely give all my tone under these huge voices when they were at the top of the stave, but I most certainly had to show consideration when they descended to the bottom of the voice even though the composer's markings still called for me to play *fortissimo*. Had I followed these injunctions I should have been too loud for my singers and would have given them such discomfort that they would have been impelled to force their tone.

The problem of balance is further complicated: it is not a *sine qua non* that because a voice is big it will stand more weight from the pianoforte. Chaliapin and Kipnis had big voices but the fact that they were deep made it incumbent on me to accompany them with discretion or my tone would have covered theirs. In volume their voices were greater far than Elisabeth Schumann's and yet her voice could stand more pianoforte tone than those basses, being a high soprano.

Therefore the *tessitura* of the voice or instrument has to be considered. We find a parallel with the violin and violoncello, for the violin's notes lie in the treble and high treble, and though it is but a quarter the size of its big brother, its tones are less likely to be submerged.

One essential difference for the pianist between playing for the singer and playing for the strings must be explained. With the singer, it is the accompanist who is responsible for procuring a just balance of tone between his pianoforte and the voice. If a graph could be made of the respective tonal weights of singer and accompanist it would be seen that they are identical: at least they ought to be for a perfect balance. (I am speaking generally, though there are, of course, exceptions to this rule.) But in instrumental sonatas the situation for the pianist is different in that responsibility for obtaining a balance of tone is shared, the players do not necessarily seek to match one another in volume: here, the composer wishes the violin to predominate and the pianoforte to recede; there, it is the violinist who must make way and allow the pianist to take the floor. In this respect the pianist in a permanent duo has an advantage over the accompanist (by a permanent duo I mean a pair who arrange to work as a team, only accepting engagements together, never changing partners) for the accompanist playing with all and sundry cannot pick his violinist or violoncellist. He may find himself with a player who saws away regardless of the pianoforte part. I, for instance, have had the vexation in Brahms's E minor Sonata of being unable to hear my lovely melody – clearly marked *dolce* – because the 'cellist played his parenthetical and repetitive bass notes so loudly. Should I struggle to make myself heard above him and make the entire phrase *forte*? This thought flashes through my mind at the very performance since the question at issue did not arise at rehearsal. If I obstinately adhere to the composer's instructions and remain true to the spirit of the music, playing *piano* against my partner's outrageous *forte*, I should read in the paper on the following day: 'There was not sufficient support from the pianoforte.' I once asked Lionel Tertis what were his tactics with a pianist who played too loudly for his viola and he said, 'I play softer than ever.'

*

One of the most tiresome tasks that comes the accompanist's way is that of transposition. For the benefit of those of my readers who do not know what it means to have to 'transpose' a piece of music (how I envy them) I must explain that though your score is printed in one key you actually play it in another.

At recitals and in recordings with singers I am transposing half the time and so is every other accompanist. Singers make the most unreasonable requests at times with little idea of the stress they are imposing. To play, for instance, Wolf's *Nachtzauber* a tone down or *Zur Warnung* a tone up are complicated assignments, for the songs bristle with accidentals and unexpected progressions. Being asked to make these transpositions I should always require a little time to work on them. (A little time? I flatter myself.)

Difficult though *Night's Magic* and *Warning* are to *transpose* they are not difficult to *play* once your brain is functioning in the new key. On the other hand a song may be easy to transpose in terms of transposition, let us say from G natural to G flat, but if it is a fast moving piece of music it will involve a change of fingering necessitating some preparation.

It is history that a violinist playing the Kreutzer Sonata with Brahms found the pianoforte a half-tone flat, whereupon he asked Brahms to transpose the entire work a half-tone higher to save him from tuning down his strings. The fact that Brahms accomplished this prodigious feat proves what a giant of a musician he was, though a still, small voice within me asks, 'Did he play *all* the notes?' If he did it was a miracle of physical facility which enabled his fingers and hands to adapt themselves without preparation to the different fingering and hand positions that the new key involved. Many a good musician reading the Beethoven Sonata away from the pianoforte – as one reads a newspaper – could transpose the work in his mind into A flat or A sharp, but to *play* it in those strange keys would mean much labour for the notes would no longer be 'under the hand'.

Schubert's *Liebesbotschaft* was originally written in the key of G for high voice. In this key the accompanist can make the little brook ripple softly and sweetly; his fingers literally flop into position with ease. But voices of a lower compass also want to sing this charming song and, the *tessitura* of the original key being too high for them, the song is published in other keys, for example in E flat. But the mere fact that it is *printed* in the new key is of little help to the accompanist, for he could have transposed it into any key. But the point is this, his hand no longer flops naturally into position; technically the song has become more difficult to play. Of course, the accompanist can 'cover' the notes somehow, but can he make the song ripple as softly and as smoothly as it rippled in the original key? The song once easy must now be practised anew and refingered. And yet the audience is unaware of these difficulties; they know only that for some unaccountable reason the brooklet has become a torrent and is thundering and heaving and bumping over the rocks.

As a young man I was gifted with what is known as 'perfect pitch', and this was rather an impediment than an advantage to me when I had to transpose: playing a piece of music in B flat, when my eyes saw the page printed in C natural, upset my ears and brain, I found my fingers subconsciously wandering back to the tones I could hear with my inner ear – the tones that I saw on the printed page.

During my 'perfect pitch' period, a singer with whom I frequently worked asked me to transpose a song down one tone from A flat to G flat. There was a top A flat at the end of the song, and he was frightened of it, so I undertook this transposition having several hours to study it before our concert. It was not a difficult change to make except for one stretch of some dozen or so bars in the middle of the song – bars of startling modulations which were crawling with pestiferous accidentals. At the performance I embarked on the transposed song with quiet confidence, but when I approached this dark forest of quick-moving double-sharps and double-flats I became nervous – in fact I lost myself. I beat and hacked my way through the undergrowth and got entangled. When I emerged breathless into the clearing I found, to my horror, that I was now playing the accompaniment not one tone *lower*, but one tone *higher* than the original key. This nearly killed my colleague, for he now had to sing a top B flat instead of the G flat he had bargained for. A nasty guilty feeling still steals over me when I recollect his bulging eyes, swelling neck, and the awful noise he made as he flung himself, like a fish out of water, at a note that was beyond his reach.

This was the end of a beautiful friendship.

The gradual loss of perfect pitch has been an advantage to me as an accompanist, since it makes the act of transposing less hazardous for me – and for the singer.

*

I have only touched in this chapter on one or two of the absorbing questions with which the accompanist has to deal and of course I have expressed a purely personal opinion : not everyone will agree with me. Many an accompanist will feel that my approach to *Wanderers Nachtlied* is exaggerated out of all proportion to a piece of music that a child could play : some singers (of the older school ?) might scout the thought that the accompanist's tone should equal theirs in volume : some 'cellists will aver that the pianist can never play softly enough. Be all this as it may I have attempted at all times to practise what I have herein preached ; for better or for worse.

27

Psychic Bid

IN a television interview on the Ed Murrow programme, Mme Maria Callas and Sir Thomas Beecham declared that, facing the public, the performer must have the inner conviction that what he was going to do he could do better than anybody else in the world.

This is going too far. I am certain that Pablo Casals does not tell himself how marvellous he is; he is humbly praying that he will do justice to the music he is about to play. A man who walks on to the platform convinced that there is nobody like unto him is not a serious artist, he is a pompous jackass.

The term *prima donna* – literally first lady (of an opera company) – has unfortunately become debased and it is now universally applied, metaphorically, to men or women who consider themselves as superior persons, better than others. It is these people who are known to the layman as 'temperamental'; again a much abused term.

Every artist has passion, poetry, fire, tenderness – in one word temperament – in varying degrees, but when I am asked in an awed whisper, 'Is Madame X temperamental?' I know perfectly well what the nonsensical question means. It may be taken for granted, strangely enough, that it applies to a singer and it would be safe to assume too, in nine cases out of ten, that it applies to a woman. Nobody would ask if Gioconda de Vito were temperamental since she is a violinist but they would ask if Elisabeth Schwarzkopf or Victoria de los Angeles were. Another distinction: there would be no question of Eileen Farrell or Kathleen Ferrier being temperamental because they are respectively American and English. The true intent of the question would be better expressed thus: 'Is Madame X well-behaved?' for, apparently, if the answer is in the negative, then Madame X is 'temperamental'. To deserve this rich and magical delineation, a person has to have the following qualifications it would seem: he, sorry, *she* must be rude, pugnacious, capable at any moment of flying into screaming and uncontrollable rage, she must break contracts and, in short, be thoroughly unreliable. Of necessity she must be a 'foreigner'.

As a rule these ill-mannered people (or temperamental, if you insist) are the most difficult to deal with since they are unbalanced. Their music like their lives lacks a basic rhythm, and they are as a rule poor musicians. Perhaps an inferiority complex is at the root of their peculiarities.

I am aware that every living person under the sun considers himself a good, nay, infallible judge of character. I do not claim infallibility but I am right half the time and manage to get a fair idea of the functioning of the minds of my working partners. The accompanist must endeavour to do this since his art is to a great extent an unselfish one ; his life is spent listening to and considering the other fellow. Your solo pianist, on the contrary, is the complete individualist. As for the conductor, he would be hard put to it if he concerned himself with the mental processes of the players under him : to put it more succinctly, he does not give a damn. Chamber music (the string quartet, the violin sonata, the Lieder cycle) demands an intimate cooperation and understanding between the performers. With a permanent ensemble this presents little difficulty but with the accompanist who works with scores of artists during a single season it is indeed a problem. Yet I find this one of the most exciting aspects of my work, getting to know my colleague through the music.

At the first rehearsal the experienced accompanist soon learns the quality of his partner, the standard of his musicianship, whether he is serious or superficial. He gets, too, some knowledge of the man's character : is he conceited or modest, coarse or refined? Is he excitable and nervous, or calm and restrained? Hot or cold? These considerations have as much bearing on the harmony between singer and accompanist as have the more technical questions of ensemble.

As a young man it was very natural that I should defer to my colleague when a matter arose for discussion at a rehearsal, for generally I would be his junior in years and in experience.

He would also be a figure of fame whom I would regard at our initial meeting with some awe. He was always right and I was always wrong. Always? Well not quite, for I remember a passage in Richard Strauss's *Traum durch die Dämmerung* when I had to wait after a comma in the musical phrase for my singer to sound his note, since my chord was due on the half beat *after* his note. He waited for me – I waited for him. He strode majestically to the piano, looked at the score over my shoulder, and asked why I waited. I replied that I had to wait since my entry was half a beat later than his. 'I sing it exactly as it is written,' he said, 'and your chord comes first.' I therefore played it first but it was wrong. This sort of thing happened frequently when I was feeling my way; I even had the experience of the singer forgetting the words in public, breaking down completely, and turning deliberately to glare at me so that it might be patent to all that the accident was of my doing.

With added years and widening reputation, however, the accompanist's psychological problems increase. The indignities he had to stomach in his youth cannot now be tolerated. His handling of that little situation in the Strauss song described above depends largely now on the musicality of his partner, perhaps a word will be enough to put the singer right or perhaps the phrase will need to be repeated half a dozen times before it is secure. Possibly the singer is incapable of mastering this condemned spot and the accompanist must use his judgement as to whether to persist or give it up as a bad job.

The accompanist has to know when to advise, when to accept advice, when to attack and when to retreat. If your partner, perhaps the proud owner of a magnificent voice, is musically crude and commits grave errors of musical taste, you have to ask yourself the question – is it worth the fight to put them right? The concert is one week hence, you have never previously met one another, can you possibly make the transformation in time? Once again you abandon the chase. You feel guilty about it but there is nothing to be gained in unsettling the singer before the event, when time is so short. On the other hand, if the young singer or violinist is an artist of considerable promise you owe it to him, and your conscience, to work and work again, until he has overcome his difficulty.

Advice, however, has to be tendered tactfully in some cases, for you can easily rob your colleague of what little confidence he may have. While it may be aiming too high for a member of the Diplomatic Corps to aspire to being an accompanist, the latter most certainly has to be a diplomat. (Indeed the beautiful idea occurs to me that if some of these distinguished Dips really studied the art of accompaniment they might become much more successful diplomats.)

So far so good, but what happens at the concert when through nervousness or force of habit the singer falls back into the error you have striven so hard to correct? The answer is unequivocal: *the singer is always right on the night*. Every good accompanist is a life saver on more occasions than is generally recognized and if I give two instances of my own propensities in this valiant pastime it is not to single myself out above my fellows.

Misha Léon, a tenor very much in vogue in my youth, included *The Cloths of Heaven* by Thomas Dunhill in his English group: it is a song that strays charmingly through a succession of keys and, to my surprise, I heard my singer in an unaccompanied phrase sing this whole phrase one tone lower than it should have been. I jumped with him and transposed the rest of the song. We started in the key of E flat and finished in D flat.

The Holmesdale Fine Arts Club in Reigate, Surrey, engaged me to play with a violoncellist a programme of contemporary music. The President of the Society requested that we include Frank Bridge's *Mélodie* which we learned specially for the occasion. At the concert we were halfway down the first page when our paths diverged and it slowly dawned on me that I did not know where on earth my 'cellist was: suddenly I heard the open C string (the 'cello's lowest note) played *fortissimo*. 'Heavens,' thought I, 'this long C comes on the last page.' I quickly turned several pages – eloquent pages destined to be unheard – until I found and joined my drowning partner who was still hanging on to her note for dear life. 'That *Mélodie* was the gem of the evening,' we were afterwards told.

But my best life-saving story came from Elena Gerhardt and is a testimonial to Coenraad V. Bos's coolness and resourcefulness. They were performing Wolf's *Lied vom Winde* (*Song of the Wind*) and Elena's memory played her false for once and she omitted a huge slice from the middle of the song. As smoothly as you please Bos bridged the gap and to Elena's surprise they finished together. The audience, bless their hearts, were so thrilled with the performance that they insisted on it being repeated. 'Won't they be bewildered', whispered Bos to Elena before he began again, 'to find the song has become much longer.' In truth, the first attack of wind had been a short one.

Although no voice producer, the experienced accompanist is a discerning critic and the young singer would do well to visit him at least six months before her recital for him to assess her capabilities and confer over the choice of programme. The singing teacher is not always the best judge of what is suited to his pupil, while the accompanist can often see things in truer perspective.

'Why did Gerald Moore allow her to sing Brahms's *Zigeunerlieder*?' wrote one critic the morning after a Wigmore Hall recital. The critic had good cause to question the judgement of this particular choice for the Gipsy Songs need a big full-blooded voice with vigorous piano playing whereas my singer had a small sweet lyrical quality quite incapable of 'filling out' the music. Naturally my playing had to be reduced in size and the sum total of it all proved but a caricature of what these songs should be. Why then did I not counsel the young lady to alter her choice? Because I was not consulted: the programme had been chosen by her teacher and was a *fait accompli*, in print before our first rehearsal.

I would not like it to be thought that I am constantly handing out advice in an Olympian way to all the artists who have the misfortune to cross my path. On the contrary I learn something from nearly everyone for whom I play. The accompanist cannot be inflexible and he finds, to his amazement, there are hundreds of ways of interpreting one simple piece of music. When my colleague is a fine and sensitive musician I listen carefully to what he says. If we are not in accord – it may be a question of mood, phrasing, dynamics, colour, tempo – then I compromise. I find most often that my partner is prepared to compromise too and we come, without trouble, to a happy understanding. Sometimes he will stick to his guns, will not budge, and I have sufficient respect for him to capitulate ungrudgingly, knowing that his ideas are born of his own inner convictions and are by no means illogical.

Elena Gerhardt, for instance, found my tempo for Schubert's *Liebesbotschaft* far too fast. I did indeed state my opinion which is that the rippling 32nds in my treble represented the rippling stream and that the song's time signature was two beats to the bar and not four but I did not pursue the argument with a woman whom I so deeply respected. When I played this song for her I adopted the very slow speed she liked. This is the only song where we ever disagreed.

Recording *Vergebliches Ständchen* with Christa Ludwig I found her tempo too slow for my taste but on hearing the finished record I find the interpretation delightful – and the tempo is just right for this opulent voice.

One can add as an afterthought here that it would be a dull world if there were only *one* way of performing a Schubert or Brahms song. One singer on this basis would be the same as another, one accompanist – but no! I carry the preposterous premiss no further.

It is a great help, it might be supposed, towards a unanimity of ideas if the two associated artists conceive a respect – not to say personal sympathy – one for the other. But this is not to be taken for granted. Many of the people I have accompanied in the past I liked personally but I disliked playing for them; when I state that I can think of many friends with whom I am in complete disagreement musically it is not to imply that I am right and they are wrong, it is simply stating a fact. Yet strangely enough I remember good performances with some for whom I could not say I felt great warmth of heart; Szigeti was not the man to inspire that feeling nor was Ida

Haendel, yet I greatly enjoyed making music with them: but then they are both superb violinists and that is the main consideration.

But how could one begin to like a conceited young man who told me, as I related earlier, that if the London public liked Kreisler, then he would play in the Kreisler manner?

A pretentious young man is difficult to cope with. Dame Myra Hess quite disinterestedly championed a young violinist some years ago, who seemed to show promise. The boy had his chance when Max Rostal, his teacher, had a slight accident: he was called in to fill the breach to play Beethoven's Violin Concerto. By chance James Agate, the dramatic critic, was at the concert. He went mad over the boy, had a large picture of him inserted in the *Daily Express*, and wrote the most fulsome notice in which he described the performance as liquid bliss and almost credited the player with genius. This article had a wonder that was twofold; firstly it took up a lot of space when newspapers were severely restricted in size (it was during the war), secondly it was a so-called musical criticism written by a man who was a self-confessed amateur where music was concerned. I remonstrated with him, saying that this hysterical publicity – far in excess of anything Menuhin or Heifetz, recent visitors to England, had received – might harm a young and undoubtedly talented boy who was still only in the student stage. That my fears were not groundless was proved some time later when the youngster came to me to rehearse for a London recital; he had all the airs and graces of a prima donna and when my wife saw him off the premises she expressed the hope that we had had a profitable rehearsal; 'Yes,' said he with a complacent smile, 'poor Gerald had to go through it.' I had to explain, when told of this, that his meaning was that I had been purified seven times in the fire of his genius.

As a footnote to the above I must, in justice, add that this young man himself 'had to go through it'; he did not find that the world was waiting for the sunrise. After the Agate explosion had died down he had a long and hard struggle which had its effect on him. He is now modest and, through dint of sheer hard work, has emerged as a gifted and sincere musician.

I repeat; the finer and the more serious the artist, the greater his modesty when approaching his work. Set Svanholm, that superb Siegfried, Loge, Tristan, with scores of operatic triumphs behind him, came to rehearse *Die schöne Müllerin* with me; he had not previously performed the cycle in public. His first words to me were, 'Tell me all – say anything you want to me.' My reaction was not one of pride at my own importance, nor did I glow at the implied acknowledgement of my authority: on the contrary I felt an increased respect for Svanholm.

The eternal problem for the performer is the settling of his own mental equilibrium, the striking of a happy mean between conceit and self-confidence, between self-satisfaction and a sober valuation of his worth.

Undoubtedly there is some truth in the Callas-Beecham apophthegm for it is assuredly necessary for the artist to think well of himself or he would never dare make an exhibition of himself before an audience. Let us remember when we witness an artist on the platform radiating the most sublime self-assurance that in reality he may be extremely modest and nervous, that he has donned this cloak of self-complacency to disguise his fright. For my part I am aware, when acknowledging applause, that I wear my warmest smile when I know that I have played badly; the smile helps me to walk off the stage and masks my fury. A bad performance haunts the artist like a nightmare for days and days and the memory of it is only erased by a good performance. All the same the too introspective artist is in a bad way as I discovered on my American tour with John Coates when I was thrown into a precarious state of nervousness that all but unbalanced me. The most vigilant self-criticism of course is necessary, but the time comes when the artist must tell himself he is good or he will go under.

It is a fight.

28

Acoustics, Lighting and Air-conditioning

FRITZ KREISLER, who must have put a girdle round the world many times, has declared that the itinerant musician on his wanderings saw only a town's railway station, hotel, and concert hall. And indeed an artist unpacks his tail coat and flies straight to the hall when on tour, for he is anxious to practise and is consumed with an itch to foresee some of the thousand and one difficulties which will crop up at the evening performance.

How are the acoustics?

It is impossible to assess them in this large empty space – the accompanist suggests his piano lid should be slightly opened, the singer feels it should be closed. Some halls, it is disconcerting to find, present problems whether full or empty, and I can think of several, large and resonant as railway stations, where a phrase one has finished playing comes echoing back. Science has made some strides in this respect as the modern halls in Götteberg, Stuttgart, and London show us. But is there any new hall today better than the Mozarteum in Salzburg, the Residenzsaal in Munich, or the old Queen's Hall in London? Oddly enough the most perfect place I know for sound owes nothing to science – the Patio de los Arrayanes in the Alhambra, Granada where you sing and play with the sky for your ceiling.

How is the lighting?

Here the artist decides for himself what he wants, for it is fatal to leave this to the discretion of the electrician as I did on one occasion at the Edinburgh Festival. Through no fault of my own since my lecture recital for children was arranged at the very last moment, I was unable to visit the hall in advance. The electrician used his imagination, he went mad; when I sat down to play he flooded me with light, but every time I stood up to speak he plunged me in darkness so that it was difficult for me to hold the attention of my youthful audience. Electricians are a touchy race and this particular one must have found me loathsome to behold in full face.

A lights rehearsal is an urgent necessity though Dame Nellie Melba on her last tour of U.S.A. and Canada never bothered about it until after her concert had started. She tested the lighting effects while her assisting artists were performing: during the first group of violoncello solos with which Beatrice Harrison opened, lights were raised and lowered, spots, foots, flashed on and off until the diva was satisfied with the result. That 'cellist and audience were disturbed was of small moment: Dame Nellie was not personally inconvenienced.

Apart from these matters of sound and light, however, the layman might be surprised at the jinxes that await the innocent performer.

It is impossible to foresee everything, as John McCormack discovered when we arrived one Sunday afternoon at a cinema (it was the only hall in the town able to accommodate a large audience) during his wartime tour on behalf of the Red Cross. We heard records being played to while away the time until the concert began, records amplified to a deafening degree. We Lilliputians were bludgeoned by the Brobdingnagian voice of Beniamino Gigli; a hundred tenors in the chorus would have sounded puny beside it.

'Take that damned thing off,' snarled the Irish tenor to the man operating the machine in the wings.

'What! In the middle of a song?'

'Stop it at once or I will smash the machine.'

I had every sympathy with John: what sort of effect would his voice make on an audience that had been reduced to a coma by this gigantic amplification?

I too have had my shocks. I was booked with a violinist for a sonata recital in Gloucester, and Dr Herbert Sumsion, chairman of the music society there, telephoned me in London some days before the event to ask me if I minded playing on a Steinway. Far from minding, I assured him, I loved the Steinway; it was my delight. I added, however, that for this concert it was important that I had a piano that could be opened on a small stick. No doubt our conversation was a trifle blurred by faulty telephone wires for when I walked out on to the platform at the concert not having paid a pre liminary visit to the hall, I found my piano was – a small Steck, which Dr Sumsion had procured with great difficulty and some expense. It was, doubtless, a nice little piano but it was a baby-grand and could not be compared with the large concert-sized pianoforte I had expected to play on – the Stein way which was now lying on its side, strapped up.

The story is told that Ferruccio Busoni touring Spain walked out to perform in some smallish town without having given a passing glance at the stage; after all, his own instrument went with him from place to place, what need had he to worry? After bowing gravely to his audience – they must have been mystified – he turned to his piano to find that it was still in its packing case.

Of course Busoni and I (never before have I been mentioned in the same breath as this colossus) would have been forewarned had we reconnoitred the field of battle before the engagement.

In the course of this recommended preliminary investigation I try the piano, have it placed in the required position; make sure that the piano stool is the right height (the tuner will come later and alter it, naturally) and will take the strain on a even keel. Some stools see-saw dizzily from side to side according to the vigour of the pivoting pianist.

Then I announce that I want a page-turner.

If you wish to know about the gentle art of turning pages, I am the very man to tell you. For more years than I care to remember I have had obliging men or women sitting on my left turning over the leaves of my music too early so that I have to guess at the three or four measures which my inexorable colleague has hidden from view (the moving page having turned, not all my piety nor wit could lure it back); or – far more frequently – turning too late through the turner's desire to hear the very last note of the page sounding clearly in his ears before he permits me to see what is coming next. (Meaning, of course, that I have to make a rough guess at what lies overpage and may momentarily become lost.) These slow-coaches, all the same, provide the less reverent members of the audience with some amusement because they see the accompanist going red in the face, bobbing his head up and down to indicate he wants the page turned, and they hope he is going to have a fit. To one such helper I addressed myself very quietly after one movement of a violin sonata ; 'If you cannot read the music, why don't you turn the page when I nod my head?' 'Because', replied he with some heat, 'your head is bobbing up and down all the time.'

I used at one time to prefer turning the pages myself, not in a sonata where it is impossible but in an atmospheric cycle of songs such as *Die Winterreise* or *Dichterliebe*. Time after time at the end of a song all hushed and tranquil, Strauss's *Morgen* for instance, with the singer perfectly still and with the accompanist's fingers glued to the keys, giving the impression of movelessness – and holding his last chord until the tone dies away – only one person is moving on the platform, and indeed in the whole hall – the page-turner : breathing heavily he leans forward before I have concluded my *Nachspiel*, picks up the programme to see what follows, and searches for the next song, disturbing the eye by his movements and the ear by the rustling and shuffling of pages. More than once, having played my final chord I have released my left hand – keeping my sustaining pedal down to hold the tone – and flung my arm out like a bar to stifle the movement which my fidget was about to make.

Why did I not give him full instructions before the concert? Because, I suppose, I was too distrait, too absorbed in giving myself treatment, persuading myself that all would be well with me when I was by no means so certain about it. If my wits are about me I show him the music in advance and tell him not to move at the end of a cycle or a song until the applause starts. He may shuffle to his heart's content during the hubbub.

Just before the last few notes of a page are played your ideal turner turns the page quickly – and he turns the page at the top right-hand corner. He must stand up to do it – for if he remains seated he has to turn the page at the bottom of the music and his right hand and arm will obstruct the player's movements. If the turner is corpulent the pianist may find his left hand imprisoned between stomach and keys. A long course of training is necessary.

The good page-turner is a blessing and a bad one a curse. Why then have I lost the confidence of youth when I dispensed with this gillie of the keyboard? Because I have had one or two unfortunate experiences. With the air-conditioning of modern concert halls I find, especially on the platform, the most subtle little zephyrs wafting around and they concentrate cleverly on my score. Directed by some gremlin or imp these friendly little blasts get to work – when there is no one beside me – and after I have turned the page, gently waft it back again. Page fifteen, for instance, though I have turned it, dislikes lying on page fourteen and, while my two hands are busily engaged on the keys, I have seen the rebellious page slowly rise from slumber and start to turn back to the place it found more comfortable. With not a hand to hold it the page begins its slow rotation from left to right – but should I not have been prepared for this when it happened while practising at home? No, it did not happen in the privacy of my studio – no draughts there; this devil of a page stored it up for the concert when it knows two thousand eyes will be directed to the platform. But in the meantime – God help me – the page slowly rises from its bed nor can I release one hand for a second to slap it back. I must provide a counterblast and begin with my breath – puffing like a grampus – to blow at the fluttering sheet, taking care to maintain a steady pressure of wind before the puffing angle becomes too acute. It has to be calculated very nicely but it takes up all your attention. The singer is dimly aware that something unusual is going on but you do not tell him of your troubles when you quit the stage, though you hear him complaining to the hall manager that the wind blows around him from all directions.

Fischer-Dieskau made his New York début with Schubert's *Die Winterreise* and, as in the past with this cycle, I turned the pages myself. The very quick-moving song *Erstarrung* (*Numbness*) caught me on the hop; I had not a second in

which my left hand could be spared to turn the page. Fischer-
Dieskau's copy had been turned at terrific speed by others
before me and was hanging by a thread and this was the
moment when this slender umbilical cord broke, the page slid
down on to the keys – rested for a moment on the back of my
left hand, and started fluttering in a long looping descent to
the floor. I grabbed it as a dog catches a bouncing ball, still
weaving triplets with my right hand. Nothing could disturb
that mighty young man Fischer-Dieskau, but I was disturbed,
and in the next song, *Der Lindenbaum* (*Lime Tree*), I gave a
very sloppy performance of the beautiful but difficult introduction.

But the breeze that frolics so playfully with my pages is a
menace to the singer. It is a mystery to me how ladies can
endure it. If a man were to wear an off the shoulder evening
gown the cold would kill him. Dora Labette, however, was
equal to any emergency. I played for her in a perishingly cold
hall where she sang like an angel and was a vision of love-
liness. As I cowered over the fire in the artists' room I asked
her how she managed to keep warm in her diaphanous gown.
For answer she raised her skirt and revealed a pair of corduroy
trousers pinned up well above her satin slippers.

Since the moral predicated in this chapter concerns the
advisability of paying a preliminary visit to the hall, it may
not be altogether out of place if I mention the feminine
toilette.

Every woman likes to feel that her gown makes a pleasing
picture against the curtains or draperies that decorate her
stage and she makes the unpleasant discovery that the red or
green or black frock she had intended to wear looks ghastly
in this light or with that background. A state of emergency
exists; women friends or willing chambermaids are called
in to cope with the situation. Extemporaneous measures have to
be taken.

This is where I pay my tribute to the pin.

Pins were the bane of my life when I was an infant. 'Please,
mother, no safety pins,' I wailed when being dressed up in a
silk blouse and velvet breeches for a party. Some of my prima

donnas dare not share my childhood prejudices; their gowns, hurriedly draped with apparent grace round the shoulders, bust, waist, the admiration of all, would disintegrate without the nimble pin. The strength of a pin has to be heard to be believed. When I step with all my weight on a singer's train, as she sprints for the pianoforte in the centre of the platform, something has to go. The poor dear stops dead in her tracks, of course, probably cursing me under her breath though still smiling happily at the public – but the damage is done. I hear a rending sound but there is no evidence that I can see of any damage. The pin has done its duty. Whether it would stand up to further and more severe tests I do not know for I have made it a habit never to tread on a lady's train more than once during the course of a single evening.

29

Behind the Scenes

In those days when I accepted engagements with anybody and appeared almost every other night at the Wigmore Hall playing for the quaking and inexperienced, I adopted a nonchalant demeanour in the artists' room to give the impression that I was un-nervous and had confidence in my colleague. I learned then not to talk too much. Perhaps I was feeling half dead with fatigue through working with other people and recording all day, but I did not boast about it. The unwisdom of indulging in these heroics had been impressed on me when Mengelberg, conductor of the Amsterdam Concertgebouw, was at the Queen's Hall with an English orchestra. Sharing his artists' room with his first violinist, he was infuriated when this gentleman arrived, flung himself down in an armchair and declared he was exhausted. 'Do you know, I have been teaching every moment since our rehearsal this morning until a half hour ago. I am tired out.' Of course he was, but what was the point of talking about it? Did he expect Mengelberg to commiserate? Far from it, the conductor complained bitterly to the management and demanded of them what sort of playing could they expect from the orchestra when their leader was exhausted before the concert had even begun?

Scenes that take place in the artists' room might rudely disillusion the waiting audience did it know of them, but Harold Craxton's experience is the one that I like best of all. He was playing for a very fine baritone. The Wigmore Hall manager, a predecessor of Mr H. T. Brickell, was in the habit of dining at Pagani's Restaurant, returning to his office, and resting there until the end of the artist's first group. The sound of Gabriel's trumpet would not have penetrated to this sequestered den. A thump on the floor from the box office, situated over the managerial sanctum, usually signified that this first group was over, and imagining he heard this signal one evening – it was about a quarter or ten minutes before nine – he roused himself, bustled through the hall to the artists' room, and congratulated Craxton's singer with effusion: 'I have never heard you in such splendid form. That group was a joy. Don't wait too long. The critics are still there and seem very happy. Strike while the iron's hot.' The baritone's eyes popped out of his head with astonishment. 'But I haven't started my concert yet.' Unbeknownst to the poor manager the recital was billed to commence not at the usual hour of eight-thirty but at eight forty-five p.m.

Unlike the Green Room of many provincial halls in England, that of the Wigmore Hall is invariably warm and comfortable though, until recently, the amenities were by no means all that could be desired. 'Leaving the room' was an uncomfortable expedition: one had to quit the warmth, pass down a draughty corridor, descend stone steps by the emergency exit doors in order to visit the icy lavatory. These offices, or to be more accurate this office, was shared by both lady and gentleman artists: turn by turn, of course, not together. A reconstruction has taken place now and a hole has been cut in the floor of the Green Room leading direct to the washrooms below, but it is still decidedly chilly down there. While on this charming subject I would observe that the Men's Lounge, as it is called in America, is no misnomer, for every room in each building is of uniform temperature and one can, without endangering one's health, lounge there: at least you can if the atmosphere is congenial to you. Not so in England, you hasten in and out as fast as possible. Before his recital at Wigmore Hall, Norman Farrow, the American baritone, emerged from the lower regions white of face and shivering: 'I am no more hypochondriacal than any other singer,' he said, 'but, gee, if I go down to the Men's Lounge again I'll sure catch pneumonia.' Anxious to convince me, he added, 'I could see my breath down there as if I were smoking a cigar.' I tried to assure him with my English complacency that that was quite in order; 'In England we insist that the rooms where we must expose ourselves, the lavatory, bathroom, and bedroom, should be the coldest rooms in the house.'

The experienced professional gives instructions that nobody be admitted to his artists' room prior to his appearance so that he may compose his thoughts and perhaps practise a little. But the débutante is misunderstood if she attempts to deny entry to all her friends and relations. To them the affair is a fiesta, an excuse for the gathering of the clan. It is of paramount importance to them, having made the supreme sacrifice of coming to hear her, that the poor girl should be aware that they are present, and they will burst in on her privacy and – especially if she be a singer – blow their cigar smoke in her face. I quickly ushered these bores out when I was on the scene. The time for these *réunions* should be after the concert.

Even the famous are not averse to seeing their friends when their work is over but their obligation to the public does not finish with their final encore. There are few people living who are not flattered by the request for an autograph and it may be taken as axiomatic that when they do not want this signature of yours, they do not want you. And so the artist, tired and perspiring, often finds himself signing programmes and autograph books for half an hour or more at the end of a concert ; he is barely thanked, it is taken for granted.

John Coates, in company with many distinguished soloists at a Three Choirs Festival in Hereford, had an autograph book pushed under his nose. 'But young man, you have my signature here already.' 'Really, sir, what is your name, sir ?'

I appreciate seeing friends after the concert if they have something encouraging to say to me but if they can find nothing felicitous to say I would rather they left me alone. One lady brought me down to earth with a bump. She usually accompanied Jelli d'Aranyi but as she had been indisposed I was asked to act as her substitute. She sat in the audience and came to speak to me afterwards ; we had not met for years. 'Gerald,' she exclaimed, opening her arms to embrace me, 'it is simply wonderful –' she paused and I hung my head modestly in expectation of a handsome compliment – 'how well you *look*.' Now if on such an occasion a fellow artist confines his remarks to your health and your beauty, it is another way of telling you that you played like a pig: this is tactfully understood. I endeavoured to parry this body blow by pretending to ignore it. 'What a thrilling thing Ravel's *Tzigane* is! It is the first time I have ever played it.' 'My dear, I could *hear*,' then relentlessly following up her attack, 'But it can really be a most effective piece of music.' When I had picked myself up off the floor she had gone.

Apropos of this little episode and to digress momentarily from post-concert considerations, I must confess to having enjoyed my little revenge. The same lady telephoned me years later to say she had started to read my *Unashamed Accompanist* when staying with friends but had had no time to finish it and would I present her with a copy. The 'My dear, I could *hear*' still rankled – the elephant never forgets – and I coldly informed her that the publishers were already issuing another edition and she should have no difficulty in obtaining it from any bookseller.

In these days after a recital I like to return to my home or hotel, change into my dressing gown, sit with my wife, and enjoy my whisky and soda in a comfortable armchair. I am not saying every man must do as I do: some like parties, some dislike whisky and soda, some prefer other men's wives. Each to his taste. Sticking fairly consistently to this habit I find I am ready for my work the following morning; I follow Sir Henry Wood's example. Sir Henry was complimented by a young friend at the end of a strenuous season of Promenade Concerts on his physical fitness and how did he manage it? 'What do I do? Why,' said Timbers, as he was affectionately nicknamed by his orchestra, 'I go home after a concert, have a good supper with half a bottle of wine, followed by a cigar. Not like young X. What does he do? Goes home and drinks hot milk. Milk makes you so *adagio*.'

My disappearing act after a concert is quite well known but, not to give a false picture, I must own in self-defence that I am by no means an anchorite, I find parties delightful if they do not interfere with my work: given this proviso I am ready to make whoopee and enjoy myself to the full.

30

Press Gang

SOME years ago Sir Thomas Beecham wrote a series of weekly articles for the *Sunday Times* on musical matters dear to him. I was agog one Sunday when I read that in the following weekly issue of the paper Sir Thomas's contribution would be entitled 'The Immodesty of Critics'. I smacked my lips in anticipation. Here is a man, thought I, in an unassailable position, his niche in the world of music unique, who will lay about him with gusto, who will give a Roland for an Oliver. Alas, I was doomed to disappointment for the article that appeared bore a different title, and the subject matter had nothing whatsoever to do with critics. What had happened to the promised – and one must presume, prepared – essay? That the great man suddenly became pusillanimous is unthinkable. Were his strictures impolitic? I can offer no explanation.

Beecham's defection was regrettable to me because it is so delightful to see the biter bit. Yet, in truth, I bear no grudge against the critics who, by and large, have been extremely indulgent with me.

The critics, incorruptibles, of our great national newspapers and periodicals are deep-thinking, discerning writers who have spent their lives in the service and study of music in its composition and performance. They are the ones who keep abreast of world scholarship in musicological matters. Their general knowledge, as Ernest Newman said, is inevitably and understandably deeper than that of the practising musician whose entire time is devoted to the preparation and performance of his own specialized duties. They will study twenty works while the practising musician is striving to master one.

I do not know how long exactly it took Geza Anda to get the second piano concerto of Bartok into his brain and then into his fingers but I should hazard several months. Your critic reads the score, plays the work again and again on his gramophone and arrives at a very clear and just appreciation of it. He has learned the Bartok in as many days as it took the pianist months and is quite competent to criticize the composition and its execution.

The territory these men cover is vast. That we should agree with their every word is out of the question nor would they expect it for they are human beings and make mistakes. But they stimulate our imagination, our curiosity, seek to guide us, and to maintain our standard; they keep abreast of the times and tell us what is happening (because we ourselves cannot possibly find the time to survey the scene), they remind us what we owe to tradition. These men we respect. There are occasions when their presence is a spur and an inspiration. My irreverent title to these lines does not embrace them, it alludes to the army of press men on the cheaper papers of London, our big cities, and provincial towns, whose ignorance is a threat to the musical life (and how delicate this is!) of their readers as well as an impertinence to those they criticize.

The cruellest criticisms I have ever had were made by men who could not play a single note on any musical instrument – even the penny whistle. They were the arbiters of elegance, could have shown us all how to do it if only they had been *able* to play, sing or conduct. They were the ones who had all the temperament, fire, poetry, and imagination. Of course there was no proof that they possessed all these virtues, one simply had to take their word for it. 'They are the ones', wrote Martin Cooper, 'who demand a perfection which is, in the last resort, hardly more desirable than it is achievable.'

'Knowing an art without any personal experience of its practical problems is a very doubtful form of culture' (I again quote Mr Cooper): 'and it is significant that the most persistent perfectionists are without exception non-practisers of the art, amateurs and connoisseurs with no practical experience of music making.'

Anyone who can hold a pen feels qualified to criticize and to criticize cruelly. There is nothing on earth to prevent a young journalist from sleeping through a Casals performance of a Bach Suite or Rubinstein's playing of a Beethoven Sonata and dismissing it the following morning as disappointing. This hypothetical case of artists grown old in the service of music being subject to the correction of a young man with little or no knowledge often happens, but the practising musician has to endure it. This sort of thing does not occur in our responsible journals but the fact that it appears in cold print at all is sufficiently bad for the health.

A contributor on a Brighton paper after a Victoria de los Angeles recital in the Dome (I omit his raving over her glorious singing – nobody could fail to recognize this) wrote, 'Gerald Moore identified himself completely with the Schubert songs, but of the two artists only the singer was authentic in the Spanish music : here Moore was *ersatz*.'

Now this reads, if you have not been to the concert to judge for yourself, as discerning criticism. I took the trouble to find out who the writer was. He was a boy just out of his teens : possibly the nearest he had ever been to the coast of Spain was to Dieppe on a day trip. What would have satisfied this carping critic? Obviously it would have to be nothing less than the accompanist whom Miss Victoria de los Angeles engages to play for her in Spain. Who then is her partner when she sings in Madrid, Barcelona, at the Festivals of Granada, Seville, Cordoba, San Sebastian, Santander? I hardly dare mention it, but the answer is the *ersatz* Moore.

It is so facile to pronounce that one must be Spanish to play the music of Granados and Falla, German or Austrian to understand Mozart, Beethoven, Schubert. Must one be English to get to the heart of Britten, Vaughan Williams, Berkeley, Rawsthorne? Should Samuel Barber be labelled 'For Americans only'?

When Toscanini visited London in the thirties, bringing the New York Philharmonic for a series of concerts, Elgar's *Enigma Variations* were included in the programme and an electrifying and memorable performance he gave of it. One paper, however, made the comment, 'It was very fine but was it English?' : the meaning being that it was not *echt* Elgar. The suggestion that the writer has a deeper understanding of Elgar than Toscanini is beside the point, what really does matter is the implication that unless you are English you cannot interpret Elgar. To warn all foreign artists that they must keep off the grass, that Elgar is sacrosanct and far too subtle to be understood except by those who are born within a certain radius of Worcester, is to do the composer a disservice. James A. Forsyth who asked his readers this question was a gentleman with little knowledge of music; a close friend of Hamilton Harty, it was a matter of principle with him not to praise other conductors too highly.

On the other hand the life of a serious music critic is arduous and worrying. It is a great responsibility. He cannot commit himself to paper day after day, week after week, without making a few slips. The late and much respected Fox-Strangways, for example, dismissed with opprobrium a violin and piano sonata by Eugene Goossens which he said in his notice he was hearing for the first time. He quite forgot he had warmly praised the same work several months earlier. Both notices had appeared in the *Observer*, Albert Sammons being the performer on each occasion. When Sammons showed these contradictory valuations to him, Fox-Strangways was extremely annoyed. But how could the poor man, living night after night in concert halls, possibly bear in mind everything he had heard? Perhaps he was feeling out of sorts when he listened to the work on the second occasion: though this conclusion does not console the composer.

I have attended many a concert or opera for my pleasure and asked myself how, were I a critic, would I put down on paper a just appreciation of what I had heard? It would be beyond me. But it was not only on the grounds of my incompetence that I refused to write a criticism on a fellow-artist in an American journal. You cannot umpire a game and be one of the players: it is not fair to jump from one side of the fence to the other. At Salzburg some years ago I lunched with Irmgard Seefried and with her was Erik Werba who has become her permanent accompanist. Now Werba at that time had never heard me play except on records, though he told me Irmgard and our mutual friend Helga Mott had praised me to the skies. Yet I felt ill at ease when Seefried told me that it was he, a fellow-accompanist, who would be writing the criticism of my concert that evening with Elisabeth Schwarzkopf for the Viennese papers. How would he listen? Had I been in his position I am afraid I should have paid more attention to the pianist than an impartial critic ought: again, being always with Irmgard Seefried, would not his loyalty and admiration for her colour his judgement when listening to another singer? Werba is a fine musician and we are the best of friends and as I did not read his reviews I am certainly not accusing him of bias. I am only saying how most people – and certainly I – would have felt in his place.

It was for these considerations that I declined to write for this American journal. It did not seem to me to be playing the game. There should be an *esprit de corps* with musicians just as, in the critics' camp, there is honour among – ahem – them. Wolves do not rend each other.

I am still 'one of the boys' and hope to continue thus for a few years.

Since my theme is that of Press comment (not to be confused with enlightened criticism) I would like to quote one *Daily Telegraph* notice which gave me the greatest pleasure. It read:

'Mr Gerald Moore and his partner Mr Bertie Meyer, sitting North and South respectively, won first prize at the Savage Club Duplicate Bridge Tournament held last week.'

31

Modern Recording

In the old days when recording was an adventure, the singer roared into the trumpet and the pianist thrashed his keyboard with never a care in the world: provided the one sang in tune and the other was an accurate marksman all was well. Listening to the finished reproduction weeks after the gramophone session when the wax had been processed my principal concern was, had I played any wrong notes? And that was as far as self-criticism needed to go, for it was all too obvious that every piece of music had to be emitted in a healthy *forte*. Moreover, the final result was such a rough approximation that it had a twofold effect: it deadened the artist's conscience and it aroused no interest in the serious music critic.

What a different state of affairs today! Every record is reviewed in numberless periodicals and newspapers by knowledgeable writers who do not shrink from making comparisons: 'While A's singing of this cycle is far better than B's or C's, it is inferior to D's.' The critic is only expressing a personal opinion but his judgement is made on the exact reproduction, the truest mirror, reflecting every minute inflexion, nuance, that A, B, C or D have made.

Far more important than this consideration, however, is the effect that tape recording has on the progress of the artist, for now he can listen to himself, can hear the weaknesses he suspected nakedly exposed.

It is all the fault of that confounded microphone; it picks up that which is imperceptible to the human ear, chronicles its evidence on the tape, and is now plainly heard. I now hear (for I must concentrate on my part, leaving the singer to worry over his) that I am guilty of that habit, so beloved by amateurs, of non-synchronization of the hands – the left hand anticipating the right: it is only by a minute fraction but I cannot condone what I would not pass in a pupil. Now comes that fearful passage which has given me so much trouble : I had hoped that the uncertainties and flaws would have been camouflaged by that convenient refuge the sustaining pedal, but it is not so. 'Can you use a little less pedal there? It sounds rather muddy,' says the recording manager. Even an accompaniment that I have performed in public for years, love deeply, imagined I treated eloquently, has sounded humdrum when played back to me ; the too sudden swelling or diminution of tone, unshapely *ritardandi* or *accelerandi*, the subtle *rubato* on which I prided myself, are all exaggerated and contrive to distort and over-sentimentalize the music.

Maggie Teyte in her autobiography, *Star on the Door* (Putnam), says, 'No one can mistake Gerald Moore on a record for any other pianist ... what is this unmistakable quality ? I think it is due to his mastery of the necessary weight of arm, according to the distance of the microphone.' I appreciate Maggie's compliment but the explanation is much simpler. I cannot judge my dynamics according to my distance from the microphone. Although my opinion will assuredly be canvassed, the responsibility for obtaining an even distribution of tone between me and my partner lies with the recording manager. And I will add this : when plenty of tone can be heard from my pianoforte in records I have made, when in other words there is a perfect balance, the credit should go to the man in charge.

The sensitive artist who does not face the microphone with awe is very exceptional. With me – and this despite my long experience – it amounts to fear. For one panic-stricken moment, control is lost and I fight to regain it. This is why, unless I am master of the situation, which is seldom, I am prone to hurry when I embark on a technically difficult passage as a horse loses the rhythm of his stride when he sees a big jump ahead of him.

All these weaknesses, be it observed, would largely pass unnoticed in a concert performance. True, you can make endless repetitions in the recording studio until all is well : David after assiduous practice with his sling 'holed out' in one when he slew Goliath at the first and only performance, but had he to repeat his exploit a dozen times, each effort would have been more difficult than the last. An artist can bring off an electrifying *tour de force* when inspired in public performance; he is on the crest of the wave. But in recording, this brilliant feat may not come off first time, it has to be repeated again and again and it begets a terror in the mind of the performer.

Dietrich Fischer-Dieskau – as John McCormack before him – is one of those rare beings who refuses to be intimidated by the microphone. Of all the singers I know, his attitude towards recording is the wisest: to sing one song ten or twelve times is anathema to his temperament, he may perform it two or three times but after that he will declare he has done his best and leave it at that. But when he steps up to the microphone and announces to the engineer that he is ready to start, he really means he is ready to dive off the springboard immediately and he is not kept waiting one second. There is no fussing and delaying with buzzers and red lights. When the song is finished he and I will have a short discussion and then he will announce into the microphone, 'Two corrections. I would like to repeat from Bar 24 to Bar 40 and Mr Moore wishes to repeat his *Nachspiel*, after which we would like to hear the whole song and corrections played back to us.'

In this way we recorded *Die Winterreise* – twenty-four songs – in two or perhaps three evenings. Admitting that at the end of each session we sat in the recording room listening to everything, consulting, deciding then and there what must be repeated, it is none the less a most unusual achievement on the part of a singer.

The microphone which has recorded us is also the artists' means of communication with the recording chamber and there is no reason that I can see why it should ever be disconnected. I cannot but feel that the preliminary single buzz followed by a long wait, then the two buzzes followed by a seemingly interminable wait before the red light appears, are time wasting: when the artists are poised to begin, these long delays are tiring and frustrating.

Buzzers and lights are pleasing only to the occasional onlooker who is thrilled by the mystery of it all. A third person in the studio, however, is hateful to the serious artist unless that person is involved in the proceedings. My only idiosyncrasy, if indeed it be one, is that I find the effort of concentration considerably more difficult if I feel I am being watched. At a public performance the artist puts on a show, he gives an impression of composure as he walks on to the platform. He assumes this cloak to protect himself, he seeks to put the audience at their ease – makes a pretence of being master of the situation. But in making a gramophone record he has no time or inclination to put up a defence like this. I have seen singers stand on one foot or move their arms like semaphores as they were singing ; I myself get tied up in knots when playing – I crouch over the keyboard, glaring horribly, my eyes going up to the music, now down to the keys, and then up again. I should imagine I look ludicrous in the extreme. When perpetrating these antics one does not want to be watched by some outsider. If, as happened to me, this third party of one or more persons sits within your range of vision twenty feet away, you see out of the corner of your eye the slightest movement of a hand or a handkerchief or the turning of a head and it is thoroughly distracting. These faces, dimly seen, are like large white pills. I saw one of these kibitzers nudge her companion to draw attention to the grimace I was making. They were friends of the singer, not of mine, but I had them removed and to this day they regard me, I am sure, as a stuck-up little prima donna. But they were a nuisance. Besides – the face I was pulling was one of my favourite ones.

Yehudi Menuhin, too kind-hearted to refuse, used at one time to allow some of his importunate admirers in the studio. Chairs creaked with their ecstatic shiver as the red light came on, and they could hardly be restrained from speech before the last note had been played, so anxious were they to say how marvellous it was. I have known the recorder come into the studio and ask if anyone had spoken before the red light was out as he fancied he had heard a voice, and I have had the venomous pleasure of replying, 'Yes, this lady said, "Wonderful, wonderful, wonderful".' As at that time we were recording on wax, our effort went for nought and had to be done all over again.

John McCormack with a friend in tow, whom I must confess

I could not see or hear as I played, behaved abnormally by shouting at the recorders and glaring belligerently at me. I asked him quietly what was the matter with him and he whispered with a wink, 'I am just putting on a show for my pal over there. I don't want him to think it is too easy.' Even the quietest of visitors tucked away in a dark corner makes his presence felt.

My association with His Master's Voice and Columbia Gramophone Companies has been a long one: I have seen the trumpet give way to the microphone; the record of seventy-eight revolutions per minute give way to thirty-three r.p.m.; wax discs ousted by tape; the monaural succeeded by the stereophonic record player. But the names 'Columbia' and 'H.M.V.' have also been superseded, they have been rendered indistinguishable along with the Capitol and Marconiphone Companies under the all-embracing insignia of E.M.I. What, it may be asked, do these initials represent? Truth to tell I could not have supplied an accurate answer to this question when I began writing this chapter in Texas, U.S.A.: unpractical dreamer that I am, with my head in the clouds, I realized that I must find the answer on returning to England; it is Electrical Musical Industries.

No doubt in the interests of the amalgamation, advertising slogans of individual companies had to be watered down, and this included the picture of the dog sitting before the phonograph listening to the voice of his master, surely one of the most famous slogans ever conceived.

Though Sir Ernest Fisk, one-time managing director of E.M.I., was adamant for inaction when it came to introducing the long-playing record (it is literally true that the utterance of the words 'long-playing record' was forbidden in his presence) the campaign to do away with the dog was waged with energy and relish. It almost succeeded but, I am glad to say, the offending cur is immortal and now under the present régime he looms again on hoardings and in shop windows. I have been in Greece, Bulgaria, Yugoslavia and such places where every word and hieroglyphic were strange, when suddenly my eye has been arrested by the sign of the little dog listening with pricked ear.

It gave one a friendly feeling; more than that it stood and stands for a world-famous concern with a long record of achievement behind it. (Did I say *long record*? Pace, Sir Ernest!)

I have been recording most happily with the company for over forty years. This is a good innings and I wonder if there is any other artist on the company's books who could make such a proud boast – I except conductors as they go on for ever. Had I been a well-known singer, I should have been presented with a handsome machine long ere this, but such gestures do not come the way of the accompanist. When it finally occurs to the powers that be that the 'oldest inhabitant' should receive some such token as recognition for long service, it will be too late, I shall be requiring a harp, or whatever instrument is then in vogue in the Elysian Fields.

32

Travellers' Tales

THAT musicians are eccentric in their habits I do not admit for a moment, though I am sometimes made to feel I am an oddity when I ask for a meal at 11 p.m. after a concert. Why could I not eat before the concert? Let us suppose I have been rehearsing and practising a sonata or a song cycle for weeks and wish to be fighting fit at a certain date and at a certain hour. It is unreasonable to assume I shall be keyed up to the highest pitch, to give of my very best, if I swallow a hurried dinner before making for the hall. When the digestive organs are busily engaged you are not physically or mentally at your peak, yet strangely enough you descend to earth with a bump when your effort is over, your inner man craves for fuel.

In America or across the English Channel the traveller has no difficulty in obtaining a meal at any hour of the day or night, but in my own country, apart from one or two big cities, a musician looking for a meal after his evening performance is up against it and has to make do with a cold collation: and even this has to be ordered well in advance. In fact the chief concern of the reception clerks when you sign the hotel register at noon is, 'Will you be wanting early tea tomorrow morning?'

Bernard Miles declared, 'England expects that every tourist shall be in bed by 10 p.m.' At the Edinburgh Festival members of foreign orchestras cannot obtain a modest glass of beer when their work is finished. But we are not the only country to have odd rules. On one of my few free evenings in Australia I was dining at my hotel in Adelaide when the waiter told me I must finish my wine by 7.45 p.m. or it would be removed from the table. On a Canadian train in my comfortable armchair I ordered a dry martini: it was so refreshing that I later asked the steward to repeat the dose but this could not be done because we had now proceeded from Ontario into Quebec and that particular carriage had no licence in the province of Quebec: if I moved into the next car, however, my order would be fulfilled.

Even in France, that wonderful country for travellers, there can be the occasional snag, though not, of course, where food and drink are concerned. Enid and I had one and a half days' train journey from Spain to a Festival in France. When we were shown our accommodation on arrival, I complained that I had booked a room with bath. They were sorry they had no rooms left with bath. I therefore asked them to send a chambermaid to prepare a bathroom for us but was told, 'C'est très difficile'. In short, I was forced to stand at my wash basin washing up as far as possible and then washing down as far as possible. The name of the caravanserai was Grand Hotel des Bains!

On a journey I prefer my own company with my books and papers to the chatter of an acquaintance, but nothing can be more thrilling than the chance meeting of an old friend. My overnight train from Dallas, Texas, to Indianapolis stopped at St Louis, Missouri for three hours. It was time for breakfast and I had it in the station restaurant. To my great delight Benno Moiseiwitsch whom I had not met for a couple of years was sitting at a table. Unobserved, I went up behind him and complained I had been waiting a long time for this particular table and when did he propose to move? Without knowing who was speaking to him he turned round (what a good poker player he is!) and without change of expression argued that he had no intention of hurrying over his eggs to please me. We argued vehemently and his companion, the piano tuner, was convinced there was going to be violence: his face was a study when Benno and I burst out laughing. It appeared that Benno had come from Houston and our carriages had linked up during the night. When our train left St Louis we met in the club car and journeyed on together playing gin rummy. Benno insisted on the tuner – with whom he played cards frequently – sitting next to him to watch, so that he could learn how to draw, discard, and build. I expected the tuition to be expensive for me as I am mediocre at this game. But it was Benno, the master, who paid dollars and dollars to the pupil. To my entreaties for more lessons Benno now turns a deaf ear.

Was it my meeting with Moiseiwitsch or a surfeit of gin rummy that went to my head? When I alighted at Indianapolis and waved him off to New York I was in a bemused condition and decided to get to bed early since my lecture was to take place at noon next day. Greatly disturbed during the night by revellers in the adjoining room, I roused myself in the morning in none too good a mood and ordered breakfast to be brought up to me. I just had time for a hot and cold shower before a gangling youth in a white coat appeared with my tray. One should always examine a tray, because waiters with Machiavellian cunning often omit something vital. This fellow had brought no spoons and I did not see how it was possible to eat half a grapefruit, boiled eggs, stir my coffee without one. I rang Room Service and waited for ten minutes before a different man came up grasping in his huge hand a fistful of spoons which he spilled with a clatter on my tray. 'Enough spoons, sir?' he sneered. Now my American friends are adept with a fork and only use a knife apologetically but even they have to use spoons on occasion; this seemed to be one of these occasions and I attempted to tell the waiter so, but he was gone before my argument had time to expand. After eating my cold eggs, drinking my tepid coffee, I was shaving myself when a tap came on my door. It was the first gangling youth and in his hand was a glittering array of spoons of all sizes. 'Why,' he said with a guffaw, looking at the ruins of my breakfast, 'you had spoons all the time.' I snarled 'Geddahellouderhere'.

I flew on to Toronto to stay with my brother later that day and told him of my Indianapolis misadventures. He reckons I must be mustard to travel with.

My giant friend, Bruce Boyce, confided to me, 'You English are funny people.' He finds our trains very small after the large Pullman cars of America and Canada and has to walk the swaying corridor with bowed head. To misquote Tennyson, 'And once, but once he lifted his eyes,' and he 'suddenly sweetly strangely' bumped his cranium on the lintel of the doorway to the restaurant car. Half stunned, he sank to his knees and then, pulling himself together, stumbled back to his own compart-ment with a bad cut on his forehead – his face covered with blood. 'And what did the people in my compartment do? Did they express any concern or show the slightest interest? No! They averted their eyes, and those who were reading books or newspapers buried their noses in them. Yes, you British are a funny lot.' I had to explain to Boyce how perfectly normal their behaviour was; they saw this huge chap with blood streaming from a wound and naturally took him for a gunman or desperado who should be given a wide berth.

The very mention of that word *berth* almost gives me a shudder. It takes me down to the sea in ships. In my youth I had many pleasant experiences of ocean voyages but my feelings have undergone a sea-change. I now find them boring: I am not conceited on shipboard. I recall, with disgust, returning from Brussels when our steam-packet leaving Ostend at three in the afternoon was blown by the gale across the Channel in record time but denied entrance to Dover Harbour because of the boisterous seas, not that I saw them, I was keeping watch below. Eventually we were cast ashore more dead than alive at Newhaven after twenty-four hours on the water.

If planes are grounded it is because of bad weather; if planes are grounded you take a boat when dwelling in our sea-girt land. A journey to Dublin was made under these conditions. On arrival at the port of Holyhead around midnight I went straight to my cabin on board, slipped into bed, and rang the bell for the steward. I ordered two large whiskies and gave instructions I must be wakened by a cup of tea at seven in the morning. My whiskies, accompanied by aspirin, put me straight off to sleep. 'That is the way to cross the Irish Sea,' I told the steward over my morning tea. 'I slept undisturbed the whole night, unaware of any tossing and pitching, rock'n roll.' 'No, sir, you wouldn't have felt much movement,' he answered. 'You see, we haven't cast off yet. It's been too rough.'

To Enid who had never been on a big liner before, always travelling by plane, I boasted of the heavenly time I had had as a young man on shipboard, especially the sunny voyage to

Cape Town – 'seventeen days of Paradise'. So one year we decided to travel to America by sea. Our trip coincided exactly with the equinoctial season. Gales, rain squalls, mountainous seas, and finally fog accompanied us continually. And of course the ship's siren's Banshee wailing accompanied the fog. Would you take a stroll on the deck before breakfast to imbibe the salt sea breezes? The deck is enclosed with thick glass on account of the huge seas running and you breathe in only hot air. The Mersey and Hudson rivers are pleasant enough, but the stretch of blue water in between is nauseating. Ralph and Ursula Vaughan Williams were fellow-passengers and we met often at cocktail time when Ursula would exchange picturesque confidences with us as to our respective symptoms. V.W. himself was a lion who never missed a meal. For my part, I am thoroughly happy pushing a punt on the upper reaches of the Thames but Joseph Conrad's passion for the Seven Seas leaves me cold, nor am I tempted by John Masefield's invocation to go down to them again. Not all great writers feel alike over marine affairs. The Atlantic is a wash-out so far as the Moores are concerned.

I am quite sure Eugene Ysaÿe was not a sufferer from *mal de mer* but he was not without experience of its sensation. He found himself one morning in Torquay, Devon, in company with the pianist Raoul Pugno. He had been there before and, wanting to show off his local knowledge, he took his friend to a pub and ordered two pints of raw cider. Pugno repaid the compliment and then they repaired to their hotel for lunch. It was substantial – for they were both big men – and the pianist thought the lunch was over until Ysaÿe said, 'And now a wonderful surprise for you. Garçon! Bring ze Devonshire cream.' A large dish was placed in the centre of the table, but Ysaÿe seized it, put it in front of him and said with commanding dignity to the amazed waiter, 'And one for my friend.' The couple devoured their Devonshire cream *au naturelle* with soup spoons. Their concert had to be cancelled. Devonshire cream and cider may both be indigenous to Devon but they do not make good bed-fellows.

33

Australia

IT was not until I sat down to write this chapter that I began to ask myself why did I find my tour in Australia in 1953 so exhausting?

I always view with a scornful eye the professional musician who, with the air of a martyr sacrificing his life for the sake of his insatiable public, tells you, sadly shaking his head, that he has had a terrible month with twenty-six recitals. In fact no artist need take on more work than he wishes as I am now beginning to find out. When, therefore, I state that out of my forty-nine days' sojourn in Australia I had forty-one public appearances, I do not boast about it; I confess it with some self-reproach.

I was booked for sixteen Lieder evenings with Irmgard See-fried (including two joint recitals with her husband, the violinist Wolfgang Schneiderhahn) and numerous lecture recitals. In addition I was scheduled to give a series of four or five Arm-chair Chats. Since the horror of television had not yet spread its contagion so far as Australia, these talks were to be delivered over the sound radio, all so cosy and comfortable. I had received no precise guidance as to the burden of these talks but I imagined that my theme would be music, and I prepared them accordingly. To my dismay I was told in Sydney that it was hoped my subject matter would be much more general; gossipy, amusing reminiscences were wanted along Alexander Woollcott lines. My scripts had to be rewritten. Now the process of thinking out and writing an address lasting twenty minutes takes much time and I should have been a wise man if I had either insisted on sticking to my original scheme or had cancelled them altogether. Instead, and in an effort to be obliging, I rewrote these scripts: the only time I had to map them out was late at night – for every day was filled up. To have allowed them to assume such overwhelming proportions in my mind and to prey on me as they did surely indicates that I must have been mentally jaded. I see in my engagement book that the previous year had been a full one with no time for rest or recuperation barring a short two-week Italian holiday.

Three qualities are essential in a professional musician, as my friend Mark Hambourg liked to say: the first is good health and the other two are the same. Most artists have abundant resilience, will exhaust themselves until they have no more resistance than a piece of blotting paper but, after a good night's sleep, will rise thoroughly refreshed in body and mind. Fortunately for me I have this capacity too and I anticipated my tour 'down under' with eagerness, shrugging off or unaware of any feeling of tiredness.

I had left England at the end of a bitter February and found myself four days later in Sydney where the heat hit me in the face as I stepped out of the plane – the thermometer registering 100 degrees. My nightly sleep averaged a couple of hours for three weeks. I do not attribute my insomnia, however, to this sudden transition from cold to heat – in England one is inured to all vagaries of climate – but rather to the worrying over these delightful and confounded Armchair Chats. And when people talk to me about kangaroos, wallabies, kookaburras, koala bears, I am certain they are talking nonsense for I never saw one, I was too busy.

The Australian audiences are marvellous. The huge town halls in Sydney, Melbourne, Brisbane, Adelaide were packed by an eager, enthusiastic public whenever Irmgard Seefried appeared, and in each of these cities four or more different programmes were given.

Seefried was then at her zenith. There was something reminiscent of Elisabeth Schumann about her singing (and no doubt Elisabeth had recognized this when she first heard the young soprano's New York début) which won all hearts. It is a pity, in my opinion, that Irmgard changed her method. In the effort to increase the volume of her voice, her tone has lost some of its quality; but none of this was evident in 1953 and she was an enormous success. Her animation and zest delighted everyone and we had the greatest fun travelling around together.

She found plenty of leisure in between recitals, and became as brown as a berry surf-bathing while I became paler and paler sweating over my scripts.

Under the auspices of the Australian Broadcasting Commission it is a rule that one half hour of every public concert is broadcast. With Seefried this was no problem as we had six or seven different programmes on the go, but with my lecture-recital this was embarrassing to me. As Grock, the great clown, had but one act – a masterpiece it was too – so had I. I now have five or six lectures on the go but I was more restricted in those days. Having given my all in Melbourne I would arrive next day in Ballarat to be told that they had heard my lecture broadcast from Melbourne yesterday and hoped I was going to give them something entirely new this evening. It was soon discovered that my lectures, undeniably superb, earning rave notices from the press (none of which I admit were exaggerated) were all one and the same. The kindly critics declared that my matter was so brilliant it could be heard many times to the advantage of all, but on the other hand there were those who described me as 'The A.B.C.'s problem child'. But by this time I was beyond worrying, too tired to care.

My happiest recollections were my talks to the children. Their attention, their quick reaction, their laughter were stimulating. My first Australian appearance was before 3,000 of them at the Sydney Town Hall.

Now one has to be on one's toes when addressing boys and girls ; they cannot be fooled. I have seen adult audiences swooning with rapture over an artist who was four-flushing them, performing carelessly, unmusically. They fell for his window dressing – the flourishes, the studied nonchalance. He would not have got away with it with a young audience. The head-mistress of one of England's big girls' colleges told me of the girls' enthusiasm over a young instrumentalist and how they begged her to re-engage the player the following year. In the meantime the young woman had been cordially received in Warsaw, Vienna, Paris and Berlin and her successes had gone to her head : she became a mass of affectation and when she returned to the scene of her former conquest, her airs and graces repelled the girls, they developed an instinctive dislike for her. Children quickly detect affectation or side, they resent being patronized and lose interest when they sense any lack of sincerity.

I can say quite humbly that my experiences with young Australians did me a power of good. I am grateful to them and also, I must add parenthetically, to my friend Harold Williams, the famous baritone singer, who knowing my qualms turned up at my initial appearance of the tour in Sydney 'to push me on the stage'.

The strenuous schedule mapped out for me would not have been possible without the superb organization, indeed solicitude, of the A.B.C. Arrangements were so complete that even correspondence was taken off my hands – though my letters to my wife were written by her husband in person. But I could not have attempted to answer the letters, read the musical compositions, comply with the requests that poured in on me by the hundred. One gentleman from Western Australia sent me his compositions – some twenty songs in manuscript – with the demand that I should examine and give him a detailed criticism of each: he also added, in a burst of generosity, that if Madame Seefried would care to perform any of them in public he 'would raise no objection'.

Sir Henry Irving's 'I am the public's most humble servant' is a truism brought home with a vengeance in Australia. After a recital Irmgard Seefried and I would sit at a table and a long crocodile would be marshalled by the police as hundreds of autograph hunters slowly filed past us. This was expected and there was no escape. Yet, so perverse is human nature, that when one lady, having obtained Seefried's signature, swept by me without wanting mine, I felt peeved.

It would be a vain misrepresentation were I to claim that before my coming little notice had been taken of accompanists, but it would be nearer the truth to say that no accompanist had previously been given so much publicity. The Australian papers were flooded with articles and pictures of me – the air was filled morning, noon and night with my recordings. A stranger telephoned me in my hotel to tell me that I ought to be ashamed of myself, that everybody was getting sick of the sight and the sound of my name. I asked him very patiently what he wanted me to do about it, and why did he not use a little intelligence and address his complaints to the proper quarter, the A.B.C.? It seems that advanced propaganda on the accompanist's behalf aroused resentment in some breasts though nobody vented their spleen on Irmgard Seefried whose every movement was front page news.

Such an episode as this, and there were several of them, I generally took very quietly since it is my habit when out of my own country to try to behave as courteously as I can: the reader may recall an earlier chapter wherein I offered no argument to my Australian taxi-driver when he gave me his cosmic survey beginning: 'If I were Winston Churchill . . .'

Certainly Sir Thomas Beecham would not have remained silent under such an onslaught! When he was asked by a reporter, 'What do you think of our bridge over Sydney Harbour?' he replied, 'It is far too large, it ought to be removed'.

This did not go down well with Australians.

But they had their revenge. When another reporter in an interview with the great man listened to a brilliant and learned discourse on the history of music in England from Purcell to Britten, the printed article he produced was headed by the caption, 'Famous conductor wears buttoned-boots'.

This did not go down well with Sir Thomas.

Although lazy by nature I have always been able to whip myself up to strenuous work when I knew it had to be done. I had survived physical and mental strain in the past and emerged none the worse, but the end of my Australian tour found me completely exhausted. I was driven to the airport with such a cold in the head that I knew the place for me was bed. 'It does not matter if *you* catch a cold – *you* are not a singer,' I was told. This is as may be but I was deaf in one ear for nearly two months afterwards.

I left Sydney on Saturday and arrived at Honolulu on Sunday where the plane was serviced. It was an eight-hour stop and the Airways Company provided three other men and me with a pent-house in one of the modern luxury hotels on the beach. These men were a distinguished looking trio – all white-haired, a judge of the High Court, a Harley Street specialist, and an American scientist; we dined together and I recognized that we were in American territory when the pretty Hawaiian waitress, after allowing us to examine the menu for some minutes, approached us with, 'Well, boys, made up your minds?'

Leaving Honolulu on Sunday night we arrived in San Francisco on Sunday morning – an absurdity which I have never understood – and there was Solomon at the airport to meet me.

On Monday night I was met by Trevor in New York, and he loves to tell his friends how, on taking me to the Twenty One Club, I was in a fury in a few moments. We were talking about our last meeting which had been four years earlier and I recalled a round of golf with him, his son David, and Chris Dobson when I hit the finest drive of my life. The hole where this occurred was long and difficult and your ball had to pitch in an area of about twenty square feet to be perfect; from there, given sufficient impetus, it rolled down a slight hill and gave you a good opening to a green, guarded by two streams. As my lovely new white ball rolled out of sight down the slope I experienced a thrill that it is beyond my pen to describe. Since the other three made poor drives we had to search for their balls in the rough and it was a good ten minutes before I arrived at the brow of the hill. I looked down. My ball was gone. In the distance I saw several urchins playing catch with it, and ya-hooing at me: their enjoyment was heightened by my face, purple with rage, and by my hoarse imprecations. I brandished a club threateningly in their direction but this they seemed to regard as uproariously funny. I dropped another ball and sent it in the river, and the next followed suit – fortunately these thieving magpies were too far away to see this or they would have had hysterics. I found my gorge rising as I reminded my brother of all this four years later but, nice fellow though he is, he failed to see how important it was, saying I ought to have another drink and go to bed as I must be very tired.

*

This was Coronation year. Before my departure to Australia I had written to Sir William McKie, organist and choirmaster of Westminster Abbey, to ask him if I could join the augmented choir for the great occasion, and at Melbourne I received a cable from Enid saying I had received an official invitation.

George Baker had told me that I must move heaven and earth to get into the choir if I could: 'You will never see another Coronation, please God, and the gorgeous pageantry of it will always be in your memory.'

No member of the choir could gain his ticket of admission to the Abbey for the Service unless his rehearsal ticket showed he had attended every single practice. There were three rehearsals in the Church of St Margaret's with organ and three more in the Abbey itself with full orchestra.

For the first time since I sang as a boy in St Thomas's Church in Toronto I found myself in a choir standing among some of the finest basses in the country. No longer a treble – strange as it may seem – my voice could be described as a bleating rather than a vibrant bass. Compared to such stalwarts as Norman Allin, Robert Easton, Owen Brannigan, Norman Walker, my contribution could hardly be described as overwhelming, but come what may, I was now a singer, *pro tem*, and any proffered engagement to play the piano could go hang.

It was flaming June with drenching rain and an icy wind when the choir assembled in the cloisters on Coronation Day at seven-thirty in the morning. In my thin cassock and surplice, borrowed for the occasion – pockets stuffed with the recommended raisins and bars of chocolate to sustain me – I shivered with the cold.

We supernumeraries were perched up in the rafters of the Abbey with a bird's eye view. We were tightly packed, shoulder to shoulder, and I no longer felt cold; on the contrary it became terribly hot. I found too, after sitting for some time on my unyielding bench with little room for my knees, that it was a decided relief to stand up. But standing up to sing I found it difficult to place my feet squarely into the floor space owing to the exiguity of the pew in front; moreover, the protrusion of my own wooden seat prevented me from straightening my legs. I found it a decided relief to sit down. For five hours I was in a constant state of eagerness either to sit down or to stand up.

Everybody had warned me that the pageantry and solemn splendour would be overwhelming but I was not prepared for the depth of my own emotion. The glittering fanfares, the great body of voices, all contrived to move me profoundly. The vision of our young and beautiful Queen processing slowly up the aisle in her gorgeous robes is never to be forgotten. Her entry was the signal for us to sing Parry's setting of Psalm cxxii, 'I was glad when they said unto me, We will go into the House of the Lord', and I sang my heart out with the tears trickling down my cheeks.

I required my handkerchief throughout the whole service.

I was pretty low physically at this time due, I imagine in retrospect, to the after-effects of my strenuous days and sleepless nights in, and the journeyings to and from Australia. At all events when the choir was permitted to quit their eyrie I was exhausted, had a feverish headache and was dripping with perspiration. I joined my friends George Baker and Parry Jones in the Chapter House for refreshments but soon melted from the scene and made my way home with great difficulty amid the multitude and in the unrelenting rain. I was convinced I had pneumonia and fell into bed with hot water bottles and extra blankets.

Here Enid, who had travelled across London to witness the ceremony on her father's television, found me hours later deep in the arms of Morpheus.

But there was no pneumonia. Enid talked me out of it.

34

Lecturing in America

APART from occasional engagements abroad and the odd tour here and there my professional life kept to a fairly regular course prior to 1939. I was the spider sitting in London waiting for the flies to walk into my parlour; some of them, as I have said, were most distinguished flies too. After the war, however, I began to receive more and more invitations from the continent and it was exciting to me to find, due no doubt to my many recordings, that I had some sort of reputation in Paris, Berlin, Munich and Vienna. From that time the pattern of my life underwent a considerable change. The ambition of my youth to see my name scattered as frequently as possible over the concert advertisements of *The Times* and the *Daily Telegraph* has died, since half of my life is now spent away from England. My London appearances are in consequence fewer. This is a good thing for me for it broadens my horizon and lifts me out of a certain routine which could become monotonous. It is also a good thing for the London critics who must be sick of the sight of me. Even when available for concerts in London, I have now arrived at the age or stage when I am able to pick and choose my engagements with more discrimination, being no longer interested in the Wigmore Hall début of some young unknown.

This is not a high and mighty attitude, it is plain common sense. As my concerts are now more lucrative I am able to afford the luxury of refusing those which – perhaps involving too long and tiring a journey or choking my engagement book too full for comfort – do not attract me. I have more leisure now to think and study, have more time to prepare my work. God knows I seem to need more time than ever I did before; it takes me longer to learn and longer to digest what I have learned. Time is infinitely precious to me and there is too little of it left for it to be dissipated, along with my strength, on unpromising material.

But I am not claiming to be a superior person nor do I pretend to have 'grown out' of the Wigmore Hall. I still love it and regard it as an ideal venue for an intimate recital and when brilliant young men such as Hermann Prey and Donald Bell the baritones or Eric Friedman the violinist ask me to play for them there, I do everything possible to make myself available.

The point I am labouring to make is that there is great strain attached to the accompanist's work. When I go to Berlin over the heads of German accompanists and play for Fischer-Dieskau, to Barcelona for de los Angeles, to Copenhagen for Aksel Schiotz, to Athens with Alexandra Trianti, I feel I am taking on big responsibilities. These artists must hold me in high esteem, must place great reliance on me to wish to have me on their own native soil: they expect a high standard from me and I have to work extremely hard to maintain it.

You are walking the tight-rope when you perform in public. The perfection of Heifetz is most delicately poised though the layman could not be expected to understand this. Nor would he understand why that wonderful man Casals having slipped and cut his hand exclaimed, 'Good, I shall never be able to play the 'cello again.' No doubt Casals thanked God when his hand returned to normal but his immediate reaction on seeing his lacerated left hand was one of relief.

My work is everything to me; a matter of life and death; indeed I am so anxious about my own capacity that I can sympathize with Casals's emotions even though my feelings would not have gone to such extremes as his. Is the standard I have set for myself too high? Perhaps so. In any case I cannot sit down and play to myself for my own enjoyment and I envy some of my brother professionals who will play to their friends for hours and derive as much pleasure from it as their listeners. The joy of working is one thing (hearing in my mind and imagination the colour, shape, and then striving to reproduce it in living sound) but playing for my own delectation is another. Too aware of my own limitations, I can truthfully boast when I sit on a piano stool that I am modest, though doubtless my inhibitions would be classified as inordinate conceit by a psychiatrist.

But, as I have said before, it is easier to talk than to play, and when I stand up to address an audience I am a different being from the man who sits down to accompany a singer or violinist in recital. With my lectures I am perfectly relaxed and at home. Lecturing is a side-kick with me. When I walk alone on to the stage I am responsible to no one but myself and I revel in the sensation of getting hold of my listeners, riveting their attention, communicating ideas to them, making them smile. When an audience is responsive and lively I am conscious of a wave of goodwill which flows from it and gives me strength and confidence. I feel this much more in a lecture than I do at a concert.

This is why I anticipate a lecture tour in America with relish even though it involves long and tiring journeys, and comes at the end of a season of strenuous concertizing in Europe. But I do no accompanying; I make this a rule. The Americans – Eleanor Steber, Nan Merriman, Mack Harrell – and equally fine artists from Europe have paid me the compliment of asking me to collaborate with them while in New York and though it pains me to refuse them I remain obdurate because it is such a change for me to get some relief from the concentration that I am impelled to give to my accompanying.

I have only appeared twice in America in company with a singer, with John Coates in 1926 and thirty years later with Dietrich Fischer-Dieskau on his initial tour. So now I arrive in America with no rehearsals to arrange, no anxious correspondence about programmes, no crowding of appointments: and what is more I can have my pianoforte lid opened on the long stick. I pretend to be a prima donna and Enid runs around me making out I am important.

It was in 1954 that, urged by Solomon and other friends, I resolved to try my luck with my talk in America and I booked the New York Town Hall, through the agency of Columbia Artists Management, to see what would happen.

I was a success. Well, I must have been for I have visited the U.S.A. every year for a six- or seven-week tour ever since.

Music making in America is a big industry and the artist is generally persuaded that it pays to advertise. Music magazines with circulations which percolate to every town and city have a tremendous influence. An ambitious artist wants to see his name in them. (Mr Paderewski was an exception who ignored all inducements to advertise, and one periodical, now defunct, at the conclusion of his 1916 tour vindictively devoted the centre page of their issue to setting out in detail each programme together with the town and date on which it was performed. There were thirty or more of them and the caption running across the double page in large red letters read:

'The *versatility* of Mr Paderewski.'

All the programmes were identical and that was where the shoe was intended to pinch. But what necessity had Paderewski to advertise when every hall was sold out? The cities he visited were hundreds of miles apart, why need he vary his programme since it would be heard by a completely different public at each concert?)

After my début my agents suggested that I join the throng of singers, instrumentalists and conductors whose photographs smiled happily out at the reader between the covers of a most highly respected journal. I discarded those pictures of mine which seemed to say 'See what a good boy am I', rejected those where I had attempted to appear intellectual, and finally chose one which, I persuaded myself, looked waggish. It was an expensive luxury to have my large face with newspaper clippings above and beneath and around it, from *The New York Times*, *The Philadelphia Inquirer*, *Christian Science Monitor*, *Chicago American*, *San Francisco Chronicle*, and as a *coup de grâce The Saturday Review* with Irving Kolodin's ' . . . one of the professional discourses of our time'. But my picture, seen in this galaxy of stars, all of whom were proclaimed as being unparalleled in their respective spheres, did not create the furore I had expected and I quickly retired from this form of competition.

The fact that I am an Englishman with an English accent is no impediment to me with the Americans. In England our attitude towards a visitor from abroad is contradictory; at one moment we look down our noses with disdain at 'another foreigner' and at the next we will engage him to sing or play to us, second-rater though he may be, in preference to a second-rater of our own. In America the general public, by and large, is less illogical and perhaps less insular for it greets a visiting artist without prejudice, appraising him according to his worth. But it does not shut its eyes to its own native talent as we do in England. Even such illustrious artists as Myra Hess, Solomon, Clifford Curzon, gained greater prestige in their own country after they had won their triumphs abroad. Americans do not waste time like this and I can think of many of their musicians – Leonard Bernstein, Eileen Farrell, Leontyne Price, Lawrence Tibbett, Leonard Warren, George London and others – who were honoured at home long before they won inter-national reputations.

There is a short cut in the road to fame in America – a name can be made overnight. It is only an amazing generosity of out-look that makes this possible. In fact, generosity is uniform in America.

Goodwill is put into practical effect at the expense of end-less trouble. Since all travel and hotel arrangements are meth-odically made in advance, it was an unheard-of experience for us to arrive in Atlanta, Georgia, with no place to lay our heads. All accommodation had been fully booked by a Law Convention which filled the town to overflowing. Edna Giesen, my agent, promised us that we would be looked after, and sure enough two strangers greeted us at the air terminal, planted us in a hotel (they insisted on seeing our room to ensure all was well), then drove us off to their house where we proceeded straight-away to the kitchen and helped them mix drinks and cut sandwiches. One minute we were Mr and Mrs Moore and the next Enid and Gerald. Again no time wasted.

As a boy touring Canada at a dollar a concert I had been de-pressed by the dreary sameness of the small towns in the prairie provinces: always the inevitable grain elevator at the railroad station, the same squat wooden houses, the flat, snow-covered landscape. Over forty years have passed since I saw those towns and things may now be different, sanitary arrangements im-proved, but there is still a regrettable regularity in the layout of many of the big cities in North America and Canada ; one town bears close resemblance to another with its cluster of sky-scrapers. When his American host pointed out one of these huge structures to Mr Arthur Balfour, telling him enthusiastic-ally that it was fireproof, the Englishman replied, 'What a pity!'

But who am I to talk? In my own country everything Ameri-can is regarded as *chic*, in fact our teenagers chew chiclets and wear blue jeans, our blues singers would be unacceptable did they not affect American accents, and our architects erect sky-scrapers. Worst of all we have caught on – and it is spread-ing all over Europe – to the American habit of background music : I find it difficult to indulge in the process of thinking even at the best of times, but when this slime is being poured into my ears, thought or study or reading are quite impossible. I begged my pretty American air-hostess on one occasion to switch it off and this she most obligingly did with a 'Not musical, eh?' Background music is a menace and you find it everywhere.

Uniformity, however, is not to be condemned out of hand. In every American hotel for instance, each room has its own private bath – this is taken for granted – every bed is comfort-table, hygiene and cleanliness are habitual, and so is efficiency. When I call the operator to order my breakfast she immediately replies, 'Good morning, Mr Moore,' and this when I am just one out of two thousand other guests. In only one instance is this efficiency lacking : the newsvendor – as courteous as the taxi-driver – fails to provide his customers with a trolley to roll home the Sunday papers. They weigh half a ton.

On the whole, the American visiting England is in much worse case than the English visitor to America. For one thing he finds himself being driven to his bedroom at night far earlier than is his wont. He would be advised to utilize the time before sleep descends upon him by studying our money system which is one of the most brilliant and complicated ever devised by the mind of man. It is a mystery to anyone coming from abroad. We shall never budge – '*Ils ne passeront pas*' – and shall go on dividing pounds into shillings and shillings into pence with bulldog tenacity. Tanners, bobs, florins, half-crowns, and guineas are thrown in merrily to add to the confusion. Why do I charge guineas instead of pounds? I am asked by friends from abroad and I tell them as I pocket my fee that it is just another way of squeezing extra shillings out of them. Why do we not change to the metric system? Because it is too simple. The fact that no visitor understands our currency is of inestimable advantage to us.

I have been fortunate enough to see more of America than many Americans and have penetrated the fastnesses of Wyoming and Montana – once the heart of the Wild West – and the hinterland of Nebraska. My agent was apprehensive – until she knew me better – lest my subject matter were too erudite for some of the audiences I might encounter in these States. She worried unnecessarily for I do not know the meaning of the word 'erudite' and take it to mean a pestilence of sorts.

Most of my tours have been in the winter. January, February, March, are not the most delectable months in which to fulfil a tightly packed schedule, particularly as many of my engagements are with universities and colleges. Some of the finest of these establishments in Pennsylvania, Ohio, Illinois, New York State, are miles away from the big cities. Small airports which serve them are unable to keep open after a heavy snowstorm and since many of the passenger trains are discontinued one has to go as far as possible by train and then proceed by bus and finish up with a final scramble – breathlessly talking to your reception committee – over deep virgin snow to the shelter of your college or hotel.

Even an up-to-date city such as Pittsburgh can be paralysed under these conditions. No car could make its way up the drive when I was due to make my departure from the university there. Bag in hand I waded to the street and by sheer good luck picked up a taxi, and through the ingenuity of the driver, who avoided streets where cars skidding broadside-on had caused long traffic snarls, I was delivered at the station only just in time to catch my train to Chicago. A drive of ten minutes under normal circumstances had taken forty.

These conditions obtain in most countries from time to time

and are not peculiar to America. I myself was reared on fog. But it is a pity to find oneself visiting, year after year, when it is largely snowbound, a land where the Fall season is the most beautiful in the world. So now my tours of the U.S.A. are arranged for the autumn and I may see the maple leaves, whole hillsides of them gleaming, red in the sunlight. Nor do I need rubbers (goloshes) at all unless I am sent to expatiate on the art of accompaniment to the Alaskans.

35

Caviar and Vodka

SIR ARTHUR BLISS, Master of the Queen's Musick, headed a party of English musicians on a short tour of Russia in April 1955. Sir Arthur and Trudy Bliss, Clarence Raybould conductor, Jennifer Vyvyan soprano, Phyllis Sellick and Cyril Smith duo-pianists, Alfredo Campoli violinist, Leon Goossens oboist, and I made up the group. We were to be guests of the Government of the U.S.S.R. Trudy nicknamed us collectively The Blissters, though naturally only *en famille*.

The interchange of visits between Russia and the western world is now an everyday occurrence, but this tour had some significance in that it was the very first of its kind since the war.

I could not imagine a happier party and we were better friends at the end of our visit than we were at the beginning. A companionship sprang up between us, reinforced perhaps by being in a country whose language we did not understand. Even our own names were unrecognizable to us on the placards advertising our concerts. Mine, however, because of its sheer purity and brevity was soon deciphered, for when the word MYP was read we knew we had arrived at the correct city. For MYP is pronounced MOORE and ever since then, when I run into Trudy Bliss I am hailed as Mip.

I began to realize that I was about to penetrate behind an Iron Curtain when I had filled up the complicated forms and supplied half a dozen photographs for my visa, and when told – by way of a send off from London – that Enid should write to me only if it were urgent when a letter might be sent in the diplomatic bag to the British Embassy in Moscow.

Campoli and I, owing to previous commitments, travelled a day later than the others and in consequence missed the fan-fares, the photographers, and the red carpet in Moscow. True, Campoli and I were photographed on our departure at London

Airport but as Alfredo cheerfully remarked to me as we posed, 'It will never appear in print'.

Our plane had to be diverted, owing to bad weather, to Leningrad, yet in spite of the unexpectedness of our arrival there, we were given a most cordial welcome and as we sat in the airport we heard over the radio the voice of David Oistrach, that great violinist, greeting us in the friendliest terms and praising his colleague Alfredo Campoli. Oistrach's fellow-feeling for us was shown by all the Soviet musicians we met. He, with Shostakovich, Khachaturian, Kabaleviski, and other representative artists, attended our concerts in Moscow and were charming to us. International sport so often creates bad blood, summit conferences are freezing, but the interchange of artists between countries can do nothing but good.

It must have been an effort for Oistrach to come to our appearances for, as Mrs Oistrach told me, he was teaching from morning till night nearly every day, snatching a stand-up lunch between lessons. His tours abroad are permitted only on condition that he makes up for the teaching time lost when he returns to Moscow ; nor does he complain of this.

The audiences overwhelmed us by their enthusiasm. Alexander Kipnis once told me that the Russians are inherently musical, for the crossing-sweeper and scavenger are moved by music. I would not say that en masse they are cultivated listeners for their taste is conservative in the extreme, they like above all a tune they can get their teeth into. They never tire of Tchaikovsky.

The directive that Soviet composers must write 'For the People' is a possible explanation of this conservative attitude. Their scope of appreciation is by no means inhibited, however, for of all the songs sung by Jennifer Vyvyan it was her singing of Purcell that 'stopped the show' in her joint recitals with Goossens. Campoli and I could not complain either of the splendid recognition we received after our Beethoven or Bach sonatas, but it was this violinist's dazzling virtuosity and sweetness of tone in his last group of Kreisler pieces that sent our public wild with delight. Nor would this response be any different perhaps in any other part of the world.

But I should be giving a misleading picture were I not to place on record the fact that the public listened with keenest interest and lively curiosity to works which were new and strange to their ears: Gordon Jacobs's Oboe Concerto with Goossens as its incomparable soloist, the double piano concerto of Lennox Berkeley so brilliantly performed by Phyllis Sellick and Cyril Smith, the fine playing of the Moscow and Leningrad orchestras of Vaughan Williams's *London Symphony*, Elgar's *Cockaigne*, Walton's *Portsmouth Point*.

Nevertheless, it is no reflection on the composers and performers of these works, if I say that a special distinction was attached to the Bliss Violin Concerto not only for the originality and colour of the work itself or for the extraordinary playing of Campoli in the solo part but by reason of the presence on the rostrum of the composer himself. In fact, Bliss was a winner all along the line – unless I except the few games of chess in which he indulged with some members of the Soviet Orchestras.

Although I have yet to be convinced of the virtues of Communism I can see that in Russia the artist is regarded as a person of importance, he attracts as much attention and is given as much publicity as a crack tennis player in America or in England. His emoluments too are very high, if he is in the top flight. As we grade our tennis players, so in Russia do they grade their musicians, and the fees for each grade are standardized. Thus Oistrach, Richter, Rostropovich, would naturally be in the first grade: Yampolsky, who goes everywhere with Oistrach, plays sonatas with him and is a superb pianist, would be down-graded with much lower fees because he is an accompanist.

I had some idea how the system worked when I went with Leon Goossens to do a twenty-minute recital on the radio in Moscow. Goossens, being a soloist and recognized as one of the leading oboe players in the world, was told he would receive the fee that was invariably given to artists of the first grade ; I was told that as an accompanist I should receive a lower-grade fee. Here Goossens without hesitation generously explained through an interpreter that in England I was regarded as a first-rate artist and that since we were playing duets for oboe and piano he would divide his fee equally with me. With no fuss and with no disputation the management at the radio station bowed to Lee's argument and agreed at once to pay me the same fee that they awarded to musicians of the first rank. I did one twenty-minute broadcast with Leon, another with Jennifer Vyvyan, and a third with Alfredo Campoli – and received in roubles the equivalent of £1,500. I was paid in cash at the rate of £25 per minute and walked out with the roubles, bundles of them, stuffed into my music case: it was the highest fee I have ever received in my life. When I was informed that I was not allowed to bring the roubles out of the country, a hollow tone crept into my merry laughter.

I was never aware at any time of being restricted in my movements but, of course, I only wanted to see objects and places of historical interest; in Moscow the Museum and the Bell Tower at the Kremlin; in Leningrad the Hermitage. With Alfredo, indefatigable photographer, I walked all over the place. I was not interested in seeing the workers' marvellous canteens as I know factory canteens in England and America are every bit as good, but did not risk a sceptical smile by rubbing this fact home.

We were in Kiev for the May Day celebrations and procession. For days the preparations for this festivity had been going forward, decorations and bunting filled the streets and, more striking and less pleasing to the eye, immoderately large pictures of Lenin and members of the Supreme Soviet were affixed to the buildings. These likenesses, some of them as large as a tennis court, looked grimly down on us. A scowl measuring several square feet could not be said to communicate the joy of spring. Joseph Stalin's picture was conspicuous by its almost complete absence.

We were invited to witness the procession from a special stand. It must have been tiring for the throng marching past but it was far more tiring for us since we had no seats. As for the endurance of the commentator who talked over the loud-speaker for more than four hours as a million men, women, and children filed past him, it is beyond praise; he would announce enthusiastically each batch of schoolchildren, or splendid gymnasts, each corps of glorious railway workers or farm workers, with a description of who they were and whence they came, concluding each idyll with a vociferous 'Hooray' bellowed into the microphone with deafening effect. The 'Hooray' was the recurring refrain that punctuated all his utterances nor did any of the onlookers cheer since it was thus done by proxy. Of all the marchers only the children carrying their spring flowers looked as if they were enjoying themselves.

Kiev on the river Dnieper is a fine city. It was ravaged by bombardment in the war yet hardly a trace of the damage can be seen. 'And I understand', said a lady interpreter to me when I remarked on the wonderful transformation 'that London's scars are still painfully evident.' We visited several old churches and found the steps leading to St Vladimir lined with old women holding out their hands for a few copecks. My indefatigable interpreter assured me that they were begging for the benefit of the church : I could not refrain from replying that they were certainly dressed for the part.

Despite the probability that a bigger percentage of the population wears boots and shoes than ever before, there was much poverty to be seen. When Campoli and I walked along the Nevsky Prospekt in Leningrad (we were impelled to interest ourselves in jewellery, goblets and trinkets, full-sleeved Ukrainian blouses, frills and furbelows, since our roubles were immobile) we found long queues forming outside the jewellers' shops. They filed in when the doors opened with no wherewithal to buy but merely to stand and gaze at the display. At our entry they parted courteously to give us pride of place, recognizing us as foreigners and prospective purchasers.

These were the same people who listened to our music with such rapt attention – who lived in fairyland when they attended the Bolshoi Ballet, who queued for hours – thousands at a time – to pass by Lenin's tomb in Red Square.

All the women one saw on the streets wore the same shaped hat, rather like a squashed tea-cosy ; it came in three colours, green, red, and black, and the only variation to this hat was the scarf which was generally worn by the road-sweepers and bricklayers, who were mostly women. (With the exception of several beauties in the ballet there was never an attractive woman to be seen in the streets – unless, indeed, they saw me coming and hid themselves. To be accurate, I saw one statuesque Juno with flaming golden hair who, splattered with plaster, looked magnificent as she climbed her ladder.) The men wore caps of a sombre black. Everybody looked solemn – not to say grim.

Clothes do not make the man but there is a certain satisfaction in appearing neatly even if not immaculately dressed. I was inclined to imagine that sartorial conditions might have improved since I was there but two friends, members of the Royal Ballet of London, who danced in Moscow and Leningrad in 1961, tell me that things are much the same; so much so that when our dancers flew into Moscow airport the Russian interpreters complimented them on the fine travelling clothes with which the British Government had provided them in order 'to impress us Russians'. The dancers protested again and again that their clothes were their very own but their protestations fell on unbelieving ears.

In the magnificent foyer of the Bolshoi Theatre, glittering with superb chandeliers and beautiful tapestries, the awed populace walked ankle deep on the unprotected and sumptuous carpets. No linen drugget covers these carpets to save them from the dirt brought in from the streets, for the theatre belongs to the people in the same way that Moscow's Underground Railway belongs to them. Visitors to Moscow from the provinces will go down to the Underground merely to look at it, as indeed I did. I did not travel on this subway and cannot tell if the service is frequent and up to date but the station I visited resembled a submerged cathedral with its marble pillars and floors and the total absence of advertising placards.

Nothing, it seemed to me, is too good for the people, for the masses.

But what of the person? I could not help feeling that he was a cog in a very efficient machine. A distinguished man in any profession in the U.S.S.R. provided he is a good Party Man is well catered for: he is lent, perhaps given by the Government, a flat in Moscow and a small house in the country and from the same source he is lent or given a car. Whether he is able to call anything his own I cannot say, for despite all the kindnesses that we received – the flowers, the friendliness – all the hospitality showered on us was official and took place in hotels. I never saw the inside of a private house. Of living conditions I can only speak of my own experience in hotels therefore, and I was comfortable. In Moscow, for instance, I had a suite with a grand piano – some strings in the middle octaves were missing, giving the effect of hiccups – and I was able to practise to my heart's content. The windows were lined with putty to keep out the cold of the dying winter but I cut some of it away to let in the spring warmth.

Surprisingly enough there is an air of leisureliness that reminded me of Spain ; the spirit of mañana obtains. If, before a concert, I wished to have a quick meal such as an omelette and a cup of coffee, I allowed at first half an hour for this : it is not sufficient time. I never spent less than an hour and a half in a restaurant even though my order might be a simple one. It did not pay to be in a hurry. Under no circumstances would the waiter accept a tip.

Our farewell concert in Moscow was attended by Messrs Bulganin and Khrushchev.

Unlike statesmen we had no differences to iron out, unlike sportsmen we needed no referee to see fair play. We were all bound together — Russians and Englishmen – by our love of music. We came in contact with such vast numbers of the people through the concerts, the radio and television, we were able to converse in such a friendly way – in either English or German – with so many of the young people we met that we feel our visit was highly successful.

36

Summer Festivals

I FEEL very immature when men of middle age tell me how relieved they will be when the festivities of Christmas are over and things 'have settled down to normal again'. While never losing sight of the fact that Christmas is a religious festival, I do not forget it is also a holiday season and I revel in holidays. Now if I were a successful tenor or baritone, this period, especially in England, would be spent travelling from one end of the country to the other fitting in as many oratorio engagements as I could possibly contrive: as soon as one *Messiah* had finished in the afternoon I should be bolting for the station to catch the train for my next *Messiah* in the evening.

The instrumentalist, on the other hand – unless he is an orchestral player – is carefree and can keep his fiddle or flute in its case or lock up his piano, secure in the knowledge that his services for the time being are not required.

The summer was the best time of all when I was young, for though there would be practising to do and the odd recording session, I knew that July and August would be free of concerts. I could play golf all day and bridge all night. Perhaps, after all, the reason for this blissful state of freedom for me was that few people realized what a jewel I was. Or could it be that Summer Festivals, as we know them today, had not acquired any momentum? In England alone such a mushroom growth of them has sprung up in the last thirty years that one Festival follows and overlaps another. If you are invited to appear at several of these and in addition are engaged for some of the Continental ones – each insisting on an eclectic programme involving much preparation – you find your summer is fully booked up: no close season.

But am I complaining? Would I have it otherwise? Most certainly not: besides, I have found by preparing my programmes well in advance, that in the delectable surroundings in which these concourses are invariably held, I catch up on operas and symphony concerts of which I have been deprived during the winter.

I do not swoon with ecstasy at my own playing, as I have said, but – I add this in case I have not made it clear – I adore music. Critical of my own playing, I am far less critical of others and I go with excitement as a listener and with a wide open mind. It frequently happens that I have had a blissfully happy evening drinking in a Mozart symphony or a Verdi opera only to discover, when reading the newspaper the following morning, how wrong I was and that the performance was excruciatingly bad. Perhaps I recognized at the time that the performance was below par but it did not deprive me altogether of my pleasure in the music.

In any case there is good clean fun to be had on occasion. In Venice, for instance, it may be certain I combined business with pleasure and went to the Ducal Palace to see a superb performance of Verdi's *Otello* in the courtyard. Idly turning the pages of the programme I found such a delightful outline of the plot translated into English from Boïto's libretto as would have made Shakespeare turn in his grave. In Act III, for instance, I read, 'Othello is only thinking of killing Desdemona. At the mercy of delirium he falls down fainted. Iago triumphally enjoys.'

Well, it may be fairly rough hewn but it gives a picture. But when, through the ingenuity of the printer, I read of the innocent meeting between Cassio and Desdemona that 'Iago looks with attention at the mating', the picture it conjures up is quite a different one.

The poor printer is often accused of inaccuracy ; I would rather attribute him with a highly coloured imagination. Surely it was this which led him on one English Festival programme to call Brahms's love song not *O liebliche Wangen* (O fairest cheek) but *O liebliche Wanzen*. The substitution of a z for a g made a slight difference to the meaning for the literal translation of *Wanzen* is 'bed-bug'.

The summer Festspiel is a way of life which is now universally enjoyed, for America and Canada have caught the festive spirit and I have had many invitations from across the Atlantic.

These I have had to decline regretfully since Europe is my happy hunting ground from May to September. Intermittently I find myself going to Bath, Cheltenham, and York, to Casals's own festival at Prades, to Switzerland, France, and Holland, but it is to four festivals especially that I look forward with eagerness year after year. I single these out apart from the others because I visit them with a regularity which is certainly not monotonous: they are – taken in order of the calendar – Granada, King's Lynn, Salzburg and Edinburgh. With these four I am, at the moment, a season-ticket holder.

At the Fiesta España I play for none other than Victoria de los Angeles. This year, at my own request and most reluctantly, I am missing it in order to give my undivided attention to the completion of this valuable contribution to literature.

It is only the getting-to and the coming-from Granada which is trying. Flying from London to Madrid is quite straightforward but the night has to be spent in Madrid, for Iberian Airlines arrange for the Granada plane to leave some few minutes before the plane from London is due to arrive. It is all very cunning. The same syncopation operates on your return journey.

But once there, Granada is enchanting with its flower-filled gardens and fountains of the Generalife. Here under the stars the ballet is held. There are three open-air courts for concerts in the Alhambra – the big Palacio de Carlos V for orchestras, the small but intimate Patio de los Leones, ideal for a string quartet or a Segovia recital, and the Patio de los Arrayanes.

Victoria de los Angeles sings in the Patio de los Arrayanes and at her matinée recital the elegant quadrangle is painted gold by the rays of the setting sun, filled with the gold of her voice. The Spaniards are swept into a frenzy by the singing, by the modesty and sweetness of the singer. She is their own darling Catalan.

Of a summer night the court, filled with people, can be airless. It is then that the diplomats tactlessly smoking in the front rows just below the singer have to be requested to extinguish their cigarettes. A light summer breeze is welcome except when it concentrates on my music when I am playing, but in this instance I have always been lucky for Gonzalo Soriano, the virtuoso pianist, very kindly turns the pages for me. His hand and fingers crawl crab-like down and up the tremulous page and he does it without covering the actual notes I am reading ; a species of legerdemain only possible from a man with a technique.

Only the swallows can be slightly disturbing. Until the sun goes down these swoop and wheel and flutter in the most fascinating way. One's eyes, when in the audience, are attracted by them, especially when they fold their wings tightly and squeeze themselves into the minute interstices of the Moorish architecture where they nest.

We always stay at the Alhambra Palace Hotel, high up on the hill with a magical vista of golden sun-dried plain, the Sierra Nevada range to one side and Granada spread out below. Since one hears every sound that comes up from the town, we discovered that the best time to sleep is the afternoon. At night it is impossible, for during the fiesta a fair is held. It is a mile away but the carousel goes on all night, and the blare of the roundabouts – inevitably amplified – comes into your open bedroom window as clearly as if a gramophone record were being loudly played in the next room. This goes on until 4.30 or 5 in the morning and its cessation is a signal for the cocks to start crowing.

The Spaniards keep strange hours. In summer time you lunch at three and dine at eleven. At Santander the evening concerts begin just before midnight and at a Yehudi Menuhin recital the halfway stage was not reached till well after one. Diana Menuhin complained bitterly to Felicitas Keller, our manager, that the hours were impossible. 'The concert', she said, 'will last another hour at least and we shall not be in bed before dawn.' Miss Keller endeavoured to placate her by pointing out that she could sleep in the following morning, the Spaniards retired late and they correspondingly rose late.

'Not in my hotel, they are talking in the next room at the top of their voices at seven in the morning.'

'Ah, but they are probably English.'

'They are conversing in the most fluent Spanish.'

Here the exchange ended inconclusively.

I must admit that a performance late at night makes the day a long one. My usual routine on the day of a concert is to work all the morning, walk for an hour after lunch, take an hour's rest, practise again, and then after an egg and a cup of tea I am ready to dress for the concert. But this programme cannot be followed if your concert starts at 11.30 (which in Spain means midnight or just after) instead of 8 p.m. You do not know what to do with yourself with those extra three or four hours.

Fortunately, Victoria de los Angeles has acquired the habit, after so many engagements in other countries, of starting her concerts at a reasonable hour and so she insists that her summer recitals in Spain are matinées; these begin at 8.30 p.m. or as they ought to put it, 8.30 for 9.00 p.m.

Spanish cooking is not so unattractive as many tourists think. Brilliant things are done with oil as my old friend Antoni Sala used to show me in his Chelsea days, but above all their sea-foods are delicious, especially if you are near the Mediterranean or the Atlantic coasts. In Barcelona or in the north at San Sebastian, Santander, La Coruña, Bilbao, fish of almost every description is served and most expertly cooked. The squid, dished up with its inky-blue sauce, was one speciality that I mastered but failed to understand or enjoy: Enrique Magriña owned up afterwards to hating it, while Victoria and Enid, at the urgent entreaty of their respective husbands, left their squid unmolested, free (if it were alive) to squirt its obnoxious fluid at more appreciative customers.

*

Of all the festivals in Great Britain one of the most intimate and *gemütlich* is the King's Lynn. (I do not forget Benjamin Britten's Aldeburgh but since the presiding genius there is the greatest accompanist in the world there is no call for my services.) This picturesque Norfolk town on the estuary of the Ouse has the fine medieval Guildhall of St George for its recitals, chamber music, and plays. Orchestral concerts are held in several of the old Saxon or Norman churches.

The inspiration at King's Lynn is Ruth Fermoy whose beauty is only equalled by her charm and energy. I have played for some superb artists here but the greatest joy to me was my collaboration with Ruth Fermoy herself. Somebody suggested – I do not know who it was but I feel very grateful to him or her – that she and I combine to make a piano-duet team for the benefit of the Lynnites.

Now we are both experienced musicians : Ruth had been a professional pianist up to the time of her marriage while I (shall I say with half a century behind me ?) could claim to have progressed beyond the tyro stage, yet the two of us found music for four hands the most difficult form of ensemble we had ever tackled. Unanimity with the singer presents the accompanist with no problem for the consonant gives him warning when the sung vowel, with which he synchronizes, is coming ; if need be he can watch the singer's lips. With a string player he see the bow out of the corner of his eye when attacking a note or chord, or, failing that, he can sense the exact moment when the horsehair is about to bite the gut. But with the percussive pianoforte the simultaneous striking of a chord or note with your partner is not so straightforward for there is no cautionary indication as to the precise fraction of a second when the hammer will hit the strings. We found it was not so impossible if we played strictly in time with metronomical exactitude, but two human beings do not wish to give the impression of a pianola. This is the danger of the pianoforte duet. Perhaps this form of music making is akin to madrigal singing in that the performers are apt to derive more enjoyment than the listeners. Neither of us entertained the idea of becoming a permanent team but we rehearsed conscientiously and sometimes had a third person to listen and criticize; none other than our dear but redoubtable Lionel Tertis.

With Ruth in the treble all eyes would be on her and the picture was infinitely pleasing but with me in the treble my lovely partner was hidden from view, putting the team at once at a decided disadvantage. I sometimes assured the audience that though unseen Ruth Fermoy would certainly be heard.

There was another reason why I preferred playing Secundo

rather than Primo: the player in the bass – sitting, in other words, south of the equatorial middle C – has control of the pedals. Without that sheet anchor, the sustaining pedal, I felt forsaken; it seemed unnatural to play with both feet planted squarely on the floor while uneasily tinkling away in the treble. Instinctively my foot would fumble for this pedal only to find it had another tenant.

But rehearsing could be great fun. I once ventured to say, 'I cannot hear your left hand there.'

'It is rather difficult for me to make the notes speak when you are already holding the keys down yourself.'

I was accused sometimes, not unreasonably, of occupying too much keyboard territory. There might be many instances where I would have to remove my hands quickly out of the way so as not to impede traffic, so I wrote code words on my part that my limited intelligence would instantly understand and obey, such as 'Duck' – 'Shrink' – and in *Marche Écossaise* by Debussy 'Awa' wi' ye'.

The eleventh birthday of this delightful and friendly Norfolk *réunion* occurred in 1961. Here, from time to time, has been heard the lovely singing of Kathleen Ferrier, Mattiwilda Dobbs, Elisabeth Søderstrøm and so have the voices of Edith Evans, Flora Robson and Peggy Ashcroft. We have laughed with Peter Ustinov, been transported by Beryl Grey. And, to give some idea of the informal atmosphere that obtains, we hear John Barbirolli, not only conducting the Hallé Orchestra, but playing his violoncello in the chamber-music ensemble.

Queen Elizabeth the Queen Mother attends many of the concerts and her presence is an inspiration to audience and artists alike. And always there is the Lady Fermoy herself, relaxed and charming, giving the impression that the running of a mere festival is child's play.

I have missed but one King's Lynn Festival: the first. Though how they managed to do without me I cannot imagine. As for our music for four hands, we have given it a rest, having inflicted it on the public for several years in succession. But we shall come back, perhaps in 1970, the twentieth birthday of this colourful perennial, when I shall insist on my partner playing Primo.

*

There is indeed a contrast between the Dutch landscape of the Norfolk Fens – wide and bracing – and the wooded hills, mountains and lakes of the Salzkammergut. There is no more enchanting town in Europe than Salzburg. It is seen at a disadvantage during the season, being packed tight with visitors, but I have never been there at any other time. Enid and I stay away from the madding crowd in the pretty outlying district of Parsch whence we have a twenty-minute walk under the lime trees along the bank of the Salzach river, very often in the rain, to the Festspielhaus or the Mozarteum.

We use Shanks's pony a good deal in Salzburg, for my first rehearsal there follows so closely on the heels of my King's Lynn engagements that it is impossible to make the journey by car. It is just as well that we have this exercise to work off the effects of the Kartoffeln (the potato is the most versatile vegetable ever invented but the simple boiled potato in Austria is unequalled anywhere else), of the Kaiserschmarrn and the Salzburger Nockel – all fatal for the cut of the jib, but inasmuch as my figure has gone beyond recall I have ceased to worry about it – much.

But how it rains! Even Herbert von Karajan cannot stop it. Yet your Salzburger, as your Englishman, refuses to be intimidated by the weather and each year Hofmannsthal's *Jedermann* is optimistically scheduled for performances in the Domplatz, and concerts and opera in the Courtyard of the Residenz – all of which are open-air performances. But I notice – with acknowledgement to the prudence of the management – that the Festspielhaus is kept conveniently free on the occasions of these *al fresco* events in case the weather turns sour.

I was tempted to say there is no reason why it should ever stop raining in Salzburg – and yet – when the sun shines one forgets it has ever rained at all. It is then that the little town nestling in its hills is incomparably beautiful. As Christmas follows Christmas and I receive inquiries for July or August from the Festspielhaus, I find myself longing to see it again.

So often at these festivals I meet friends who went to the orchestral rehearsal of a new symphony in the morning, to a chamber concert in the afternoon, to an opera in the evening. This was the daily routine, and with dark rings under their eyes they complain of being tired and surfeited. When I ask them why they try to hear so much, they reply that that was their reason for coming to Salzburg. It is not my way of enjoying music. We book our seats on alternate rather than consecutive nights and take the day off up the Gaisburg in between. Good concentrated listening is tiring and must be rationed otherwise the appetite may sicken.

Keeping to this pattern we come away from this Festival invigorated, and of all the visits we have made, the last one always seems to have been the best. The two stars in the most recent (1961) were Schwarzkopf and Fischer-Dieskau. I do not say this because I happened to be accompanying them in Lieder Recitals. In fact Schwarzkopf – lovely though her *Wolfabend* was – made history in *Der Rosenkavalier*. Many with a longer memory than mine who heard her Marschallin in the Neues Festspielhaus declared it to be the finest portrayal of the part they had ever experienced. I was too moved to visit her after the performance.

Fischer-Dieskau was the other highlight in his recital of Wolf's Mörike songs. He reckons that one song recital is as taxing as three operatic roles. It is a *volte-face* to sing Wolfram for a whole season as he did, to sing Fiordiligi and the Feldmarschallin for a whole season as Schwarzkopf did, and in the middle of that season to give an isolated Wolf recital. It is as if a painter working for weeks on a huge canvas abruptly transferred his attention to a miniature. With a string of concert performances or a season of undiluted opera the voice has time to settle down ; it is the sudden leap from one *genre* to another that is so hazardous : only supreme artists such as Schwarzkopf and Fischer-Dieskau can manage it.

For this reason perhaps there are only four or five Liederabends during the whole Salzburg season : islands in an ocean of opera.

But fancy going every year to this precious spot and being paid for it!

I ran into Neville Cardus one summer evening in London and he asked, 'Are you going to cricket tomorrow?' I told him, and my tone may have sounded unconcerned, that I was off to Salzburg on the morrow.

'Off to Salzburg? And you're not turning somersaults with joy?'

*

The Edinburgh Festival overlaps that of Salzburg. In fact, more than once Enid has flown home two days ahead of me to drive the car to Scotland while I, leaving immediately after my last concert in the Mozarteum, have proceeded straightway from London Airport to catch the night train up north. Sometimes I have managed to get to King's Cross station with only a few minutes to spare: a close thing even though there is no close season.

Again we follow the same tactics by picking our listening judiciously. We lived out in the country for the first few years of the Festival with our friend Dorothy Beckwith and her family in their lovely place by the Pentland Hills at Balerno. I could drive in and do my rehearsing at Rosalind and Alex Maitland's surrounded by their superb collection of pictures, and then escape from the city back to the country. But the Beckwiths without consulting us moved to Sussex and we now have Ruth D'Arcy Thompson's flat just off Princes Street where I can practise and rehearse as much as I like. Nothing disturbs me here except the maroon which is discharged daily from the castle precisely on the stroke of one. Every day, precisely at one o'clock I jump out of my skin.

The Black Salzburg was the sobriquet Carl Ebert gave to Edinburgh, nor was it meant as a disparaging comparison. Salzburg is a pretty little Christmas-card picture and the other is a majestic city but beyond the fact that each has a castle perched high up on a rock – illuminated of nights – they share few points of resemblance unless it is a predilection for rain, and the gallant staging of open-air attractions. Gallant is *le mot juste* for Edinburgh. Whereas in Salzburg, sitting in the Domplatz or the Courtyard of the Residenz with one eye on the stage and one eye on the gathering clouds you know that shelter is near at hand, at 'Auld Reekie' you go to the Military Tattoo on the Castle Esplanade prepared for any contingency with rain-coats, umbrellas, travelling rugs, and a thermos flask. There is no escape. Yet it would indeed be a weak spirit who would not think it worth while, for the swinging kilts and the martial skirling of the pipes are sights and sounds never to be forgotten. They set your heart on fire: this is just as well, it keeps out the cold.

And how cold it can be! Coming hot-foot from the south, the Scottish air – bracing and healthy, no doubt – congeals the blood at first. Poor Enrique Magriña, stepping off the plane with his wife, Victoria de los Angeles, in early September, was caught in a snow-flurry. He had come direct from the heat of Barcelona and, hatless, was wearing a tropical suit and open-meshed white shoes. It looked extremely funny. Enrique, after a moment of shocked incredulity, joined in my hearty laughter.

Compared to some of the European festivals, Edinburgh's is very young for it was inaugurated only in 1947 yet its reputation is world-wide. Every artist – be he musician, actor, dancer – has the ambition to appear there, every composer and playwright wants to be heard there.

I cannot deny that I take an immense pride in the fact that I am the only artist who has appeared at every single Edinburgh Festival since the beginning, and those musicians with whom I have associated represent a veritable league of nations. The list not only includes the names of those special beloveds of mine but several young and brilliant artists who will rejoice all hearts – and mine too – for many years to come, Elisabeth Søderstrøm, Kirsten Meyer, Mattiwilda Dobbs, Lois Marshall, Nicolai Gedda, Luigi Alva, Hermann Prey, to mention but a few. My first meeting with some of these was at Edinburgh and has resulted in continued association and warm friendship.

This international gathering of lovers of art was launched with a mighty swing by Rudolf Bing, now manager of the Metropolitan Opera Company in New York, and whose friendship I continue to enjoy. Now Lord Harewood is in charge. Under his vigorous and fearless direction it will continue to flourish. He may even get us, eventually, a new opera house.

37

Television

LIKE to recall the Chinaman who when asked to tell how it came about that he and his wife were blessed by such a large and seemingly ever increasing number of children replied, 'We no telly.'

When I alluded earlier to the horror of television, I was speaking as a performer. I enjoy television as a viewer and am not guilty of that form of snobbism which boasts of having no television set in the house. But I am not an addict and will go into the next room to see a programme which I have every reason to hope I shall enjoy, and when it is over I quit. The point is that the set is in a separate room – and this is very important. As our friend the Chinaman implied, television can be a fearful time-waster.

But what a power it has; through its medium one can visit the hearths of a million homes in the twinkling of an eye: world-wide reputations, or at least nation-wide reputations, are made overnight. Look at me, honest plodder that I am: for forty years, afar and asunder, I have been steadily pushing down the keys on my piano at thousands of concerts, building up, one would imagine, some sort of a shaky reputation: I had appeared, if that is the correct expression, on the sound radio – playing and speaking – hundreds of times, but I would not have called myself in my most extravagant moments, a famous person. Who ever heard of me? How many people knew my name? Let us say that I was known to music lovers. Well, they constitute a fractional percentage of the population of the British Isles.

Then one morning Enid and I hailed a taxi. After taking my instructions the driver said, 'Mr Moore, I would like to ask you a question when you leave my cab.' 'How does he know you?' whispered Enid. 'Television,' I answered importantly. I had had my first talk on television the previous evening.

I was no stranger to the cameras for I had accompanied Suggia, Menuhin, and other instrumentalists in short recitals ; appearances I was able to take in my stride more or less but which had created little notice. It was talking that did the trick, by talking I had become to some extent a television personality. Let me say straight away, however, that gazing directly into the eye of the camera and addressing it is a vastly different proposition from sitting down and playing accompaniments.

'All you have to remember is to be natural,' I was assured again and again by well-wishers, themselves incapable of stringing three words together in public. And indeed, according to some critics I was 'a natural' but let me say that I have never yet felt natural when on the set.

I was engaged to do a series of Armchair Chats on the lines of those that I had given in Australia, each talk to be interlaced with a certain amount of playing, and the strain of memorizing these talks accompanied by all the distractions that seem to be part and parcel of the business of television was considerable. On the sound radio you would be sitting alone with your notes and the microphone before you, with nothing to disturb your concentration. In the television studio where your concentration must be very much more intense through having to commit your script to memory there are twenty other people, at the very least, keeping you company. There are three or four cameramen each with their assistants raising or lowering their impedimenta continually or pushing them within a few feet of your nose ; there are scene-shifters, lights men, microphone men from the 'sound department' ; ladies from the make-up room looking at you with concern wondering what they can do with powder and paint to make you presentable. Then there is the studio manager in direct communication by headphones with the producer (hidden away in another room) who remits to you the producer's advice or criticism. For hours before actual transmission you rehearse your 'act' again and again : you moved too far from the chalked spot on the floor, you addressed the wrong camera, you rose unexpectedly from your chair and bumped your cranium with a painful crack on the microphone which, an inch or two above your head, dangles fish-like on the end of a rod. There are so many ways of going wrong when the rehearsal is repeated that it is small wonder the producer complains you look as grave as an undertaker and too rigid. You are still distracted by an urgent gesture behind a camera, by a stage-hand rushing on to the set to remove an offending vase of flowers, by the voices of two men arguing in a far corner. Hardened, as I have said, to practising in a concert hall where I can work away happily, oblivious of the screeching chairs being regimented in rows, of attendants loudly passing the time of day across the empty auditorium, of the song of the Hoover, I find the delicacy of my mechanism is thrown out of gear by the slightest stir of a hand or flutter of a handkerchief when recording or televising. The TV studio is pregnant with nervous bustle. I could practise through it but I cannot talk through it for my eyes are not glued to my keyboard but to the camera and I see every movement. Absolute quiet is not procured until you are just about due to go on the air when the floor manager calls vociferously, 'Quiet studio. Quiet everyone. Half a minute to go. . . . Ten seconds to go. . . . Five seconds . . .' until with a wave of the arm in your direction, as if hurling a hand grenade, he gives you the signal to start. I sometimes wish the major domo would be as assertive at rehearsal as he is before performance but perhaps he is afraid of hurting somebody's feelings for instead of the cautionary and authoritative 'Quiet everyone', his pre-rehearsal warning is less peremptory; he coos coaxingly, 'Can we have a little spot of *tranquillo*, chaps ?'

It stands to reason that at the dread moment when you are 'on' you do your very best to appear completely at ease. Perhaps you overdo it. One correspondent wrote me, 'You professed last night on television to have a deep love for Schubert but it was quite obvious to me that you had a much deeper love for Gerald Moore.' I wonder how this censor would have reacted if he could have seen the shivering, frightened soul below the urbane surface; probably he would have sat on the edge of his chair and muttered, 'This fellow is giving me the fidgets, he is not going to make it.' But the receipt of an anonymous letter is, in the long run, encouraging; one feels that an advance has been made, or at least interest aroused.

Another time, and once again to give an air of repose, I smoked a cigarette as I chatted away in my easy chair. This provoked a letter telling me that I was setting a deplorable example to young people by smoking. It is very difficult not to displease somebody.

Oddly enough I do not feel so frightened when being interviewed. Replying to questions, even when having no premonition as to their nature, perhaps unable to give the answers, is not so trying: for one thing the screen is being shared by another, neither am I speaking uninterruptedly for twenty minutes or more. I have sat many times on panels without feeling unduly harassed, though I confess to a sensation of butterflies in the stomach when hearing myself described as the Panel Expert. This happened in a quiz when Antony Hopkins was question master: being the only musician on the panel I, if you please, was the 'brain'. Hopkins, to give an instance of the puzzles I had to deal with, played one note – the D below middle C – and asked me which concerto began with that single note. It was the Beethoven violin concerto, of course, and any musician would have known it. (A friend, who was sitting among the invited audience, heard a man behind her say, as I looked down momentarily before replying, 'He has all the answers written out under the table.')

The musician, as I have indicated, finds himself performing to a vast audience, most of whom will have little knowledge and, let it be admitted, little liking for music. It is a new public. The path must be made smooth by the gentlest guidance if the unenlightened are to be won over. This is the responsibility, in the main, of the programme planners and the problems confronting them are not always appreciated. (Listening to a violin concerto, I once heard some moron in the audience ask his neighbour, 'Why is one of the violinists standing up?') Whereas a Shakespeare play well performed or a convincing crime thriller will be enjoyed alike by illiterate and intellectual, serious music had to be handled very gingerly at first in order not to frighten the great majority of viewers. This is why the explanatory talks of Sir Malcolm Sargent, Antony Hopkins, Sydney Harrison, and others (perhaps even mine) contributed so much to the softening-up process. America had to accord the same treatment to its lost sheep and they found an incomparable shepherd in the brilliant Leonard Bernstein.

For some years now we have listened to instrumental recitals on television. The average listener would certainly find the pianoforte literature of Beethoven, Schumann, Brahms well beyond his understanding but he could see with his eyes that Arrau, Curzon, Moiseiwitsch, Rubinstein, Solomon were doing magical things with their fingers and he was held; he was impressed. The act of singing, however, is not so spectacular and for a long time the idea of presenting the songs of Schubert or Fauré could not be considered.

That the British Broadcasting Corporation has made progress with their policy of gentle and persistent persuasion was proved when they conceived the idea of presenting a series of short recitals under the title of 'Great Singers of the World'. I was invited to introduce and accompany these artists. This series began in 1958 and has been continued intermittently ever since.

It was my responsibility to give a short translation of each song, for many of our guests would be singing in a foreign language – one cannot sing Sibelius or Manuel de Falla in English.

No sooner was the project announced in the press when one critic leapt into print deploring the necessity of 'explaining' a Schubert song and opining that the so-called recital would follow the usual television trend and become a chatty interview with 'and where do you travel from here?' type of conversation. Now this indignant gentleman is a cultivated musician, he is intimate with the songs of Schubert and the rest, he speaks German, but he could not appreciate the fact that 95 per cent of our audience would not understand one word in a foreign language, nor did it occur to him that their acquaintance with Schubert songs would be confined to the Serenade and the Ave Maria.

While writing these lines I received a letter from the B.B.C. informing me that they wish to transmit a song recital on every alternate Saturday night from October to March during the winter of 1961–2. Saturday night!

It is regarded by the pundits as a most valuable listening time. To have justified this, our listening figures must have increased enormously. (The B.B.C. is able to assess with uncanny accuracy the numbers of every programme's invisible audience.) This is all very encouraging.

Listeners will hear nothing but the finest music; they will certainly hear some of the loveliest voices in the world: Leontyne Price, Hans Hotter, Teresa Berganza, Gerard Souzay, Mattiwilda Dobbs, Nicolai Gedda, Elisabeth Schwarzkopf, Kim Borg, Joan Sutherland, Richard Lewis, Nan Merriman, Dietrich Fischer-Dieskau, Christa Ludwig, Teresa Stich-Randall.

The accompanist will do his best.

38

Writing as a Pastime

I BEGAN this book on 17 January 1957. On that day my pen
'heavy with destiny' – to cull the words of a certain painter, the
greatest Englishman of our age – was poised uncertainly over
the blank foolscap. I had gone alone, a week before the beginning of an American tour, to San Antonio in order to sit down
and think. This Texan city has made itself dear to me, for there
Am I Too Loud? was conceived. I wrote all day and every day
– reams of it – and daily consigned three quarters of what I
had written to the waste-paper basket (the trash-bin, to be
colloquial): only in the evenings my friends Colonel Sam Morrow and his wife Rênée carried me off to play bridge, or Wanda
and Phil Pattison took me for a short drive of a couple of hundred miles. Later in the course of this same tour I spent a long
week-end in a small Ontario town – Pembroke – refusing the
affectionate comfort of my brother Trevor's Toronto home in
order to write more. This has been the pattern of my life for
over four years wherever I have been, in fact these memoirs
have been my spare-time obsession. Now we are nearing the end
of 1961. It may be observed that my labour has been prolonged
and not altogether without pain.

Though I have not said all I intended to say I think I have
said all I ought. Lightweight though it is, this book has cost me
more effort than my two earlier sallies into print. Unlike Mr
J. B. Priestley who, referring to his gigantic literary output, said,
'I had the time' – I *made* the time. (It may be remembered I had
the temerity to couple my name with Busoni: now it is coupled
with Priestley. May I be forgiven!)

'After the fourth paragraph the writer went out for a drink,'
declared Constant Lambert studying a magazine article lacking
continuity. Between my fourth and fifth paragraphs I had concerts – several of them: and periods would come, lasting for

months, when I would be too occupied with my playing to think of putting pen to paper: always the piano had to come first.

Why then did I saddle myself with this load if it became such a burden to me? I suppose it is because I have made writing my pastime. Unlike the boy of whom my mother complained he had no hobbies, I now have plenty to keep me out of mischief, reading, gardening, bridge, cricket, but above all writing. It is a wonder I have not become a more proficient writer under the circumstances but perhaps, as they say in school reports, I am showing slight signs of improvement. I had the suspicion when duet playing with Ruth Fermoy that we performers derived more enjoyment out of it than the listeners. It is so with this book. Not even the most generous of friends will gain half so much pleasure in the reading as I had in the writing.

So far as my music is concerned I am still something of a mystery even to myself. Dragged by his mother to the keyboard, the unwilling, snivelling child was found to have talent. Why? None of my family were musical at all, and I scarcely ever approached the piano as a boy unless I were driven to it. I did not absorb music into my being until my middle twenties, this time driven on by John Coates: a retarded development. Out of this unpromising start a good musician – for I must concede myself that qualification – has emerged. Music is my be-all and end-all. I cannot imagine living any other kind of life than that which I have lived. But I wish I had come to grips with it earlier.

Let it not be imagined that this volume constitutes my *Nunc dimittis*, I am not yet resigned to being put out to grass. Having got it off my chest, I intend to attack my piano with greater zest than before, and I hope to go on playing for some time yet, God willing. I believe my work, in some ways, is better than it ever was – but wait – have I not heard elderly singers retired from the public eye make the boast 'My voice is as good as ever –'? I must be careful.

To die in harness, however, is far from my wish; I want when the time comes to slow down gradually, to make a graceful *rallentando* so as to indulge myself in a little leisure. I shall not be bored. The taste for rushing hither and thither without pause, the racing against the clock, the seeing of new sights will one day lose its relish. Already the view in my garden, surrounded as it is by chestnut trees, lime and pear and cherry, a splendid copper beech, is more pleasing to me than many a scene I have journeyed far to enjoy. Here the feud between Enid and me – the relative importance of *her* flower beds and *my* lawn – may wax unabated: here I can practise and, who knows, write a little: here I can sit and reflect, making still the odd visit abroad when invited but not careering madly from one end of the globe to the other as some octogenarian Foreign Secretaries are forced to do, with no pause to think.

Pedalling up the hill was good but it will be fun to coast down on the other side. But not too fast, please, or it will be over too soon. Unlike elderly conductors who so often adopt too quick a tempo (not pianists or violinists, *they* have to play the notes) as if to prove they are as full of vitality and force as the younger stallions, my tempo will be *commodo*, not necessarily in music but in living. I shall want time to hear more opera, more chamber music, and time at last to do some teaching: above all to see more of those I love, old friends whom I have been too busy to see (too busy!) and a bevy of young people, headed by my godchildren Wendy and Richard, and others across the way and round me where I live. Let me have leave too for the odd game of bridge at the Savile Club, to stroll along and watch cricket at Lord's (provided those young chaps out in the middle get a bit of a move on) and I shall be content.

My life has been full of excitement; keen anticipation has so often been succeeded by joyous realization, thanks to God. I have known miseries and troubles, of course, but have not tried the patience of the reader still further by retailing them. Have I indulged in more than my fair stint of grumbling in the preceding pages? Well, let it be remembered that your traditional British soldier has a grouse but is a bonny fighter. I fought pretty well and, mistakenly or not, took pride in concealing the wounds and hurts that are the inevitable lot of one who parades himself before the public.

Under the banner of Music I have, so far, campaigned faithfully. I do not boast of my prowess; I am but one of the rank and file in the great army of musicians of the world. But I held my ground: I kept my place. This is enough.

Only in my own home am I a person of consequence. Everything there revolves around me – or is made to appear to do so by one who is the most perfect of all accompanists. It is her strength and devotion that pushed me up my little hill; her faith and sunshine that sustained me when I faltered.

Index